G 24045

London
1834

Godwin, William [pseud. Edward Baldwin]

Lives of the necromancers, or an Account of the most eminent persons... who have claimed for themselves or tho whom has

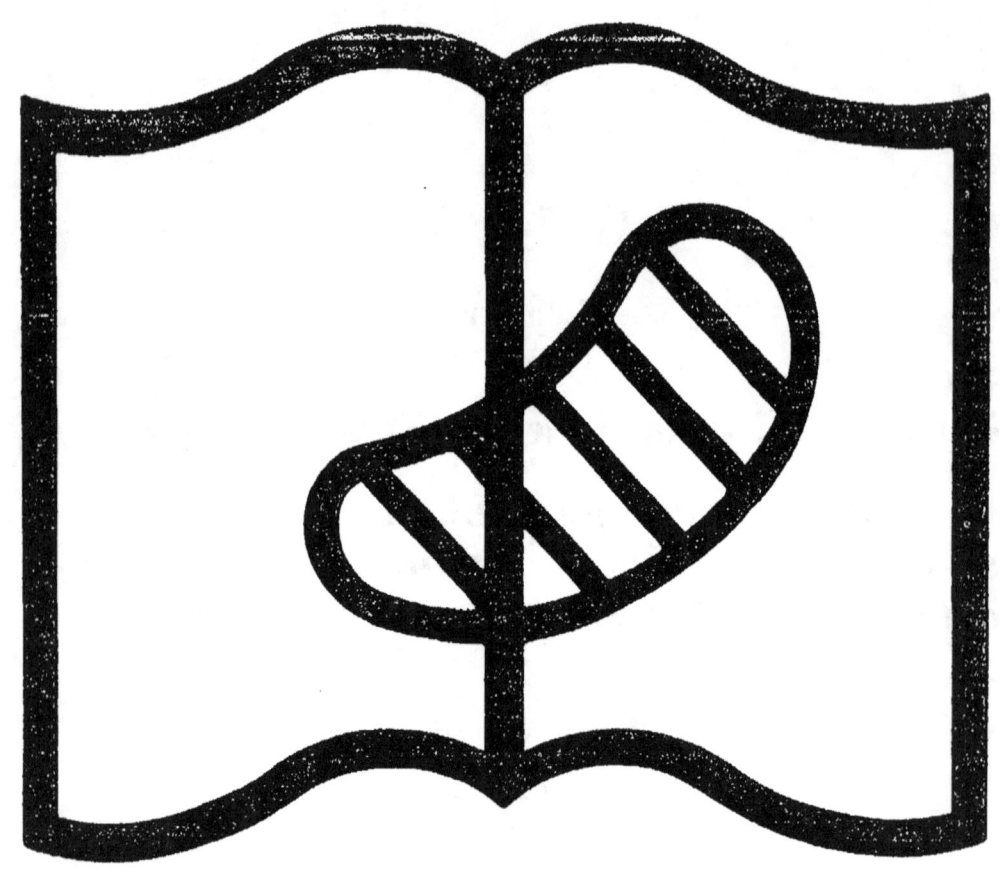

Symbole applicable
pour tout, ou partie
des documents microfilmés

Original illisible

NF Z 43-120-10

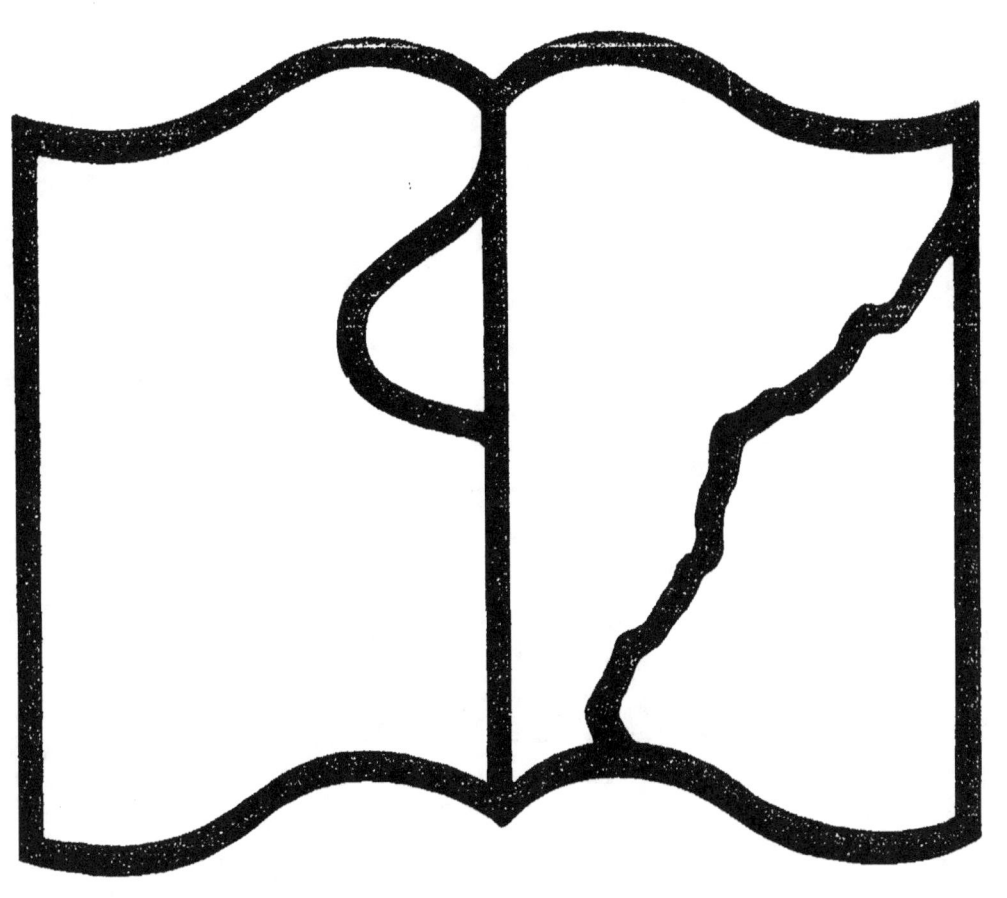

Symbole applicable
pour tout, ou partie
des documents microfilmés

Texte détérioré — reliure défectueuse

NF Z 43-120-11

LIVES

OF THE

NECROMANCERS.

BAYLIS AND LEIGHTON,
JOHNSON'S-COURT, FLEET-STREET.

LIVES

OF THE

NECROMANCERS:

OR,

AN ACCOUNT OF THE MOST EMINENT PERSONS IN SUCCESSIVE AGES, WHO HAVE CLAIMED FOR THEMSELVES, OR TO WHOM HAS BEEN IMPUTED BY OTHERS,

THE

EXERCISE OF MAGICAL POWER.

BY WILLIAM GODWIN.

LONDON:
FREDERICK J. MASON, 444, WEST STRAND.

1834.

PREFACE.

The main purpose of this book is to exhibit a fair delineation of the credulity of the human mind. Such an exhibition cannot fail to be productive of the most salutary lessons.

One view of the subject will teach us a useful pride in the abundance of our faculties. Without pride man is in reality of little value. It is pride that stimulates us to all our great undertakings. Without pride, and the secret persuasion of extraordinary talents, what man would take up the pen with a view to produce an important work, whether of imagination and poetry, or of profound science, or of acute and subtle reasoning and intellectual anatomy? It is pride in this sense that makes the great general and the consummate legislator, that animates us to tasks the most laborious, and causes us to shrink from no difficulty, and to be confounded and overwhelmed with no obstacle that can be interposed in our path.

Nothing can be more striking than the contrast between man and the inferior animals. The latter live only for the day, and see for the most part only what is immediately before them. But man lives in the past and the future. He reasons upon and improves by the past; he records the acts of a long series of generations: and he looks into future time, lays down plans which he shall be months and years in bringing to maturity, and contrives machines and delineates systems of education and government, which may gradually add to the accommodations of all, and raise the species generally into a nobler and more honourable character than our ancestors were capable of sustaining.

Man looks through nature, and is able to reduce its parts into a great whole. He classes the beings which are found in it, both animate and inanimate, delineates and describes them, investigates their properties, and records their capacities, their good and evil qualities, their dangers and their uses.

Nor does he only see all that is; but he also

images all that is not. He takes to pieces the substances that are, and combines their parts into new arrangements. He peoples all the elements from the world of his imagination. It is here that he is most extraordinary and wonderful. The record of what actually is, and has happened in the series of human events, is perhaps the smallest part of human history. If we would know man in all his subtleties, we must deviate into the world of miracles and sorcery. To know the things that are not, and cannot be, but have been imagined and believed, is the most curious chapter in the annals of man. To observe the actual results of these imaginary phenomena, and the crimes and cruelties they have caused us to commit, is one of the most instructive studies in which we can possibly be engaged. It is here that man is most astonishing, and that we contemplate with most admiration the discursive and unbounded nature of his faculties.

But, if a recollection of the examples of the credulity of the human mind may in one view supply nourishment to our pride, it still more obviously tends to teach us sobriety and humiliation. Man in his genuine and direct sphere is the disciple of reason; it is by this faculty that he draws inferences, exerts his prudence, and displays the ingenuity of machinery, and the subtlety of system both in natural and moral philosophy. Yet what so irrational as man? Not contented with making use of the powers we possess, for the purpose of conducing to our accommodation and well being, we with a daring spirit inquire into the invisible causes of what we see, and people all nature with Gods "of every shape and size" and angels, with principalities and powers, with beneficent beings who "take charge concerning us lest at any time we dash our foot against a stone," and with devils who are perpetually on the watch to perplex us and do us injury. And, having familiarised our minds with the conceptions of these beings, we immediately aspire to hold communion with them. We represent to ourselves God, as "walking in the garden with us in the cool of the day," and teach ourselves "not to forget to entertain strangers, lest by so doing we should repel angels unawares."

No sooner are we, even in a slight degree, acquainted with the laws of nature, than we frame to ourselves the idea, by the aid of some invisible ally, of suspending their operation, of calling out meteors in the sky, of commanding storms and tempests, of arresting the motion of the heavenly bodies, of producing miraculous cures upon the bodies of our fellow-men, or afflicting them with disease and death, of calling up the deceased from the silence of the grave, and compelling them to disclose " the secrets of the world unknown."

But, what is most deplorable, we are not contented to endeavour to secure the aid of God and good angels, but we also aspire to enter into alliance with devils, and beings destined for their rebellion to suffer eternally the pains of hell. As they are supposed to be of a character perverted and depraved, we of course apply to them principally for purposes of wantonness, or of malice and revenge. And, in the instances which have occurred only a few centuries back, the most common idea has been of a compact entered into by an unprincipled and impious human being with the sworn enemy of God and man, in the result of which the devil engages to serve the capricious will and perform the behests of his blasphemous votary for a certain number of years, while the deluded wretch in return engages to renounce his God and Saviour, and surrender himself body and soul to the pains of hell from the end of that term to all eternity. No sooner do we imagine human beings invested with these wonderful powers, and conceive them as called into action for the most malignant purposes, than we become the passive and terrified slaves of the creatures of our own imaginations, and fear to be assailed at every moment by beings to whose power we can set no limit, and whose modes of hostility no human sagacity can anticipate and provide against. But, what is still more extraordinary, the human creatures that pretend to these powers have often been found as completely the dupes of this supernatural machinery, as the most timid wretch that stands in terror at its expected operation; and no phenomenon has been more common than the confession of these allies of hell, that they have verily and indeed held commerce and formed plots and conspiracies with Satan.

The consequence of this state of things has been, that criminal jurisprudence and the last severities of the law have been called forth to an amazing extent to exterminate witches and witchcraft. More especially in the sixteenth century hundreds and thousands were burned alive within the compass of a small territory; and judges, the directors of the scene, a Nicholas Remi, a De Lancre, and many others, have published copious volumes, entering into a minute detail of the system and fashion of the witchcraft of the professors, whom they sent in multitudes to expiate their depravity at the gallows and the stake.

One useful lesson which we may derive from the detail of these particulars, is the folly in most cases of imputing pure and unmingled hypocrisy to man. The human mind is of so ductile a character that, like what is affirmed of charity by the apostle, it "believeth all things, and endureth all things." We are not at liberty to trifle with the sacredness of truth. While we persuade others, we begin to deceive ourselves. Human life is a drama of that sort, that, while we act our part, and endeavour to do justice to the sentiments which are put down for us, we begin to believe we are the thing we would represent.

To shew however the modes in which the delusion acts upon the person through whom it operates, is not properly the scope of this book. Here and there I have suggested hints to this purpose, which the curious reader may follow to their furthest extent, and discover how with perfect good faith the artist may bring himself to swallow the grossest impossibilities. But the work I have written is not a treatise of natural magic. It rather proposes to display the immense wealth of the faculty of imagination, and to shew the extravagances of which the man may be guilty who surrenders himself to its guidance.

It is fit however that the reader should bear in mind, that what is put down in this book is but a small part and scantling of the acts of sorcery and witchcraft which have existed in human society. They have been found in all ages and countries. The torrid zone and the frozen north have neither of them escaped from a fruitful harvest of this sort of offspring. In ages of ignorance they have been especially at home; and the races of men that have left no records behind them to tell almost that they existed, have been most of all rife in deeds of darkness, and those marvellous incidents which especially astonish the spectator, and throw back the infant reason of man into those shades and that obscurity from which it had so recently endeavoured to escape.

I wind up for the present my literary labours

with the production of this book. Nor let any reader imagine that I here put into his hands a mere work of idle recreation. It will be found pregnant with deeper uses. The wildest extravagances of human fancy, the most deplorable perversion of human faculties, and the most horrible distortions of jurisprudence, may occasionally afford us a salutary lesson. I love in the foremost place to contemplate man in all his honours and in all the exaltation of wisdom and virtue; but it will also be occasionally of service to us to look into his obliquities, and distinctly to remark how great and portentous have been his absurdities and his follies.

May 29, 1834.

CONTENTS.

	Page
INTRODUCTION	1

AMBITIOUS NATURE OF MAN . . 9
HIS DESIRE TO PENETRATE INTO FUTURITY 10
DIVINATION 11
AUGURY . . . . ib.
CHIROMANCY 12
PHYSIOGNOMY . . . . ib.
INTERPRETATION OF DREAMS . . . 13
CASTING OF LOTS 14
ASTROLOGY . . . . ib.
ORACLES 15
DELPHI 16
THE DESIRE TO COMMAND AND CONTROL
    FUTURE EVENTS 20

	Page
COMMERCE WITH THE INVISIBLE WORLD	20
SORCERY AND ENCHANTMENT	21
WITCHCRAFT	24
COMPACTS WITH THE DEVIL	25
IMPS	26
TALISMANS AND AMULETS	27
NECROMANCY	ib.
ALCHEMY	29
FAIRIES	32
ROSICRUCIANS	35
SYLPHS AND GNOMES, SALAMANDERS AND UNDINES	36

EXAMPLES OF NECROMANCY AND WITCHCRAFT FROM THE BIBLE 39

THE MAGI, OR WISE MEN OF THE EAST	44
EGYPT	46
STATUE OF MEMNON	50
TEMPLE OF JUPITER AMMON: ITS ORACLES	51
CHALDEA AND BABYLON	54
ZOROASTER	55

GREECE 57

DEITIES OF GREECE	58
DEMIGODS	62
DÆDALUS	64
THE ARGONAUTS	66
MEDEA	67
CIRCE	70
ORPHEUS	ib.
AMPHION	74
TIRESIAS	75
ABARIS	76
PYTHAGORAS	77

CONTENTS. xvii

	Page
EPIMENIDES	92
EMPEDOCLES	95
ARISTEAS	98
HERMOTIMUS	99
THE MOTHER OF DEMARATUS, KING OF SPARTA	100
ORACLES	101
INVASION OF XERXES INTO GREECE	107
DEMOCRITUS	110
SOCRATES	112

ROME	119
VIRGIL	ib.
POLYDORUS	ib.
DIDO	120
ROMULUS	122
NUMA	ib.
TULLUS HOSTILIUS	124
ACCIUS NAVIUS	ib.
SERVIUS TULLIUS	125
THE SORCERESS OF VIRGIL	127
CANIDIA	129
ERICHTHO	133
SERTORIUS	146
CASTING OUT DEVILS	150
SIMON MAGUS	ib.
ELYMAS, THE SORCERER	153
NERO	155
VESPASIAN	ib.
APOLLONIUS OF TYANA	157
APULEIUS	164
ALEXANDER THE PAPHLAGONIAN	165

REVOLUTION PRODUCED IN THE HISTORY OF NECROMANCY AND WITCHCRAFT UPON THE ESTABLISHMENT OF CHRISTIANITY ... 171
MAGICAL CONSULTATIONS RESPECTING THE LIFE OF THE EMPEROR 173

HISTORY OF NECROMANCY IN THE EAST 177
GENERAL SILENCE OF THE EAST RESPECTING INDIVIDUAL NECROMANCERS .. 185
ROCAIL 187
HAKEM, OTHERWISE MACANNA ... 188
ARABIAN NIGHTS' ENTERTAINMENTS .. 189
PERSIAN TALES 195
STORY OF A GOULE 201
ARABIAN NIGHTS 203
RESEMBLANCE OF THE TALES OF THE EAST AND OF EUROPE 204
CAUSES OF HUMAN CREDULITY ... 206

DARK AGES OF EUROPE ... 211
MERLIN 216
ST. DUNSTAN 222

COMMUNICATION OF EUROPE AND THE SARACENS 231
GERBERT, POPE SILVESTER II .... *ib.*
BENEDICT THE NINTH 234
GREGORY THE SEVENTH 235
DUFF, KING OF SCOTLAND 241

	Page
MACBETH	243
VIRGIL	249
ROBERT OF LINCOLN	252
MICHAEL SCOT	254
THE DEAN OF BADAJOZ	255
MIRACLE OF THE TUB OF WATER	257
INSTITUTION OF FRIARS	259
ALBERTUS MAGNUS	260
ROGER BACON	263
THOMAS AQUINAS	266
PETER OF APONO	268
ENGLISH LAW OF HIGH TREASON	269
ZITO	273
TRANSMUTATION OF METALS	277
ARTEPHIUS	278
RAYMOND LULLI	ib.
ARNOLD OF VILLENEUVE	281
ENGLISH LAWS RESPECTING TRANSMUTATION	282

REVIVAL OF LETTERS 285

JOAN OF ARC	286
ELEANOR COBHAM, DUCHESS OF GLOUCESTER	294
RICHARD III	297

SANGUINARY PROCEEDINGS AGAINST WITCHCRAFT . . 299

SAVONAROLA	311
TRITHEMIUS	318
LUTHER	320
CORNELIUS AGRIPPA	322
FAUSTUS	330
SABELLICUS	358
PARACELSUS	359
CARDAN	362

CONTENTS.

	Page
QUACKS, WHO IN COOL BLOOD UNDERTOOK TO OVERREACH MANKIND	364
BENVENUTO CELLINI	365
NOSTRADAMUS	372
DOCTOR DEE	373
EARL OF DERBY	398
KING JAMES'S VOYAGE TO NORWAY	399
JOHN FIAN	404
KING JAMES'S DEMONOLOGY	405
STATUTE, 1 JAMES I	407
FORMAN AND OTHERS	408
LATEST IDEAS OF JAMES ON THE SUBJECT	412
LANCASHIRE WITCHES	ib.
LADY DAVIES	418
EDWARD FAIRFAX	419
DOCTOR LAMB	ib.
URBAIN GRANDIER	421
ASTROLOGY	423
WILLIAM LILLY	426
MATTHEW HOPKINS	432
CROMWEL	437
DOROTHY MATELEY	440
WITCHES HANGED BY SIR MATTHEW HALE	443
WITCHCRAFT IN SWEDEN	448
WITCHCRAFT IN NEW ENGLAND	454

CONCLUSION 463

LIVES

OF THE

NECROMANCERS

THE improvements that have been effected in natural philosophy have by degrees convinced the enlightened part of mankind that the material universe is every where subject to laws, fixed in their weight, measure and duration, capable of the most exact calculation, and which in no case admit of variation and exception. Whatever is not thus to be accounted for is of mind, and springs from the volition of some being, of which the material form is subjected to our senses, and the action of which is in like manner regulated by the laws of matter. Beside this, mind, as well as matter, is subject to fixed laws; and thus every phenomenon and occurrence around us is rendered a topic for the speculations of sagacity and foresight. Such is the creed which science has universally prescribed to the judicious and reflecting among us.

It was otherwise in the infancy and less mature state of human knowledge. The chain of causes and consequences was yet unrecognized; and events perpetually occurred, for which no sagacity that was then in being was able to assign an original. Hence men felt themselves habitually disposed to refer many of the appearances with which they were conversant to the agency of invisible intelligences; sometimes under the influence of a benignant disposition, sometimes of malice, and sometimes perhaps from an inclination to make themselves sport of the wonder and astonishment of ignorant mortals. Omens and portents told these men of some piece of good or ill fortune speedily to befal them. The flight of birds was watched by them, as foretokening somewhat important. Thunder excited in them a feeling of supernatural terror. Eclipses with fear of change perplexed the nations. The phenomena of the heavens, regular and irregular, were anxiously remarked from the same principle. During the hours of darkness men were apt to see a supernatural being in every bush; and they could not cross a receptacle for the dead, without expecting to encounter some one of the departed uneasily wandering among graves, or commissioned to reveal somewhat momentous and deeply affecting to the survivors. Fairies danced in the moonlight glade; and something preternatural perpetually occurred to fill the living with admiration and awe.

All this gradually reduced itself into a system. Mankind, particularly in the dark and ignorant ages, were divided into the strong and the weak; the strong and weak of animal frame, when corporeal strength more decidedly bore sway than in a period of greater cultivation; and the strong and weak in reference to intellect; those who were bold, audacious and enterprising in acquiring an ascendancy over their fellow-men, and those who truckled, submitted, and were acted upon, from an innate consciousness of inferiority, and a superstitious looking up to such as were of greater natural or acquired endowments than themselves. The strong in intellect were eager to avail themselves of their superiority, by means that escaped the penetration of the multitude, and had recourse to various artifices to effect their ends. Beside this, they became the dupes of their own practices. They set out at first in their conception of things from the level of the vulgar. They applied themselves diligently to the unravelling of what was unknown; wonder mingled with their contemplation; they abstracted their minds from things of ordinary occurrence, and, as we may denominate it, of real life, till at length they lost their true balance amidst the astonishment they sought to produce in their inferiors. They felt a vocation to things extraordinary; and they willingly gave scope and line without limit to that which engendered in themselves the most gratifying sensations, at the same time that it answered the purposes of their ambition.

As these principles in the two parties, the more refined and the vulgar, are universal, and derive their origin from the nature of man, it has necessarily happened that this faith in extraordinary events, and superstitious fear of what is supernatural, has diffused itself through every climate of the world, in a certain stage of human intellect, and while refinement had not yet got the better of barbarism. The Celts of antiquity had their Druids, a branch of whose special profession was the exercise of magic. The Chaldeans and Egyptians had their wise men, their magicians and their sorcerers. The negroes have their foretellers of events, their amulets, and their reporters and believers of miraculous occurrences. A similar race of men was found by Columbus and the other discoverers of the New World in America; and facts of a parallel nature are attested to us in the islands of the South Seas. And, as phenomena of this sort were universal in their nature, without distinction of climate, whether torrid or frozen, and independently of the discordant manners and customs of different countries, so have they been very slow and recent in their disappearing. Queen Elizabeth sent to consult Dr. John Dee, the astrologer, respecting a lucky day for her coronation; King James the First employed much of his learned leisure upon questions of witchcraft and demonology, in which he fully believed; and sir Matthew Hale in the year 1664 caused two old women to be hanged upon a charge of unlawful communion with infernal agents.

The history of mankind therefore will be very imperfect, and our knowledge of the operations and eccentricities of the mind lamentably deficient, unless we take into our view what has occurred under this head. The supernatural appearances with which our ancestors conceived themselves perpetually surrounded must have had a strong tendency to cherish and keep alive the powers of the imagination, and to penetrate those who witnessed or expected such things with an extraordinary sensitiveness. As the course of events appears to us at present, there is much, though abstractedly within the compass of human sagacity to foresee, which yet the actors on the scene do not foresee: but the blindness and perplexity of short-sighted mortals must have been wonderfully increased, when ghosts and extraordinary appearances were conceived liable to cross the steps and confound the projects of men at every turn, and a malicious wizard or a powerful enchanter might involve his unfortunate victim in a chain of calamities, which no prudence could disarm, and no virtue could deliver him from. They were the slaves of an uncontrolable destiny, and must therefore have been eminently deficient in the perseverance and moral courage, which may justly be required of us in a more enlightened age. And the men (but these were few compared with the great majority of mankind), who believed themselves gifted with supernatural endowments, must have felt exempt and privileged from common rules, somewhat in the same way as the persons whom fiction has delighted to pourtray as endowed with immeasurable wealth, or with the power of rendering themselves impassive or invisible. But, whatever were their advantages or disadvantages, at any rate it is good for us to call up in review things, which are now passed away, but which once occupied so large a share of the thoughts and attention of mankind, and in a great degree tended to modify their characters and dictate their resolutions.

As has already been said, numbers of those who were endowed with the highest powers of human intellect, such as, if they had lived in these times, would have aspired to eminence in the exact sciences, to the loftiest flights of imagination, or to the discovery of means by which the institutions of men in society might be rendered more beneficial and faultless, at that time wasted the midnight oil in endeavouring to trace the occult qualities and virtues of things, to render invisible spirits subject to their command, and to effect those wonders, of which they deemed themselves to have a dim conception, but which more rational views of nature have taught us to regard as beyond our power to effect. These sublime wanderings of the mind are well entitled to our labour to trace and investigate. The errors of man are worthy to be recorded, not only as beacons to warn us from the shelves where our ancestors have made shipwreck, but even as something honourable to our nature, to shew how high a generous ambition could soar, though in forbidden paths, and in things too wonderful for us.

Nor only is this subject inexpressibly interesting, as setting before us how the loftiest and most enterprising minds of ancient days formerly busied themselves. It is also of the highest importance to an ingenuous curiosity, inasmuch as it vitally affected the fortunes of so considerable a portion of the mass of mankind. The legislatures of remote ages bent all their severity at different periods against what they deemed the unhallowed arts of the sons and daughters of reprobation. Multitudes of human creatures have been sacrificed in different ages and countries, upon the accusation of having exercised arts of the most immoral and sacrilegious character. They were supposed to have formed a contract with a mighty and invisible spirit, the great enemy of man, and to have sold themselves, body and soul, to everlasting perdition, for the sake of gratifying, for a short term of years, their malignant passions against those who had been so unfortunate as to give them cause of offence. If there were any persons who imagined they had entered into such a contract, however erroneous was their belief, they must of necessity have been greatly depraved. And it was but natural that such as believed in this crime, must have considered it as atrocious beyond all others, and have regarded those who were supposed guilty of it with inexpressible abhorrence. There are many instances on record, where the persons accused of it, either from the depth of their delusion, or, which is more probable, harassed by persecution, by the hatred of their fellow-creatures directed against them, or by torture, actually confessed themselves guilty. These instances are too numerous, not to constitute an important chapter in the legislation of past ages. And, now that the illusion has in a manner passed away from the face of the earth, we are on that account the better qualified to investigate this error in its causes and consequences, and to look back on the tempest and hurricane from which we have escaped, with chastened feelings, and a sounder estimate of its nature, its reign, and its effects.

AMBITIOUS NATURE OF MAN.

MAN is a creature of boundless ambition.

It is probably our natural wants that first awaken us from that lethargy and indifference in which man may be supposed to be plunged previously to the impulse of any motive, or the accession of any uneasiness. One of our earliest wants may be conceived to be hunger, or the desire of food.

From this simple beginning the history of man in all its complex varieties may be regarded as proceeding.

Man in a state of society, more especially where there is an inequality of condition and rank, is very often the creature of leisure. He finds in himself, either from internal or external impulse, a certain activity. He finds himself at one time engaged in the accomplishment of his obvious and immediate desires, and at another in a state in which these desires have for the present been fulfilled, and he has no present occasion to repeat those exertions which led to their fulfilment. This is the period of contemplation. This is the state which most eminently distinguishes us from the brutes. Here it is that the history of man, in its exclusive sense, may be considered as taking its beginning.

Here it is that he specially recognises in himself the sense of power. Power in its simplest acceptation, may be exerted in either of two ways, either in his procuring for himself an ample field for more refined accommodations, or in the exercise of compulsion and authority over other living creatures. In the pursuit of either of these, and especially the first, he is led to the attainment of skill and superior adroitness in the use of his faculties.

No sooner has man reached to this degree of improvement, than now, if not indeed earlier, he is induced to remark the extreme limitedness of his faculties in respect to the future; and he is led, first earnestly to desire a clearer insight into the future, and next a power of commanding those external causes upon which the events of the future depend. The first of these desires is the parent of divination, augury, chiromancy, astrology, and the consultation of oracles; and the second has been the prolific source of enchantment, witchcraft, sorcery, magic, necromancy, and alchemy, in its two branches, the unlimited prolongation of human life, and the art of converting less precious metals into gold.

HIS DESIRE TO PENETRATE INTO FUTURITY.

Nothing can suggest to us a more striking and stupendous idea of the faculties of the human mind, than the consideration of the various arts by which men have endeavoured to penetrate into the future, and to command the events of the future, in ways that in sobriety and truth are entirely out of our competence. We spurn impatiently against the narrow limits which the constitution of things has fixed to our aspirings, and endeavour by a multiplicity of ways to accomplish that which it is totally beyond the power of man to effect.

DIVINATION.

Divination has been principally employed in inspecting the entrails of beasts offered for sacrifice, and from their appearance drawing omens of the good or ill success of the enterprises in which we are about to engage.

What the divination by the cup was which Joseph practised, or pretended to practise, we do not perhaps exactly understand. We all of us know somewhat of the predictions, to this day resorted to by maid-servants and others, from the appearance of the sediment to be found at the bottom of a tea-cup. Predictions of a similar sort are formed from the unpremeditated way in which we get out of bed in a morning, or put on our garments, from the persons or things we shall encounter when we first leave our chamber or go forth in the air, or any of the indifferent accidents of life.

AUGURY.

Augury has its foundation in observing the flight

of birds, the sounds they utter, their motions whether sluggish or animated, and the avidity or otherwise with which they appear to take their food. The college of augurs was one of the most solemn institutions of ancient Rome.

CHIROMANCY.

Chiromancy, or the art of predicting the various fortunes of the individual, from an inspection of the minuter variations of the lines to be found in the palm of the human hand, has been used perhaps at one time or other in all the nations of the world.

PHYSIOGNOMY.

Physiognomy is not so properly a prediction of future events, as an attempt to explain the present and inherent qualities of a man. By unfolding his propensities however, it virtually gave the world to understand the sort of proceedings in which he was most likely to engage. The story of Socrates and the physiognomist is sufficiently known. The physiognomist having inspected the countenance of the philosopher, pronounced that he was given to intemperance, sensuality, and violent bursts of passion, all of which was so contrary to his character as universally known, that his disciples derided the physiognomist as a vain-glorious pretender. Socrates however presently put them to silence, by declaring that he had had an original propensity to all the vices imputed to him, and had only conquered the propensity by dint of a severe and unremitted self-discipline.

INTERPRETATION OF DREAMS.

Oneirocriticism, or the art of interpreting dreams, seems of all the modes of prediction the most inseparable from the nature of man. A considerable portion of every twenty-four hours of our lives is spent in sleep; and in sleep nothing is at least more usual, than for the mind to be occupied in a thousand imaginary scenes, which for the time are as realities, and often excite the passions of the mind of the sleeper in no ordinary degree. Many of them are wild and rambling; but many also have a portentous sobriety. Many seem to have a strict connection with the incidents of our actual lives; and some appear as if they came for the very purpose to warn us of danger, or prepare us for coming events. It is therefore no wonder that these occasionally fill our waking thoughts with a deep interest, and impress upon us an anxiety of which we feel it difficult to rid ourselves. Accordingly, in ages when men were more prone to superstition, than at present, they sometimes constituted a subject of earnest anxiety and inquisitiveness; and we find among the earliest exercises of the art of prediction, the interpretation of dreams to have occupied a principal place, and to have been as it were reduced into a science.

CASTING OF LOTS.

The casting of lots seems scarcely to come within the enumeration here given. It was intended as an appeal to heaven upon a question involved in uncertainty, with the idea that the supreme Ruler of the skies, thus appealed to, would from his omniscience supply the defect of human knowledge. Two examples, among others sufficiently remarkable, occur in the Bible. One of Achan, who secreted part of the spoil taken in Jericho, which was consecrated to the service of God, and who, being taken by lot, confessed, and was stoned to death[a]. The other of Jonah, upon whom the lot fell in a mighty tempest, the crew of the ship enquiring by this means what was the cause of the calamity that had overtaken them, and Jonah being in consequence cast into the sea.

ASTROLOGY.

Astrology was one of the modes most anciently and universally resorted to for discovering the fortunes of men and nations. Astronomy and astrology went hand in hand, particularly among the

[a] Joshua, vii. 16, *et seq.*

people of the East. The idea of fate was most especially bound up in this branch of prophecy. If the fortune of a man was intimately connected with the position of the heavenly bodies, it became evident that little was left to the province of his free will. The stars overruled him in all his determinations; and it was in vain for him to resist them. There was something flattering to the human imagination in conceiving that the planets and the orbs on high were concerned in the conduct we should pursue, and the events that should befal us. Man resigned himself to his fate with a solemn, yet a lofty feeling, that the remotest portions of the universe were concerned in the catastrophe that awaited him. Beside which, there was something peculiarly seducing in the apparently profound investigation of the professors of astrology. They busied themselves with the actual position of the heavenly bodies, their conjunctions and oppositions; and of consequence there was a great apparatus of diagrams and calculation to which they were prompted to apply themselves, and which addressed itself to the eyes and imaginations of those who consulted them.

ORACLES.

But that which seems to have had the greatest vogue in times of antiquity, relative to the prediction of future events, is what is recorded of oracles.

Finding the insatiable curiosity of mankind as to what was to happen hereafter, and the general desire they felt to be guided in their conduct by an anticipation of things to come, the priests pretty generally took advantage of this passion, to increase their emoluments and offerings, and the more effectually to inspire the rest of their species with veneration and a willing submission to their authority. The oracle was delivered in a temple, or some sacred place; and in this particular we plainly discover that mixture of nature and art, of genuine enthusiasm and contriving craft, which is so frequently exemplified in the character of man.

DELPHI.

The oracle of Apollo at Delphi is the most remarkable; and respecting it we are furnished with the greatest body of particulars. The locality of this oracle is said to have been occasioned by the following circumstance. A goat-herd fed his flocks on the acclivity of mount Parnassus. As the animals wandered here and there in pursuit of food, they happened to approach a deep and long chasm which appeared in the rock. From this chasm a vapour issued; and the goats had no sooner inhaled a portion of the vapour, than they began to play and frisk about with singular agility. The goat-herd, observing this, and curious to discover the cause, held his head over the chasm; when, in a short time, the fumes having ascended to his brain, he threw himself into a variety of strange attitudes, and uttered words, which probably he did not understand himself, but which were supposed to convey a prophetic meaning.

This phenomenon was taken advantage of, and a temple to Apollo was erected on the spot. The credulous many believed that here was obviously a centre and focus of divine inspiration. On this mountain Apollo was said to have slain the serpent Python. The apartment of the oracle was immediately over the chasm from which the vapour issued. A priestess delivered the responses, who was called Pythia, probably in commemoration of the exploit which had been performed by Apollo. She sat upon a tripod, or three-legged stool, perforated with holes, over the seat of the vapours. After a time, her figure enlarged itself, her hair stood on end, her complexion and features became altered, her heart panted and her bosom swelled, and her voice grew more than human. In this condition she uttered a number of wild and incoherent phrases, which were supposed to be dictated by the God. The questions which were offered by those who came to consult the oracle were then proposed to her, and her answers taken down by the priest, whose office was to arrange and methodize them, and put them into hexameter verse, after which they were delivered to the votaries. The priestess could only be consulted on one day in every month.

Great ingenuity and contrivance were no doubt required to uphold the credit of the oracle; and no less boldness and self-collectedness on the part of those by whom the machinery was conducted. Like the conjurors of modern times, they took care to be extensively informed as to all such matters respecting which the oracle was likely to be consulted. They listened probably to the Pythia with a superstitious reverence for the incoherent sentences she uttered. She, like them, spent her life in being trained for the office to which she was devoted. All that was rambling and inapplicable in her wild declamation they consigned to oblivion. Whatever seemed to bear on the question proposed they preserved. The persons by whom the responses were digested into hexameter verse, had of course a commission attended with great discretionary power. They, as Horace remarks on another occasion*, divided what it was judicious to say, from what it was prudent to omit, dwelt upon one thing, and slurred over and accommodated another, just as would best suit the purpose they had in hand. Beside this, for the most part they clothed the apparent meaning of the oracle in obscurity, and often devised sentences of ambiguous interpretation, that might suit with opposite

* De Arte Poetica, v. 150.

issues, whichever might happen to fall out. This was perfectly consistent with a high degree of enthusiasm on the part of the priest. However confident he might be in some things, he could not but of necessity feel that his prognostics were surrounded with uncertainty. Whatever decisions of the oracle were frustrated by the event, and we know that there were many of this sort, were speedily forgotten; while those which succeeded, were conveyed from shore to shore, and repeated by every echo. Nor is it surprising that the transmitters of the sentences of the God should in time arrive at an extraordinary degree of sagacity and skill. The oracles accordingly reached to so high a degree of reputation, that, as Cicero observes, no expedition for a long time was undertaken, no colony sent out, and often no affair of any distinguished family or individual entered on, without the previously obtaining their judgment and sanction. Their authority in a word was so high, that the first fathers of the Christian church could no otherwise account for a reputation thus universally received, than by supposing that the devils were permitted by God Almighty to inform the oracles with a more than human prescience, that all the world might be concluded in idolatry and unbelief[b], and the necessity of a Saviour be made more apparent. The gullibility of man is one of the most prominent features of our nature. Various

---

[b] Romans, xi. 32.

periods and times, when whole nations have as it were with one consent run into the most incredible and the grossest absurdities, perpetually offer themselves in the page of history; and in the records of remote antiquity it plainly appears that such delusions continued through successive centuries.

THE DESIRE TO COMMAND AND CONTROL FUTURE EVENTS.

Next to the consideration of those measures by which men have sought to dive into the secrets of future time, the question presents itself of those more daring undertakings, the object of which has been by some supernatural power to control the future, and place it in subjection to the will of the unlicensed adventurer. Men have always, especially in ages of ignorance, and when they most felt their individual weakness, figured to themselves an invisible strength greater than their own; and, in proportion to their impatience, and the fervour of their desires, have sought to enter into a league with those beings whose mightier force might supply that in which their weakness failed.

COMMERCE WITH THE INVISIBLE WORLD.

It is an essential feature of different ages and countries to vary exceedingly in the good or ill construction, the fame or dishonour, which shall attend upon the same conduct or mode of behaviour. In Egypt and throughout the East, especially in the early periods of history, the supposed commerce with invisible powers was openly professed, which, under other circumstances, and during the reign of different prejudices, was afterwards carefully concealed, and barbarously hunted out of the pale of allowed and authorised practice. The Magi of old, who claimed a power of producing miraculous appearances, and boasted a familiar intercourse with the world of spirits, were regarded by their countrymen with peculiar reverence, and considered as the first and chiefest men in the state. For this mitigated view of such dark and mysterious proceedings the ancients were in a great degree indebted to their polytheism. The Romans are computed to have acknowledged thirty thousand divinities, to all of whom was rendered a legitimate homage; and other countries in a similar proportion.

SORCERY AND ENCHANTMENT.

In Asia, however, the Gods were divided into two parties, under Oromasdes, the principle of good, and Arimanius, the principle of evil. These powers were in perpetual contention with each other, sometimes the one, and sometimes the other gaining the superiority. Arimanius and his legions were therefore scarcely considered as entitled to the homage of mankind. Those who were actuated by benevolence, and who desired to draw down blessings upon their fellow-creatures, addressed themselves to the principle of good; while such unhappy beings, with whom spite and ill-will had the predominance, may be supposed often to have invoked in preference the principle of evil. Hence seems to have originated the idea of sorcery, or an appeal by incantations and wicked arts to the demons who delighted in mischief.

These beings rejoiced in the opportunity of inflicting calamity and misery on mankind. But by what we read of them we might be induced to suppose that they were in some way restrained from gratifying their malignant intentions, and waited in eager hope, till some mortal reprobate should call out their dormant activity, and demand their aid.

Various enchantments were therefore employed by those unhappy mortals whose special desire was to bring down calamity and plagues upon the individuals or tribes of men against whom their animosity was directed. Unlawful and detested words and mysteries were called into action to conjure up demons who should yield their powerful and tremendous assistance. Songs of a wild and maniacal character were chaunted. Noisome scents and the burning of all unhallowed and odious things were resorted to. In later times books and formulas of a terrific character were commonly employed, upon the reading or recital of which the prodigies resorted to began to display themselves. The heavens were darkened; the thunder rolled; and fierce and blinding lightnings flashed from one corner of the heavens to the other. The earth quaked and rocked from side to side. All monstrous and deformed things shewed themselves, " Gorgons, and Hydras, and Chimeras dire," enough to cause the stoutest heart to quail. Lastly, devils, whose name was legion, and to whose forms and distorted and menacing countenances superstition had annexed the most frightful ideas, crowded in countless multitudes upon the spectator, whose breath was flame, whose dances were full of terror, and whose strength infinitely exceeded every thing human. Such were the appalling conceptions which ages of bigotry and ignorance annexed to the notion of sorcery, and with these they scared the unhappy beings over whom this notion had usurped an ascendancy into lunacy, and prepared them for the perpetrating flagitious and unheard-of deeds.

The result of these horrible incantations was not less tremendous, than the preparations might have led us to expect. The demons possessed all the powers of the air, and produced tempests and shipwrecks at their pleasure. " Castles toppled on their warder's heads, and palaces and pyramids sloped their summits to their foundations;" forests and mountains were torn from their roots, and cast into the sea. They inflamed the passions of men, and caused them to commit the most unheard-of excesses. They laid their ban on those who enjoyed the most prosperous health, condemned them to peak and pine, wasted them into a melancholy atrophy, and finally consigned them to a premature grave. They breathed a new and unblest life into beings in whom existence had long been extinct, and by their hateful and resistless power caused the sepulchres to give up their dead.

WITCHCRAFT.

Next to sorcery we may recollect the case of witchcraft, which occurs oftener, particularly in modern times, than any other alleged mode of changing by supernatural means the future course of events. The sorcerer, as we shall see hereafter, was frequently a man of learning and intellectual abilities, sometimes of comparative opulence and respectable situation in society. But the witch or wizard was almost uniformly old, decrepid, and nearly or altogether in a state of penury. The functions however of the witch and the sorcerer were in a great degree the same. The earliest account of a witch, attended with any degree of detail, is that of the witch of Endor in the Bible, who among other things, professed the power of calling up the dead upon occasion from the peace of the sepulchre. Witches also claimed the faculty of raising storms, and in various ways disturbing the course of nature. They appear in most cases to have been brought into action by the impulse of private malice. They occasioned mortality of greater or less extent in man and beast. They blighted the opening prospect of a plentiful harvest. They covered the heavens with clouds, and sent abroad withering and malignant blasts. They undermined the health of those who were so unfortunate as to incur their animosity, and caused them to waste away gradually with incurable disease. They were notorious two or three centuries ago for the power of the "evil eye." The vulgar, both great and small, dreaded their displeasure, and sought, by small gifts, and fair speeches, but insincere, and the offspring of terror only, to avert the pernicious consequences of their malice. They were famed for fabricating small images of wax, to represent the object of their persecution; and, as these by gradual and often studiously protracted degrees wasted before the fire, so the unfortunate butts of their resentment perished with a lingering, but inevitable death.

COMPACTS WITH THE DEVIL.

The power of these witches, as we find in their earliest records, originated in their intercourse with "familiar spirits," invisible beings who must be supposed to be enlisted in the armies of the prince of darkness. We do not read in these ancient memorials of any league of mutual benefit entered into between the merely human party, and his or her supernatural assistant. But modern times have amply supplied this defect. The witch or sorcerer could not secure the assistance of the demon but by a sure and faithful compact, by which the human party obtained the industrious and vigilant service of his familiar for a certain term of years, only on condition that, when the term was expired, the demon of undoubted right was to obtain possession of the indentured party, and to convey him irremissibly and for ever to the regions of the damned. The contract was drawn out in authentic form, signed by the sorcerer, and attested with his blood, and was then carried away by the demon, to be produced again at the appointed time.

IMPS.

These familiar spirits often assumed the form of animals, and a black dog or cat was considered as a figure in which the attendant devil was secretly hidden. These subordinate devils were called Imps. Impure and carnal ideas were mingled with these theories. The witches were said to have preternatural teats from which their familiars sucked their blood. The devil also engaged in sexual intercourse with the witch or wizard, being denominated *incubus*, if his favourite were a woman, and *succubus*, if a man. In short, every frightful and loathsome idea was carefully heaped up together, to render the unfortunate beings to whom the crime of witchcraft was imputed the horror and execration of their species.

TALISMANS AND AMULETS.

As according to the doctrine of witchcraft, there were certain compounds, and matters prepared by rules of art, that proved baleful and deadly to the persons against whom their activity was directed, so there were also preservatives, talismans, amulets and charms, for the most to be worn about the person, which rendered him superior to injury, not only from the operations of witchcraft, but in some cases from the sword or any other mortal weapon. As the poet says, he that had this,

> Might trace huge forests and unhallowed heaths,—
> Yea there, where very desolation dwells,
> By grots and caverns shagged with horrid shades,

nay, in the midst of every tremendous assailant, "might pass on with unblenched majesty," uninjured and invulnerable.

NECROMANCY.

Last of all we may speak of necromancy, which

has something in it that so strongly takes hold of the imagination, that, though it is one only of the various modes which have been enumerated for the exercise of magical power, we have selected it to give a title to the present volume.

There is something sacred to common apprehension in the repose of the dead. They seem placed beyond our power to disturb. " There is no work, nor device, nor knowledge, nor wisdom in the grave."

> After life's fitful fever they sleep well :
> Nor steel, nor poison,
> Malice domestic, foreign levy, nothing,
> Can touch them further.

Their remains moulder in the earth. Neither form nor feature is long continued to them. We shrink from their touch, and their sight. To violate the sepulchre therefore for the purpose of unholy spells and operations, as we read of in the annals of witchcraft, cannot fail to be exceedingly shocking. To call up the spirits of the departed, after they have fulfilled the task of life, and are consigned to their final sleep, is sacrilegious. Well may they exclaim, like the ghost of Samuel in the sacred story, " Why hast thou disquieted me?"

There is a further circumstance in the case, which causes us additionally to revolt from the very idea of necromancy, strictly so called. Man is a mortal, or an immortal being. His frame either wholly " returns to the earth as it was, or his spirit," the thinking principle within him, " to God who gave it." The latter is the prevailing sentiment of mankind in modern times. Man is placed upon earth in a state of probation, to be dealt with hereafter according to the deeds done in the flesh. " Some shall go away into everlasting punishment; and others into life eternal." In this case there is something blasphemous in the idea of intermedding with the state of the dead. We must leave them in the hands of God. Even on the idea of an interval, the " sleep of the soul" from death to the general resurrection, which is the creed of no contemptible sect of Christians, it is surely a terrific notion that we should disturb the pause, which upon that hypothesis, the laws of nature have assigned to the departed soul, and come to awake, or to " torment him before the time."

ALCHEMY.

To make our catalogue of supernatural doings, and the lawless imaginations of man, the more complete, it may be further necessary to refer to the craft, so eagerly cultivated in successive ages of the world of converting the inferior metals into gold, to which was usually joined the *elixir vitæ*, or universal medicine, having the quality of renewing the youth of man, and causing him to live for ever. The first authentic record on this subject is an edict of Dioclesian about three hundred years after

Christ, ordering a diligent search to be made in Egypt for all the ancient books which treated of the art of making gold and silver, that they might without distinction be consigned to the flames. This edict however necessarily presumes a certain antiquity to the pursuit; and fabulous history has recorded Solomon, Pythagoras and Hermes among its distinguished votaries. From this period the study seems to have slept, till it was revived among the Arabians after a lapse of five or six hundred years.

It is well known however how eagerly it was cultivated in various countries of the world for many centuries after it was divulged by Geber. Men of the most wonderful talents devoted their lives to the investigation; and in multiplied instances the discovery was said to have been completed. Vast sums of money were consumed in the fruitless endeavour; and in a later period it seems to have furnished an excellent handle to vain and specious projectors, to extort money from those more amply provided with the goods of fortune than themselves.

The art no doubt is in itself sufficiently mystical, having been pursued by multitudes, who seemed to themselves ever on the eve of consummation, but as constantly baffled when to their own apprehension most on the verge of success. The discovery indeed appears upon the face of it to be of the most delicate nature, as the benefit must wholly depend upon its being reserved to one or a very few, the object being unbounded wealth, which is nothing unless confined. If the power of creating gold is diffused, wealth by such diffusion becomes poverty, and every thing after a short time would but return to what it had been. Add to which, that the nature of discovery has ordinarily been, that, when once the clue has been found, it reveals itself to several about the same period of time.

The art, as we have said, is in its own nature sufficiently mystical, depending on nice combinations and proportions of ingredients, and upon the addition of each ingredient being made exactly in the critical moment, and in the precise degree of heat, indicated by the colour of the vapour arising from the crucible or retort. This was watched by the operator with inexhaustible patience; and it was often found or supposed, that the minutest error in this respect caused the most promising appearances to fail of the expected success. This circumstance no doubt occasionally gave an opportunity to an artful impostor to account for his miscarriage, and thus to prevail upon his credulous dupe to enable him to begin his tedious experiment again.

But, beside this, it appears that those whose object was the transmutation of metals, very frequently joined to this pursuit the study of astrology, and even the practice of sorcery. So much delicacy and nicety were supposed to be required in the process for the transmutation of metals, that it could not hope to succeed but under a favourable conjunction of the planets; and the most flourishing pretenders to the art boasted that they had also a familiar intercourse with certain spirits of supernatural power, which assisted them in their undertakings, and enabled them to penetrate into things undiscoverable to mere human sagacity, and to predict future events.

FAIRIES.

Another mode in which the wild and erratic imagination of our ancestors manifested itself, was in the creation of a world of visionary beings of a less terrific character, but which did not fail to annoy their thoughts, and perplex their determinations, known by the name of Fairies.

There are few things more worthy of contemplation, and that at the same time tend to place the dispositions of our ancestors in a more amiable point of view, than the creation of this airy and fantastic race. They were so diminutive as almost to elude the organs of human sight. They were at large, even though confined to the smallest dimensions. They "could be bounded in a nutshell, and count themselves kings of infinite space."

> Their midnight revels, by a forest-side
> Or fountain, the belated peasant saw,
> Or dreamed he saw, while overhead the moon
> Sat arbitress, and nearer to the earth
> Wheeled her pale course—they, on their mirth and dance
> Intent, with jocund music charmed his ear;
> At once with joy and fear his heart rebounds.

Small circles marked the grass in solitary places, the trace of their little feet, which, though narrow, were ample enough to afford every accommodation to their pastime.

The fairy tribes appear to have been every where distinguished for their patronage of truth, simplicity and industry, and their abhorrence of sensuality and prevarication. They left little rewards in secret, as tokens of their approbation of the virtues they loved, and by their supernatural power afforded a supplement to pure and excellent intentions, when the corporeal powers of the virtuous sank under the pressure of human infirmity. Where they conceived displeasure, the punishments they inflicted were for the most part such as served moderately to vex and harass the offending party, rather than to inflict upon him permanent and irremediable evils.

> Their airy tongues would syllable men's names
> On sands, and shores, and desert wildernesses.

They were supposed to guide the wandering lights, that in the obscurity of the night beguiled the weary traveller "through bog, through bush, through brake, through briar." But their power of evil only extended, or was only employed, to vex those who by a certain obliquity of conduct gave occasion for their reproofs. They besides pinched and otherwise tormented the objects of their displeasure; and, though the mischiefs they executed were not of the most vital kind, yet, coming from a supernatural enemy, and being inflicted by invisible hands, they could not fail greatly to disturb and disorder those who suffered from them.

There is at first sight a great inconsistency in the representations of these imaginary people. For the most part they are described to us as of a stature and appearance, almost too slight to be marked by our grosser human organs. At other times however, and especially in the extremely popular tales digested by M. Perrault, they shew themselves in indiscriminate assemblies, brought together for some solemn festivity or otherwise, and join the human frequenters of the scene, without occasioning enquiry or surprise. They are particularly concerned in the business of summarily and without appeal bestowing miraculous gifts, sometimes as a mark of special friendship and favour, and sometimes with a malicious and hostile intention. — But we are to consider that spirits

> Can every form assume; so soft
> And uncompounded is their essence pure;
> Not tied or manacled with joint or limb,
> Like cumbrous flesh; but, in what shape they choose,
> Dilated or condensed, bright or obscure,
> Can execute their airy purposes,
> And works of love or enmity fulfil.

And then again, as their bounties were shadowy, so were they specially apt to disappear in a moment, the most splendid palaces and magnificent exhibitions vanishing away, and leaving their disconcerted dupe with his robes converted into the poorest rags, and, instead of glittering state, finding himself suddenly in the midst of desolation, and removed no man knew whither.

One of the mischiefs that were most frequently imputed to them, was the changing the beautiful child of some doating parents, for a babe marked with ugliness and deformity. But this idea seems fraught with inconsistency. The natural stature of the fairy is of the smallest dimensions; and, though they could occasionally dilate their figure so as to imitate humanity, yet it is to be presumed that this was only for a special purpose, and, that purpose obtained, that they shrank again habitually into their characteristic littleness. The change therefore can only be supposed to have been of one human child for another.

ROSICRUCIANS.

Nothing very distinct has been ascertained respecting a sect, calling itself Rosicrucians. It is said to have originated in the East from one of the crusaders in the fourteenth century; but it attracted at least no public notice till the beginning of the seventeenth century. Its adherents appear to have imbibed their notions from the Arabians, and claimed the possession of the philosopher's stone, the art of transmuting metals, and the *elixir vitæ*.

SYLPHS AND GNOMES, SALAMANDERS AND UNDINES.

But that for which they principally excited public attention, was their creed respecting certain elementary beings, which to grosser eyes are invisible, but were familiarly known to the initiated. To be admitted to their acquaintance it was previously necessary that the organs of human sight should be purged by the universal medicine, and that certain glass globes should be chemically prepared with one or other of the four elements, and for one month exposed to the beams of the sun. These preliminary steps being taken, the initiated immediately had a sight of innumerable beings of a luminous substance, but of thin and evanescent structure, that people the elements on all sides of us. Those who inhabited the air were called Sylphs; and those who dwelt in the earth bore the name of Gnomes; such as peopled the fire were Salamanders; and those who made their home in the waters were Undines. Each class appears to have had an extensive power in the elements to which they belonged. They could raise tempests in the air, and storms at sea, shake the earth, and alarm the inhabitants of the globe with the sight of devouring flames. These appear however to have been more formidable in appearance than in reality. And the whole race was subordinate to man, and particularly subject to the initiated. The gnomes, inhabitants of the earth and the mines, liberally supplied to the human beings with whom they conversed, the hidden treasures over which they presided. The four classes were some of them male, and some female; but the female sex seems to have preponderated in all.

These elementary beings, we are told, were by their constitution more long-lived than man, but with this essential disadvantage, that at death they wholly ceased to exist. In the mean time they were inspired with an earnest desire for immortality; and there was one way left for them, by which this desire might be gratified. If they were so happy as to awaken in any of the initiated a passion the end of which was marriage, then the sylph who became the bride of a virtuous man, followed his nature, and became immortal; while on the other hand, if she united herself to an immoral being and a profligate, the husband followed the law of the wife, and was rendered entirely mortal. The initiated however were required, as a condition to their being admitted into the secrets of the order, to engage themselves in a vow of perpetual chastity as to women. And they were abundantly rewarded by the probability of being united to a sylph, a gnome, a salamander, or an undine, any one of whom was inexpressibly more enchanting than the most beautiful woman, in addition to which her charms were in a manner perpetual, while a wife of our own nature is in a short time destined to wrinkles, and all the other disadvantages of old age. The initiated of course enjoyed a beatitude infinitely greater than that which falls to the lot of ordinary mortals, being conscious of a perpetual commerce with these wonderful beings from whose society the vulgar are debarred, and having such associates unintermittedly anxious to perform their behests, and anticipate their desires[*].

We should have taken but an imperfect survey of the lawless extravagancies of human imagination, if we had not included a survey of this sect. There is something particularly soothing to the fancy of an erratic mind, in the conception of being conversant with a race of beings the very existence of which is unperceived by ordinary mortals, and thus entering into an infinitely numerous and variegated society, even when we are apparently swallowed up in entire solitude.

The Rosicrucians are further entitled to our special notice, as their tenets have had the good fortune to furnish Pope with the beautiful machinery with which he has adorned the Rape of the Lock. There is also, of much later date, a wild and poetical fiction for which we are indebted to the same source, called Undine, from the pen of Lamotte Fouquet.

[*] Comte de Gabalis.

EXAMPLES OF NECROMANCY AND WITCHCRAFT FROM THE BIBLE.

THE oldest and most authentic record from which we can derive our ideas on the subject of necromancy and witchcraft, unquestionably is the Bible. The Egyptians and Chaldeans were early distinguished for their supposed proficiency in magic, in the production of supernatural phenomena, and in penetrating into the secrets of future time. The first appearance of men thus extraordinarily gifted, or advancing pretensions of this sort, recorded in Scripture, is on occasion of Pharoah's dream of the seven years of plenty, and seven years of famine. At that period the king " sent and called for all the magicians of Egypt and all the wise men; but they could not interpret the dream[a]," which Joseph afterwards expounded.

Their second appearance was upon a most memorable occasion, when Moses and Aaron, armed with miraculous powers, came to a subsequent king of Egypt, to demand from him that their countrymen might be permitted to depart to another tract of the world. They produced a miracle as the evidence of their divine mission: and the king, who was also named Pharoah,

---

[a] Genesis, xli. 8, 25, &c.

"called before him the wise men and the sorcerers of Egypt, who with their enchantments did in like manner" as Moses had done; till, after some experiments in which they were apparently successful, they at length were compelled to allow themselves overcome, and fairly to confess to their master, "This is the finger of God[b]!"

The spirit of the Jewish history loudly affirms, that the Creator of heaven and earth had adopted this nation for his chosen people, and therefore demanded their exclusive homage, and that they should acknowledge no other God. It is on this principle that it is made one of his early commands to them, "Thou shalt not suffer a witch to live[c]." And elsewhere the meaning of this prohibition is more fully explained: "There shall not be found among you any one that useth divination, or an observer of times, or an enchanter, or a witch, or a charmer, or a consulter with familiar spirits, or a wizard, or a necromancer[d]: these shall surely be put to death; they shall stone them with stones[e]."

The character of an enchanter is elsewhere more fully illustrated in the case of Balaam, the soothsayer, who was sent for by Balak, the king of Moab, that he might "curse the people of Israel. The messengers of the king came to Balaam with the rewards of divination in their hand[f];" but the

---

[b] Exodus, vii. 11; viii. 19.   [c] Ibid, xxii. 18.
[d] Deuteronomy, xviii. 10, 11.   [e] Leviticus, xx. 27.
[f] Numbers, xxii. 5, 6, 7.

soothsayer was restrained from his purpose by the God of the Jews, and, where he came to curse, was compelled to bless. He therefore " did not go, as at other times, to seek for enchantments[k]," but took up his discourse, and began, saying, " Surely there is no enchantment against Jacob, neither is there any divination against Israel[h]!"

Another example of necromantic power or pretension is to be found in the story of Saul and the witch of Endor. Saul, the first king of the Jews, being rejected by God, and obtaining " no answer to his enquiries, either by dreams, or by prophets, said to his servants, seek me a woman that has a familiar spirit. And his servants, said, Lo, there is a woman that has a familiar spirit at Endor." Saul accordingly had recourse to her. But, previously to this time, in conformity to the law of God, he " had cut off those that had familiar spirits, and the wizards out of the land;" and the woman therefore was terrified at his present application. Saul re-assured her; and in consequence the woman consented to call up the person he should name Saul demanded of her to bring up the ghost of Samuel. The ghost, whether by her enchantments or through divine interposition we are not told, appeared, and prophesied to Saul, that he and his son should fall in battle on the succeeding day[l], which accordingly came to pass.

[k] Numbers, xxiv. 1.   [h] Ibid, xxiii. 23.
[l] 1 Sam. xxviii. 6, *et seq.*

Manasseh, a subsequent king in Jerusalem, "observed times, and used enchantments, and dealt with familiar spirits and wizards, and so provoked God to anger[k]."

It appears plainly from the same authority, that there were good spirits and evil spirits. "The Lord said, Who shall persuade Ahab, that he may go up, and fall before Ramoth Gilead? And there came a spirit, and stood before the Lord, and said, I will persuade him: I will go forth, and be a lying spirit in the mouth of all his prophets. And the Lord said, Thou shalt persuade him[l]."

In like manner, we are told, "Satan stood up against Israel, and provoked David to number the people; and God was displeased with the thing, and smote Israel, so that there fell of the people seventy thousand men[m]."

Satan also, in the Book of Job, presented himself before the Lord among the Sons of God, and asked and obtained leave to try the faithfulness of Job by " putting forth his hand," and despoiling the patriarch of " all that he had."

Taking these things into consideration, there can be no reasonable doubt, though the devil and Satan are not mentioned in the story, that the serpent who in so crafty a way beguiled Eve, was in reality no other than the malevolent enemy of mankind under that disguise.

[k] 2 Kings, xxi. 6.   [l] 1 Kings, xxii. 20, *et seqq.*
[m] 1 Chron. xxi. 1, 7, 14.

We are in the same manner informed of the oracles of the false Gods; and an example occurs of a king of Samaria, who fell sick, and who " sent messengers, and said to them, Go, and enquire of Baalzebub, the God of Ekron, whether I shall recover of this disease." At which proceeding the God of the Jews was displeased, and sent Elijah to the messengers to say, " Is it because there is not a God in Israel, that you go to enquire of Baalzebub, the God of Ekron? Because the king has done this, he shall not recover; he shall surely die"."

The appearance of the Wise Men of the East again occurs in considerable detail in the Prophecy of Daniel, though they are only brought forward there, as discoverers of hidden things, and interpreters of dreams. Twice, on occasion of dreams that troubled him, Nebuchadnezzar, king of Babylon, " commanded to be called to him the magicians, and the astrologers, and the sorcerers, and the Chaldeans" of his kingdom, and each time with similar success. They confessed their incapacity; and Daniel, the prophet of the Jews, expounded to the king that in which they had failed. Nebuchadnezzar in consequence promoted Daniel to be master of the magicians. A similar scene occurred in the court of Belshazzar, the son of Nebuchadnezzar, in the case of the hand-writing on the wall.

" 2 Kings, i. 2, 3, 4.

It is probable that the Jews considered the Gods of the nations around them as so many of the fallen angels, or spirits of hell, since, among other arguments, the coincidence of the name of Beelzebub, the prince of devils[n], with Baalzebub, the God of Ekron, could scarcely have fallen out by chance.

It seemed necessary to enter into these particulars, as they occur in the oldest and most authentic records from which we can derive our ideas on the subject of necromancy, witchcraft, and the claims that were set up in ancient times to the exercise of magcial power. Among these examples there is only one, that of the contention for superiority between Moses and the Wise Men of Egypt in which we are presented with their pretensions to a visible exhibition of supernatural effects.

THE MAGI, OR WISE MEN OF THE EAST.

The Magi, or Wise Men of the East, extended their ramifications over Egypt, Babylonia, Persia, India, and probably, though with a different name, over China, and indeed the whole known world. Their profession was of a mysterious nature. They laid claim to a familiar intercourse with the Gods. They placed themselves as mediators between heaven and earth, assumed the prerogative of re-

---

[n] Matthew, xii. 24.

vealing the will of beings of a nature superior to man, and pretended to shew wonders and prodigies that surpassed any power which was merely human.

To understand this, we must bear in mind the state of knowledge in ancient times, where for the most part the cultivation of the mind, and an acquaintance with either science or art, were confined to a very small part of the population. In each of the nations we have mentioned, there was a particular caste or tribe of men, who, by the prerogative of their birth, were entitled to the advantages of science and a superior education, while the rest of their countrymen were destined to subsist by manual labour. This of necessity gave birth in the privileged few to an overweening sense of their own importance. They scarcely regarded the rest of their countrymen as beings of the same species with themselves; and, finding a strong line of distinction cutting them off from the herd, they had recourse to every practicable method for making that distinction still stronger. Wonder is one of the most obvious means of generating deference; and, by keeping to themselves the grounds and process of their skill, and presenting the results only, they were sure to excite the admiration and reverence of their contemporaries. This mode of proceeding further produced a re-action upon themselves. That which supplied and promised to supply to them so large a harvest of honour and fame, unavoidably became precious in their eyes. They pursued their discoveries with avidity, because few had access to their opportunities in that respect, and because, the profounder were their researches, the more sure they were of being looked up to by the public as having that in them which was sacred and inviolable. They spent their days and nights in these investigations. They shrank from no privation and labour. At the same time that in these labours they had at all times an eye to their darling object, an ascendancy over the minds of their countrymen at large, and the extorting from them a blind and implicit deference to their oracular decrees. They however loved their pursuits for the pursuits themselves. They felt their abstraction and their unlimited nature, and on that account contemplated them with admiration. They valued them (for such is the indestructible character of the human mind) for the pains they had bestowed on them. The sweat of their brow grew into a part as it were of the intrinsic merit of the articles; and that which had with so much pains been attained by them, they could not but regard as of inestimable worth.

EGYPT.

The Egyptians took the lead in early antiquity, with respect to civilisation and the stupendous productions of human labour and art, of all other known nations of the world. The pyramids stand by themselves as a monument of the industry of mankind. Thebes, with her hundred gates, at each of which we are told she could send out at once two hundred chariots and ten thousand warriors completely accoutred, was one of the noblest cities on record. The whole country of Lower Egypt was intersected with canals giving a beneficent direction to the periodical inundations of the Nile; and the artificial lake Moeris was dug of a vast extent, that it might draw off the occasional excesses of the overflowings of the river. The Egyptians had an extraordinary custom of preserving their dead, so that the country was peopled almost as numerously with mummies prepared by extreme assiduity and skill, as with the living.

And, in proportion to their edifices and labours of this durable sort, was their unwearied application to all the learning that was then known. Geometry is said to have owed its existence to the necessity under which they were placed of every man recognising his own property in land, as soon as the overflowings of the Nile had ceased. They were not less assiduous in their application to astronomy. The hieroglyphics of Egypt are of universal notoriety. Their mythology was of the most complicated nature. Their Gods were infinitely varied in their kind; and the modes of their worship not less endlessly diversified. All these particulars still contributed to the abstraction of their studies, and the loftiness of their pretensions to knowledge.

They perpetually conversed with the invisible world, and laid claim to the faculty of revealing things hidden, of foretelling future events, and displaying wonders that exceeded human power to produce.

A striking illustration of the state of Egypt in that respect in early times, occurs incidentally in the history of Joseph in the Bible. Jacob had twelve sons, among whom his partiality for Joseph was so notorious, that his brethren out of envy sold him as a slave to the wandering Midianites. Thus it was his fortune to be placed in Egypt, where in the process of events he became the second man in the country, and chief minister of the king. A severe famine having visited these climates, Jacob sent his sons into Egypt to buy corn, where only it was to be found. As soon as Joseph saw them, he knew them, though they knew not him in his exalted situation; and he set himself to devise expedients to settle them permanently in the country in which he ruled. Among the rest he caused a precious cup from his stores to be privily conveyed into the corn-sack of Benjamin, his only brother by the same mother. The brothers were no sooner departed, than Joseph sent in pursuit of them; and the messengers accosted them with the words, "Is not this the cup in which my lord drinketh, and whereby also he divineth? Ye have done evil in taking it away*." They brought the

* Genesis, xliv. 5.

strangers again into the presence of Joseph, who addressed them with severity, saying, " What is this deed that ye have done? Wot ye not that such a man as I could certainly divine[b]?"

From this story it plainly appears, that the art of divination was extensively exercised in Egypt, that the practice was held in honour, and that such was the state of the country, that it was to be presumed as a thing of course, that a man of the high rank and distinction of Joseph should professedly be an adept in it.

In the great contention for supernatural power between Moses and the magicians of Egypt, it is plain that they came forward with confidence, and did not shrink from the debate. Moses's rod was turned into a serpent; so were their rods: Moses changed the waters of Egypt into blood; and the magicians did the like with their enchantments: Moses caused frogs to come up, and cover the land of Egypt; and the magicians also brought frogs upon the country. Without its being in any way necessary to enquire how they effected these wonders, it is evident from the whole train of the narrative, that they must have been much in the practice of astonishing their countrymen with their feats in such a kind, and, whether it were delusion, or to whatever else we may attribute their success, that they were universally looked up to for the extraordinariness of their performances.

[b] Genesis, xliv. 15.

While we are on this subject of illustrations from the Bible, it may be worth while to revert more particularly to the story of Balaam. Balak the king of Moab, sent for Balaam that he might come and curse the invaders of his country; and in the sequel we are told, when the prophet changed his curses into a blessing, that he did not "go forth, as at other times, to seek for enchantments." It is plain therefore that Balak did not rely singly upon the eloquence and fervour of Balaam to pour out vituperations upon the people of Israel, but that it was expected that the prophet should use incantations and certain mystical rites, upon which the efficacy of his foretelling disaster to the enemy principally depended.

STATUE OF MEMNON.

The Magi of Egypt looked round in every quarter for phenomena that might produce astonishment among their countrymen, and induce them to believe that they dwelt in a land which overflowed with the testimonies and presence of a divine power. Among others the statue of Memnon, erected over his tomb near Thebes, is recorded by many authors. Memnon is said to have been the son of Aurora, the Goddess of the morning; and his statue is related to have had the peculiar faculty of uttering a melodious sound every morning when touched by the first beams of day, as if to salute his mother; and every night at sunset to have imparted another sound, low and mournful, as lamenting the departure of the day. This prodigy is spoken of by Tacitus, Strabo, Juvenal and Philostratus. The statue uttered these sounds, while perfect; and, when it was mutilated by human violence, or by a convulsion of nature, it still retained the property with which it had been originally endowed. Modern travellers, for the same phenomenon has still been observed, have asserted that it does not owe its existence to any prodigy, but to a property of the granite, of which the statue or its pedestal is formed, which, being hollow, is found in various parts of the world to exhibit this quality. It has therefore been suggested, that the priests, having ascertained its peculiarity, expressly formed the statue of that material, for the purpose of impressing on it a supernatural character, and thus being enabled to extend their influence with a credulous people[a].

TEMPLE OF JUPITER AMMON: ITS ORACLES.

Another of what may be considered as the wonders of Egypt, is the temple of Jupiter Ammon in the midst of the Great Desert. This temple was situated at a distance of no less than twelve days' journey from Memphis, the capital of the Lower Egypt. The principal part of this space consisted of one

[a] Brewster on Natural Magic, Letter IX.

immense tract of moving sand, so hot as to be intolerable to the sole of the foot, while the air was pregnant with fire, so that it was almost impossible to breathe in it. Not a drop of water, not a tree, not a blade of grass, was to be found through this vast surface. It was here that Cambyses, engaged in an impious expedition to demolish the temple, is said to have lost an army of fifty thousand men, buried in the sands. When you arrived however, you were presented with a wood of great circumference, the foliage of which was so thick that the beams of the sun could not pierce it. The atmosphere of the place was of a delicious temperature; the scene was every where interspersed with fountains; and all the fruits of the earth were found in the highest perfection. In the midst was the temple and oracle of the God, who was worshipped in the likeness of a ram. The Egyptian priests chose this site as furnishing a test of the zeal of their votaries; the journey being like the pilgrimage to Jerusalem or Mecca, if not from so great a distance, yet attended in many respects with perils more formidable. It was not safe to attempt the passage but with moderate numbers, and those expressly equipped for expedition.

Bacchus is said to have visited this spot in his great expedition to the East, when Jupiter appeared to him in the form of a ram, having struck his foot upon the soil, and for the first time occasioned that supply of water, with which the place was ever after plentifully supplied. Alexander the Great in a subsequent age undertook the same journey with his army, that he might cause himself to be acknowledged for the son of the God, under which character he was in all due form recognised. The priests no doubt had heard of the successful battles of the Granicus and of Issus, of the capture of Tyre after a seven months' siege, and of the march of the great conqueror in Egypt, where he carried every thing before him.

Here we are presented with a striking specimen of the mode and spirit in which the oracles of old were accustomed to be conducted. It may be said that the priests were corrupted by the rich presents which Alexander bestowed on them with a liberal hand. But this was not the prime impulse in the business. They were astonished at the daring with which Alexander with a comparative handful of men set out from Greece, having meditated the overthrow of the great Persian empire. They were astonished with his perpetual success, and his victorious progress from the Hellespont to mount Taurus, from mount Taurus to Pelusium, and from Pelusium quite across the ancient kingdom of Egypt to the Palus Mareotis. Accustomed to the practice of adulation, and to the belief that mortal power and true intellectual greatness were the same, they with a genuine enthusiastic fervour regarded Alexander as the son of their God, and acknowledged him as such.—

Nothing can be more memorable than the way in which belief and unbelief hold a divided empire over the human mind, our passions hurrying us into belief, at the same time that our intervals of sobriety suggest to us that it is all pure imposition.

CHALDEA AND BABYLON.

The history of the Babylonish monarchy not having been handed down to us, except incidentally as it is touched upon by the historians of other countries, we know little of those anecdotes respecting it which are best calculated to illustrate the habits and manners of a people. We know that they in probability preceded all other nations in the accuracy of their observations on the phenomena of the heavenly bodies. We know that the Magi were highly respected among them as an order in the state; and that, when questions occurred exciting great alarm in the rulers, "the magicians, the astrologers, the sorcerers, and the Chaldeans," were called together, to see whether by their arts they could throw light upon questions so mysterious and perplexing, and we find sufficient reason, both from analogy, and from the very circumstance that sorcerers are specifically named among the classes of which their Wise Men consisted, to believe that the Babylonian Magi advanced no dubious pretensions to the exercise of magical power.

ZOROASTER.

Among the Chaldeans the most famous name is that of Zoroaster, who is held to have been the author of their religion, their civil policy, their sciences, and their magic. He taught the doctrine of two great principles, the one the author of good, the other of evil. He prohibited the use of images in the ceremonies of religion, and pronounced that nothing deserved homage but fire, and the sun, the centre and the source of fire, and these perhaps to be venerated not for themselves, but as emblematical of the principle of all good things. He taught astronomy and astrology. We may with sufficient probability infer his doctrines from those of the Magi, who were his followers. He practised enchantments, by means of which he would send a panic among the forces that were brought to make war against him, rendering the conflict by force of arms unnecessary. He prescribed the use of certain herbs as all-powerful for the production of supernatural effects. He pretended to the faculty of working miracles, and of superseding and altering the ordinary course of nature.—There was, beside the Chaldean Zoroaster, a Persian known by the same name, who is said to have been a contemporary of Darius Hystaspes.

GREECE.

THUS obscure and general is our information respecting the Babylonians. But it was far otherwise with the Greeks. Long before the period, when, by their successful resistance to the Persian invasion, they had rendered themselves of paramount importance in the history of the civilised world, they had their poets and annalists, who preserved to future time the memory of their tastes, their manners and superstitions, their strength, and their weakness. Homer in particular had already composed his two great poems, rendering the peculiarities of his countrymen familiar to the latest posterity. The consequence of this is, that the wonderful things of early Greece are even more frequent than the record of its sober facts. As men advance in observation and experience, they are compelled more and more to perceive that all the phenomena of nature are one vast chain of uninterrupted causes and consequences: but to the eye of uninstructed ignorance every thing is astonishing, every thing is unexpected. The remote generations of mankind are in all cases full of prodigies: but it is the fortune of Greece to have preserved its early adventures, so as to render the beginning pages of its history one mass of impossible falshoods.

DEITIES OF GREECE.

The Gods of the Greeks appear all of them once to have been men. Their real or supposed adventures therefore make a part of what is recorded respecting them. Jupiter was born in Crete, and being secreted by his mother in a cave, was suckled by a goat. Being come to man's estate, he warred with the giants, one of whom had an hundred hands, and two others brethren, grew nine inches every month, and, when nine years old, were fully qualified to engage in all exploits of corporeal strength. The war was finished, by the giants being overwhelmed with the thunderbolts of heaven, and buried under mountains.

Minerva was born from the head of her father, without a mother; and Bacchus, coming into the world after the death of his female parent, was inclosed in the thigh of Jupiter, and was thus produced at the proper time in full vigour and strength. Minerva had a shield, in which was preserved the real head of Medusa, that had the property of turning every one that looked on it into stone. Bacchus, when a child, was seized on by pirates with the intention to sell him for a slave: but he waved a spear, and the oars of the sailors were turned into vines, which climbed the masts, and spread their clusters over the sails; and tigers, lynxes and panthers, appeared to swim round the ship, so terrifying the crew that they leaped overboard, and were changed into dolphins. Bacchus, in his maturity, is described as having been the conqueror of India. He did not set out on this expedition like other conquerors, at the head of an army. He rode in an open chariot, which was drawn by tame lions. His attendants were men and women in great multitudes, eminently accomplished in the arts of rural industry. Wherever he came, he taught men the science of husbandry, and the cultivation of the vine. Wherever he came, he was received, not with hostility, but with festivity and welcome. On his return however, Lycurgus, king of Thrace, and Pentheus, king of Thebes, set themselves in opposition to the improvements which the East had received with the most lively gratitude; and Bacchus, to punish them, caused Lycurgus to be torn to pieces by wild horses, and spread a delusion among the family of Pentheus, so that they mistook him for a wild boar which had broken into their vineyards, and of consequence fell upon him, and he expired amidst a thousand wounds.

Apollo was the author of plagues and contagious diseases; at the same time that, when he pleased, he could restore salubrity to a climate, and health and vigour to the sons of men. He was the father of poetry, and possessed in an eminent degree the gift of foretelling future events. Hecate, which was one of the names of Diana, was distinguished as the Goddess of magic and enchantments. Venus was the Goddess of love, the most irresistible and omnipotent impulse of which the heart of man is susceptible. The wand of Mercury was endowed with such virtues, that whoever it touched, if asleep, would start up into life and alacrity, and, if awake, would immediately fall into a profound sleep. When it touched the dying, their souls gently parted from their mortal frame; and, when it was applied to the dead, the dead returned to life. Neptune had the attribute of raising and appeasing tempests: and Vulcan, the artificer of heaven and earth, not only produced the most exquisite specimens of skill, but also constructed furniture that was endowed with a self-moving principle, and would present itself for use or recede at the will of its proprietor. Pluto, in perpetrating the rape of Proserpine, started up in his chariot through a cleft of the earth in the vale of Enna in Sicily, and, having seized his prize, disappeared again by the way that he came.

Ceres, the mother of Proserpine, in her search after her lost daughter, was received with peculiar hospitality by Celeus, king of Eleusis. She became desirous of remunerating his liberality by some special favour. She saw his only child laid in a cradle, and labouring under a fatal distemper. She took him under her protection. She fed him with milk from her own breast, and at night covered him with coals of fire. Under this treatment he not only recovered his strength, but shot up miraculously into manhood, so that what in other men is the effect of years, was accomplished in Triptolemus in as many hours. She gave him for a gift the art of agriculture, so that he is said to have been the first to teach mankind to sow and to reap corn, and to make bread of the produce.

Prometheus, one of the race of the giants, was peculiarly distinguished for his proficiency in the arts. Among other extraordinary productions he formed a man of clay, of such exquisite workmanship, as to have wanted nothing but a living soul to cause him to be acknowledged as the paragon of the world. Minerva beheld the performance of Prometheus with approbation, and offered him her assistance. She conducted him to heaven, where he watched his opportunity to carry off on the tip of his wand a portion of celestial fire from the chariot of the sun. With this he animated his image; and the man of Prometheus moved, and thought, and spoke, and became every thing that the fondest wishes of his creator could ask. Jupiter ordered Vulcan to make a woman, that should surpass this man. All the Gods gave her each one a several gift: Venus gave her the power to charm; the Graces bestowed on her symmetry of limb, and elegance of motion; Apollo the accomplishments of vocal and instrumental music; Mercury the art of persuasive speech; Juno a multitude of rich and gorgeous ornaments;

and Minerva the management of the loom and the needle. Last of all, Jupiter presented her with a sealed box, of which the lid was no sooner unclosed, than a multitude of calamities and evils of all imaginable sorts flew out, only Hope remaining at the bottom.

Deucalion was the son of Prometheus and Pyrrha, his niece. They married. In their time a flood occurred, which as they imagined destroyed the whole human race; they were the only survivors. By the direction of an oracle they cast stones over their shoulders; when, by the divine interposition, the stones cast by Deucalion became men, and those cast by Pyrrha women. Thus the earth was re-peopled.

I have put down a few of these particulars, as containing in several instances the qualities of what is called magic, and thus furnishing examples of some of the earliest occasions upon which supernatural powers have been alleged to mix with human affairs.

DEMIGODS.

The early history of mortals in Greece is scarcely separated from that of the Gods. The first adventurer that it is perhaps proper to notice, as his exploits have I know not what of magic in them, is Perseus, the founder of the metropolis and kingdom of Mycenæ. By way of rendering his birth illustrious, he is said to have been the son of Jupiter, by Danae, the daughter of Acrisius, king of Argos. The king, being forewarned by an oracle that his daughter should bear a son, by whose hand her father should be deprived of life, thought proper to shut her up in a tower of brass. Jupiter, having metamorphosed himself into a shower of gold, found his way into her place of confinement, and became the father of Perseus. On the discovery of this circumstance, Acrisius caused both mother and child to be inclosed in a chest, and committed to the waves. The chest however drifted upon the lands of a person of royal descent in the island of Seriphos, who extended his care and hospitality to both. When Perseus grew to man's estate, he was commissioned by the king of Seriphos to bring him the head of Medusa, one of the Gorgons. Medusa had the wonderful faculty, that whoever met her eyes was immediately turned into stone; and the king, who had conceived a passion for Danae, sent her son on this enterprise, with the hope that he would never come back alive. He was however favoured by the Gods; Mercury gave him wings to fly, Pluto an invisible helmet, and Minerva a mirror-shield, by looking in which he could discover how his enemy was disposed, without the danger of meeting her eyes. Thus equipped, he accomplished his undertaking, cut off the head of the Gorgon, and pursed it in a bag. From this exploit he proceeded to visit Atlas, king of Mauritania, who refused him hospitality, and in revenge Perseus turned him into stone. He next rescued Andromeda, daughter of the king of Ethiopia, from a monster sent by Neptune to devour her. And, lastly, returning to his mother, and finding the king of Seriphos still incredulous and obstinate, he turned him likewise into a stone.

The labours of Hercules, the most celebrated of the Greeks of the heroic age, appear to have had little of magic in them, but to have been indebted for their success to a corporal strength, superior to that of all other mortals, united with an invincible energy of mind, which disdained to yield to any obstacle that could be opposed to him. His achievements are characteristic of the rude and barbarous age in which he lived: he strangled serpents, and killed the Erymanthian boar, the Nemæan lion, and the Hydra.

DÆDALUS.

Nearly contemporary with the labours of Hercules is the history of Pasiphae and the Minotaur; and this brings us again within the sphere of magic. Pasiphae was the wife of Minos, king of Crete, who conceived an unnatural passion for a beautiful white bull, which Neptune had presented to the king. Having found the means of gratifying her passion, she became the mother of a monster, half-man and half-bull, called the Minotaur. Minos was desirous of hiding this monster from the observation of mankind, and for this purpose applied to Dædalus, an Athenian, the most skilful artist of his time, who is said to have invented the axe, the wedge, and the plummet, and to have found out the use of glue. He first contrived masts and sails for ships, and carved statues so admirably, that they not only looked as if they were alive, but had actually the power of self-motion, and would have escaped from the custody of their possessor, if they had not been chained to the wall.

Dædalus contrived for Minos a labyrinth, a wonderful structure, that covered many acres of ground. The passages in this edifice met and crossed each other with such intricacy, that a stranger who had once entered the building, would have been starved to death before he could find his way out. In this labyrinth Minos shut up the Minotaur. Having conceived a deep resentment against the people of Athens, where his only son had been killed in a riot, he imposed upon them an annual tribute of seven noble youths, and as many virgins to be devoured by the Minotaur. Theseus, son of the king of Athens, put an end to this disgrace. He was taught by Ariadne, the daughter of Minos, how to destroy the monster, and furnished with a clue by which afterwards to find his way out of the labyrinth.

Dædalus for some reason having incurred the displeasure of Minos, was made a prisoner by him in his own labyrinth. But the artist being never at an end of his inventions, contrived with feathers and wax to make a pair of wings for himself, and escaped. Icarus, his son, who was prisoner along with him, was provided by his father with a similar equipment. But the son, who was inexperienced and heedless, approached too near to the sun in his flight; and, the wax of his wings being melted with the heat, he fell into the sea and was drowned.

THE ARGONAUTS.

Contemporary with the reign of Minos occurred the expedition of the Argonauts. Jason, the son of the king of Iolchos in Thessaly, was at the head of this expedition. Its object was to fetch the golden fleece, which was hung up in a grove sacred to Mars, in the kingdom of Colchis, at the eastern extremity of the Euxine sea. He enlisted in this enterprise all the most gallant spirits existing in the country, and among the rest Hercules, Theseus, Orpheus and Amphion. After having passed through a multitude of perils, one of which was occasioned by the Cyanean rocks at the entrance of the Euxine, that had the quality of closing upon every vessel which attempted to make its way between them and crushing it to pieces, a danger that could only be avoided by sending a dove before as their harbinger, they at length arrived.

MEDEA.

The golden fleece was defended by bulls, whose hoofs were brass, and whose breath was fire, and by a never-sleeping dragon that planted itself at the foot of the tree upon which the fleece was suspended. Jason was prepared for his undertaking by Medea, the daughter of the king of the country, herself an accomplished magician, and furnished with philtres, drugs and enchantments. Thus equipped, he tamed the bulls, put a yoke on their necks, and caused them to plough two acres of the stiffest land. He killed the dragon, and, to complete the adventure, drew the monster's teeth, sowed them in the ground, and saw an army of soldiers spring from the seed. The army hastened forward to attack him; but he threw a large stone into the midst of their ranks, when they immediately turned from him, and, falling on each other, were all killed with their mutual weapons.

The adventure being accomplished, Medea set out with Jason on his return to Thessaly. On their arrival, they found Æson, the father of Jason, and Pelias, his uncle, who had usurped the throne, both old and decrepid. Jason applied to Medea, and asked her whether among her charms she had none to make an old man young again. She replied she had: she drew the impoverished and watery blood from the body of Æson; she infused the juice of certain potent herbs into his veins; and he rose from the operation as fresh and vigorous a man as his son.

The daughters of Pelias professed a perfect willingness to abdicate the throne of Iolchos; but, before they retired, they requested Medea to do the same kindness for their father which she had already done for Æson. She said she would. She told them the method was to cut the old man in pieces, and boil him in a kettle with an infusion of certain herbs, and he would come out as smooth and active as a child.

The daughters of Pelias a little scrupled the operation. Medea, seeing this, begged they would not think she was deceiving them. If however they doubted, she desired they would bring her the oldest ram from their flocks, and they should see the experiment. Medea cut up the ram, cast in certain herbs, and the old bell-wether came out as beautiful and innocent a he-lamb as was ever beheld. The daughters of Pelias were satisfied. They divided their father in pieces; but he was never restored either to health or life.

From Iolchos, upon some insurrection of the people, Medea and Jason fled to Corinth. Here they lived ten years in much harmony. At the end of that time Jason grew tired of his wife, and fell in love with Glauce, daughter of the king of Corinth. Medea was greatly exasperated with his infidelity, and, among other enormities, slew with her own hand the two children she had borne him before his face. Jason hastened to punish her barbarity; but Medea mounted a chariot drawn by fiery dragons, fled through the air to Athens, and escaped.

At Athens she married Ægeus, king of that city. Ægeus by a former wife had a son, named Theseus, who for some reason had been brought up obscure, unknown and in exile. At a suitable time he returned home to his father with the intention to avow his parentage. But Medea was beforehand with him. She put a poisoned goblet into the hands of Ægeus at an entertainment he gave to Theseus, with the intent that he should deliver it to his son. At the critical moment Ægeus cast his eyes on the sword of Theseus, which he recognised as that which he had delivered with his son, when a child, and had directed that it should be brought by him, when a man, as a token of the mystery of his birth. The goblet was cast away; the father and son rushed into each other's arms; and Medea fled from Athens in her chariot drawn by dragons through the air, as she had years before fled from Corinth.

CIRCE.

Circe was the sister of Æetes and Pasiphae, and was, like Medea, her niece, skilful in sorcery. She had besides the gift of immortality. She was exquisitely beautiful; but she employed the charms of her person, and the seducing grace of her manners to a bad purpose. She presented to every stranger who landed in her territory an enchanted cup, of which she intreated him to drink. He no sooner tasted it, than he was turned into a hog, and was driven by the magician to her sty. The unfortunate stranger retained under this loathsome appearance the consciousness of what he had been, and mourned for ever the criminal compliance by which he was brought to so melancholy a pass.

ORPHEUS.

Cicero[a] quotes Aristotle as affirming that there was no such man as Orpheus. But Aristotle is at least single in that opinion. And there are too many circumstances known respecting Orpheus, and which have obtained the consenting voice of all antiquity, to allow us to call in question his existence. He was a native of Thrace, and from that country migrated into Greece. He travelled into Egypt for the purpose of collecting there the information necessary to the accomplishment of his ends. He died a violent death; and, as is almost

[a] De Natura Deorum, Lib. I, c. 38.

universally affirmed, fell a sacrifice to the resentment and fury of the women of his native soil[b].

Orpheus was doubtless a poet; though it is not probable that any of his genuine productions have been handed down to us. He was, as all the poets of so remote a period were, extremely accomplished in all the arts of vocal and instrumental music. He civilised the rude inhabitants of Greece, and subjected them to order and law. He formed them into communities. He is said by Aristophanes[c] and Horace[d] to have reclaimed the savage, man, from slaughter, and an indulgence in food that was loathsome and foul. And this has with sufficient probability been interpreted to mean, that he found the race of men among whom he lived cannibals, and that, to cure them the more completely of this horrible practice, he taught them to be contented to subsist upon the fruits of the earth[e]. Music and poetry are understood to have been made specially instrumental by him to the effecting this purpose. He is said to have made the hungry lion and the famished tiger obedient to his bidding, and to put off their wild and furious natures.

This is interpreted by Horace[f] and other recent expositors to mean no more than that he reduced

[b] Plato, De Republica, Lib. X, *sub finem*.
[c] Βατραχος, v. 1032.   [d] De Arte Poetica, v. 391.
[e] Memoires de l'Academie des Inscriptions, Tom. V, p. 117.
[f] De Arte Poetica, v. 391, 2, 3.

the race of savages as he found them, to order and civilisation. But it was at first perhaps understood more literally. We shall not do justice to the traditions of these remote times, if we do not in imagination transport ourselves among them, and teach ourselves to feel their feelings, and conceive their conceptions. Orpheus lived in a time when all was enchantment and prodigy. Gifted and extraordinary persons in those ages believed that they were endowed with marvellous prerogatives, and acted upon that belief. We may occasionally observe, even in these days of the dull and the literal, how great is the ascendancy of the man over the beast, when he feels a full and entire confidence in that ascendancy. The eye and the gesture of man cannot fail to produce effects, incredible till they are seen. Magic was the order of the day; and the enthusiasm of its heroes was raised to the highest pitch, and attended with no secret misgivings. We are also to consider that, in all operations of a magical nature, there is a wonderful mixture of frankness and *bonhommie* with a strong vein of cunning and craft. Man in every age is full of incongruous and incompatible principles; and, when we shall cease to be inconsistent, we shall cease to be men.

It is difficult fully to explain what is meant by the story of Orpheus and Eurydice; but in its circumstances it bears a striking resemblance to what has been a thousand times recorded respecting the calling up of the ghosts of the dead by means of sorcery. The disconsolate husband has in the first place recourse to the resistless aid of music[k]. After many preparatives he appears to have effected his purpose, and prevailed upon the powers of darkness to allow him the presence of his beloved. She appears in the sequel however to have been a thin and a fleeting shadow. He is forbidden to cast his eyes on her; and, if he had obeyed this injunction, it is uncertain how the experiment would have ended. He proceeds however, as he is commanded, towards the light of day. He is led to believe that his consort is following his steps. He is beset with a multitude of unearthly phenomena. He advances for some time with confidence. At length he is assailed with doubts. He has recourse to the auricular sense, to know if she is following him. He can hear nothing. Finally he can endure this uncertainty no longer; and, in defiance of the prohibition he has received, cannot refrain from turning his head to ascertain whether he is baffled, and has spent all his labour in vain. He sees her; but no sooner he sees her, than she becomes evanescent and impalpable; farther and farther she retreats before him; she utters a shrill cry, and endeavours to articulate; but she grows more and more imperceptible; and in the conclusion he is left with the scene around him in all respects the same as it

[k] Virgil, Georgica, Lib. IV. v. 464, et seqq.

had been before his incantations. The result of the whole that is known of Orpheus, is, that he was an eminently great and virtuous man, but was the victim of singular calamity.

We have not yet done with the history of Orpheus. As has been said, he fell a sacrifice to the resentment and fury of the women of his native soil. They are affirmed to have torn him limb from limb. His head, divided from his body, floated down the waters of the Hebrus, and miraculously, as it passed along to the sea, it was still heard to exclaim in mournful accents, Eurydice, Eurydice[h]! At length it was carried ashore on the island of Lesbos[i]. Here, by some extraordinary concurrence of circumstances, it found a resting-place in a fissure of a rock over-arched by a cave, and, thus domiciliated, is said to have retained the power of speech, and to have uttered oracles. Not only the people of Lesbos resorted to it for guidance in difficult questions, but also the Asiatic Greeks from Ionia and Ætolia; and its fame and character for predicting future events even extended to Babylon[k].

AMPHION.

The story of Amphion is more perplexing than that of the living Orpheus. Both of them turn in

[h] Georgica, iv, 525. [i] Metamorphoses, xi, 55.
[k] Philostratus, Heroica, cap. v.

a great degree upon the miraculous effects of music. Amphion was of the royal family of Thebes, and ultimately became ruler of the territory. He is said, by the potency of his lyre, or his skill in the magic art, to have caused the stones to follow him, to arrange themselves in the way he proposed, and without the intervention of a human hand to have raised a wall about his metropolis[a]. It is certainly less difficult to conceive the savage man to be rendered placable, and to conform to the dictates of civilisation, or even wild beasts to be made tame, than to imagine stones to obey the voice and the will of a human being. The example however is not singular; and hereafter we shall find related that Merlin, the British enchanter, by the power of magic caused the rocks of Stonehenge, though of such vast dimensions, to be carried through the air from Ireland to the place where we at present find them.—Homer mentions that Amphion, and his brother Zethus built the walls of Thebes, but does not describe it as having been done by miracle[b].

TIRESIAS.

Tiresias was one of the most celebrated soothsayers of the early ages of Greece. He lived in the times of Oedipus, and the war of the seven chiefs against Thebes. He was afflicted by the

[a] Horat, de Arte Poetica, v. 394. Pausanias.
[b] Odyssey, Lib. XI, v. 262.

Gods with blindness, in consequence of some displeasure they conceived against him; but in compensation they endowed him beyond all other mortals with the gift of prophecy. He is said to have understood the language of birds. He possessed the art of divining future events from the various indications that manifest themselves in fire, in smoke, and in other ways[a], but to have set the highest value upon the communications of the dead, whom by spells and incantations he constrained to appear and answer his enquiries[b]; and he is represented as pouring out tremendous menaces against them, when they shewed themselves tardy to attend upon his commands[c].

ABARIS.

Abaris, the Scythian, known to us for his visit to Greece, was by all accounts a great magician. Herodotus says[a], that he is reported to have travelled over the world with an arrow, eating nothing during his journey. Other authors relate that this arrow was given to him by Apollo, and that he rode upon it through the air, over lands, and seas, and all inaccessible places[b]. The time in which he flourished is very uncertain, some having represented him as having constructed the Palla-

[a] Statius, Thebais, Lib. X. v. 599. [b] Ibid, Lib. IV, v. 599.
[c] Ibid, Lib. IV, v. 409. *et seqq.*
[a] Lib. IV, c. 36. [b] Iamblichus.

dium, which, as long as it was preserved, kept Troy from being taken by an enemy[c], and others affirming that he was familiar with Pythagoras, who lived six hundred years later, and that he was admitted into his special confidence[d]. He is said to have possessed the faculty of foretelling earthquakes, allaying storms, and driving away pestilence; he gave out predictions wherever he went; and is described as an enchanter, professing to cure diseases by virtue of certain words which he pronounced over those who were afflicted with them[e].

PYTHAGORAS.

The name of Pythagoras is one of the most memorable in the records of the human species; and his character is well worthy of the minutest investigation. By this name we are brought at once within the limits of history properly so called. He lived in the time of Cyrus and Darius Hystaspes, of Croesus, of Pisistratus, of Polycrates, tyrant of Samos, and Amasis, king of Egypt. Many hypotheses have been laid down respecting the precise period of his birth and death; but, as it is not to our purpose to enter into any lengthened discussions of that sort, we will adopt at once the statement that appears to be the most

[c] Julius Firmicus, *apud* Scaliger, in Eusebium.
[d] Iamblichus, Vita Pythagoræ.   [e] Plato, Charmides.

probable, which is that of Lloyd[a], who fixes his birth about the year before Christ 586, and his death about the year 506.

Pythagoras was a man of the most various accomplishments, and appears to have penetrated in different directions into the depths of human knowledge. He sought wisdom in its retreats of fairest promise, in Egypt and other distant countries[b]. In this investigation he employed the earlier period of his life, probably till he was forty, and devoted the remainder to such modes of proceeding, as appeared to him the most likely to secure the advantage of what he had acquired to a late posterity[c].

He founded a school, and delivered his acquisitions by oral communication to a numerous body of followers. He divided his pupils into two classes, the one neophytes, to whom was explained only the most obvious and general truths, the other who were admitted into the entire confidence of the master. These last he caused to throw their property into a common stock, and to live together in the same place of resort[d]. He appears to have spent the latter half of his life in that part of Italy, called Magna Græcia, so denominated in some degree from the numerous colonies of Grecians by whom it was planted, and partly perhaps

[a] Chronological Account of Pythagoras and his Contemporaries.   [b] Laertius, Lib. VIII, c. 3.
[c] Lloyd, *ubi supra*.   [d] Iamblichus, c. 17

from the memory of the illustrious things which Pythagoras achieved there[e]. He is said to have spread the seeds of political liberty in Crotona, Sybaris, Metapontum, and Rhegium, and from thence in Sicily to Tauromenium, Catana, Agrigentum and Himera[f]. Charondas and Zaleucus, themselves famous legislators, derived the rudiments of their political wisdom from the instructions of Pythagoras[g].

But this marvellous man in some way, whether from the knowlege he received, or from his own proper discoveries, has secured to his species benefits of a more permanent nature, and which shall outlive the revolutions of ages, and the instability of political institutions. He was a profound geometrician. The two theorems, that the internal angles of every right-line triangle are equal to two right angles[h], and that the square of the hypothenuse of every right angled triangle is equal to the sum of the squares of the other two sides[i], are ascribed to him. In memory of the latter of these discoveries he is said to have offered a public sacrifice to the Gods; and the theorem is still known by the name of the Pythagorean theorem. He ascertained from the length of the Olympic course, which was understood to have measured six hundred of

[e] Iamblichus, c. 29.
[f] Ibid, c. 7.
[g] Laertius, c. 15.
[h] Ibid, c. 11.
[i] Plutarchus, Symposiaca, Lib. VIII, Quæstio 2.

Hercules's feet, the precise stature of that hero[k]. Lastly, Pythagoras is the first person, who is known to have taught the spherical figure of the earth, and that we have antipodes[l]; and he propagated the doctrine that the earth is a planet, and that the sun is the centre round which the earth and the other planets move, now known by the name of the Copernican system[m].

To inculcate a pure and a simple mode of subsistence was also an express object of pursuit to Pythagoras. He taught a total abstinence from every thing having had the property of animal life. It has been affirmed, as we have seen[n], that Orpheus before him taught the same thing. But the claim of Orpheus to this distinction is ambiguous; while the theories and dogmas of the Samian sage, as he has frequently been styled, were more methodically digested, and produced more lasting and unequivocal effects. He taught temperance in all its branches, and a resolute subjection of the appetites of the body to contemplation and the exercises of the mind; and, by the unremitted discipline and authority he exerted over his followers, he caused his lessons to be constantly observed. There was therefore an edify-

[k] Aulus Gellius, Lib. I, c. 1, from Plutarch.
[l] Laertius, c. 19.
[m] Bailly, Histoire de l'Astronomie, Lib. VIII, § 3.
[n] Plutarchus, de Esu Carnium. Ovidius, Metamorphoses, Lib. XV. Laertius, c. 12.

ing and an exemplary simplicity that prevailed as far as the influence of Pythagoras extended, that won golden opinions to his adherents at all times that they appeared, and in all places[o].

One revolution that Pythagoras worked, was that, whereas, immediately before, those who were most conspicuous among the Greeks as instructors of mankind in understanding and virtue, styled themselves sophists, professors of wisdom, this illustrious man desired to be known only by the appellation of a philosopher, a lover of wisdom[p]. The sophists had previously brought their denomination into discredit and reproach, by the arrogance of their pretensions, and the imperious way in which they attempted to lay down the law to the world.

The modesty of this appellation however did not altogether suit with the deep designs of Pythagoras, the ascendancy he resolved to acquire, and the oracular subjection in which he deemed it necessary to hold those who placed themselves under his instruction. This wonderful man set out with making himself a model of the passive and unscrupulous docility which he afterwards required from others. He did not begin to teach till he was forty years of age, and from eighteen to that period he studied in foreign countries, with the resolution to submit to all his teachers enjoined, and to make himself master of their least communicated

[o] Iamblichus, c. 16. [p] Laertius, c. 6.

and most secret wisdom. In Egypt in particular, we are told that, though he brought a letter of recommendation from Polycrates, his native sovereign, to Amasis, king of that country, who fully concurred with the views of the writer, the priests, jealous of admitting a foreigner into their secrets, baffled him as long as they could, referring him from one college to another, and prescribing to him the most rigorous preparatives, not excluding the rite of circumcision[q]. But Pythagoras endured and underwent every thing, till at length their unwillingness was conquered, and his perseverance received its suitable reward.

When in the end Pythagoras thought himself fully qualified for the task he had all along had in view, he was no less strict in prescribing ample preliminaries to his own scholars. At the time that a pupil was proposed to him, the master, we are told, examined him with multiplied questions as to his principles, his habits and intentions, observed minutely his voice and manner of speaking, his walk and his gestures, the lines of his countenance, and the expression and management of his eye, and, when he was satisfied with these, then and not till then admitted him as a probationer[r]. It is to be supposed that all this must have been personal. As soon however as this was over, the master was withdrawn from the sight of

---

[q] Clemens Alexandrinus, Stromata, Lib. I, p. 302.
[r] Iamblichus, c. 17.

the pupil; and a noviciate of three and five, in all eight years[s], was prescribed to the scholar, during which time he was only to hear his instructor from behind a curtain, and the strictest silence was enjoined him through the whole period. As the instructions Pythagoras received in Egypt and the East admitted of no dispute, so in his turn he required an unreserved submission from those who heard him: αυτος ιφη, "the master has said it," was deemed a sufficient solution to all doubt and uncertainty[t].

To give the greater authority and effect to his communications Pythagoras hid himself during the day at least from the great body of his pupils, and was only seen by them at night. Indeed there is no reason to suppose that any one was admitted into his entire familiarity. When he came forth, he appeared in a long garment of the purest white, with a flowing beard, and a garland upon his head. He is said to have been of the finest symmetrical form, with a majestic carriage, and a grave and awful countenance[u]. He suffered his followers to believe that he was one of the Gods, the Hyperborean Apollo[w], and is said to have told Abaris that he assumed the human form, that he might the better invite men to an easiness of approach and to confidence in him[x]. What how-

[s] Laertius, c. 8. Iamblichus, c. 17.
[t] Cicero de Natura Deorum, Lib. I, c. 5.
[u] Laertius, c. 9.   [w] Ibid.   [x] Iamblichus, c. 19.

ever seems to be agreed in by all his biographers, is that he professed to have already in different ages appeared in the likeness of man: first as Æthalides, the son of Mercury; and, when his father expressed himself ready to invest him with any gift short of immortality, he prayed that, as the human soul is destined successively to dwell in various forms, he might have the privilege in each to remember his former state of being, which was granted him. From Æthalides he became Euphorbus, who slew Patroclus at the siege of Troy. He then appeared as Hermotimus, then Pyrrhus, a fisherman of Delos, and finally Pythagoras. He said that a period of time was interposed between each transmigration, during which he visited the seat of departed souls; and he professed to relate a part of the wonders he had seen[y]. He is said to have eaten sparingly and in secret, and in all respects to have given himself out for a being not subject to the ordinary laws of nature[z].

Pythagoras therefore pretended to miraculous endowments. Happening to be on the sea-shore when certain fishermen drew to land an enormous multitude of fishes, he desired them to allow him to dispose of the capture, which they consented to, provided he would name the precise number they had caught. He did so, and required that they should throw their prize into the sea again, at the

[y] Laertius, c. 1.   [z] Ibid, c. 18.

same time paying them the value of the fish^a. He tamed a Daunian bear by whispering in his ear, and prevailed on him henceforth to refrain from the flesh of animals, and to feed on vegetables. By the same means he induced an ox not to eat beans, which was a diet specially prohibited by Pythagoras; and he called down an eagle from his flight, causing him to sit on his hand, and submit to be stroked down by the philosopher[b]. In Greece, when he passed the river Nessus in Macedon, the stream was heard to salute him with the words " Hail, Pythagoras!" When Abaris addressed him as one of the heavenly host, he took the stranger aside, and convinced him that he was under no mistake, by exhibiting to him his thigh of gold: or, according to another account, he used the same sort of evidence at a certain time, to satisfy his pupils of his celestial descent[d]. He is said to have been seen on the same day at Metapontum in Italy, and at Tauromimium in Sicily, though these places are divided by the sea, so that it was conceived that it would cost several days to pass from one to the other[e]. In one instance he absented himself from his associates in Italy for a whole year; and when he appeared again, related that he had passed that time in the infernal re-

[a] Iamblichus, c. 8. [b] Ibid, c. 13.
[c] Laertius, c. 9. Iamblichus, c. 28.
[d] Laertius, c. 9. Iamblichus, c. 18. [e] Ibid, c. 28.

gions, describing likewise the marvellous things he had seen[f]. Diogenes Laertius, speaking of this circumstance affirms however that he remained during this period in a cave, where his mother conveyed to him intelligence and necessaries, and that, when he came once more into light and air, he appeared so emaciated and colourless, that he might well be believed to have come out of Hades.

The close of the life of Pythagoras was, according to every statement, in the midst of misfortune and violence. Some particulars are related by Iamblichus[g], which, though he is not an authority beyond all exception, are so characteristic as seem to entitle them to the being transcribed. This author is more circumstantial than any other in stating the elaborate steps by which the pupils of Pythagoras came to be finally admitted into the full confidence of the master. He says, that they passed three years in the first place in a state of probation, carefully watched by their seniors, and exposed to their occasional taunts and ironies, by way of experiment to ascertain whether they were of a temper sufficiently philosophical and firm. At the expiration of that period they were admitted to a noviciate, in which they were bound to uninterrupted silence, and heard the lectures of the master, while he was himself

[f] Laertius, c. 21.   [g] Iamblichus, c. 17.

concealed from their view by a curtain. They were then received to initiation, and required to deliver over their property to the common stock. They were admitted to intercourse with the master. They were invited to a participation of the most obscure theories, and the abstrusest problems. If however in this stage of their progress they were discovered to be too weak of intellectual penetration, or any other fundamental objection were established against them, they were expelled the community; the double of the property they had contributed to the common stock was paid down to them; a head-stone and a monument inscribed with their names were set up in the place of meeting of the community; they were considered as dead; and, if afterwards they met by chance any of those who were of the privileged few, they were treated by them as entirely strangers.

Cylon, the richest man, or, as he is in one place styled, the prince, of Crotona, had manifested the greatest partiality to Pythagoras. He was at the same time a man of rude, impatient and boisterous character. He, together with Perialus of Thurium, submitted to all the severities of the Pythagorean school. They passed the three years of probation, and the five years of silence. They were received into the familiarity of the master. They were then initiated, and delivered all their wealth into the common stock. They were however ultimately pronounced deficient in intellectual power, or for some other reason were not judged worthy to continue among the confidential pupils of Pythagoras. They were expelled. The double of the property they had contributed was paid back to them. A monument was set up in memory of what they had been; and they were pronounced dead to the school.

It will easily be conceived in what temper Cylon sustained this degradation. Of Perialus we hear nothing further. But Cylon, from feelings of the deepest reverence and awe for Pythagoras, which he had cherished for years, was filled even to bursting with inextinguishable hatred and revenge. The unparalleled merits, the venerable age of the master whom he had so long followed, had no power to control his violence. His paramount influence in the city insured him the command of a great body of followers. He excited them to a frame of turbulence and riot. He represented to them how intolerable was the despotism of this pretended philosopher. They surrounded the school in which the pupils were accustomed to assemble, and set it on fire. Forty persons perished in the flames[h]. According to some accounts Pythagoras was absent at the time. According to others he and two of his pupils escaped. He retired from Crotona to Metapontum. But the hostility which had broken out in the former city, followed him there. He took

[h] Iamblichus, c. 35. Laertius, c. 21.

refuge in the Temple of the Muses. But he was held so closely besieged that no provisions could be conveyed to him; and he finally perished with hunger, after, according to Laertius, forty days' abstinence[i].

It is difficult to imagine any thing more instructive, and more pregnant with matter for salutary reflection, than the contrast presented to us by the character and system of action of Pythagoras on the one hand, and those of the great enquirers of the last two centuries, for example, Bacon, Newton and Locke, on the other. Pythagoras probably does not yield to any one of these in the evidences of true intellectual greatness. In his school, in the followers he trained resembling himself, and in the salutary effects he produced on the institutions of the various republics of Magna Græcia and Sicily, he must be allowed greatly to have excelled them. His discoveries of various propositions in geometry, of the earth as a planet, and of the solar system as now universally recognised, clearly stamp him a genius of the highest order.

Yet this man, thus enlightened and philanthropical, established his system of proceeding upon narrow and exclusive principles, and conducted it by methods of artifice, quackery and delusion. One of his leading maxims was, that the great and fundamental truths to the establishment of which

[i] Laertius, c. 21.

he devoted himself, were studiously to be concealed from the vulgar, and only to be imparted to a select few, and after years of the severest noviciate and trial. He learned his earliest lessons of wisdom in Egypt after this method, and he conformed through life to the example which had thus been delivered to him. The severe examination that he made of the candidates previously to their being admitted into his school, and the years of silence that were then prescribed to them, testify this. He instructed them by symbols, obscure and enigmatical propositions, which they were first to exercise their ingenuity to expound. The authority and dogmatical assertions of the master were to remain unquestioned; and the pupils were to fashion themselves to obsequious and implicit submission, and were the furthest in the world from being encouraged to the independent exercise of their own understandings. There was nothing that Pythagoras was more fixed to discountenance, than the communication of the truths upon which he placed the highest value, to the uninitiated. It is not probable therefore that he wrote any thing: all was communicated orally, by such gradations, and with such discretion, as he might think fit to adopt and to exercise.

Delusion and falsehood were main features of his instruction. With what respect therefore can we consider, and what manliness worthy of his high character and endowments can we impute to, his discourses delivered from behind a curtain, his hiding himself during the day, and only appearing by night in a garb assumed for the purpose of exciting awe and veneration? What shall we say to the story of his various transmigrations? At first sight it appears in the light of the most audacious and unblushing imposition. And, if we were to yield so far as to admit that by a high-wrought enthusiasm, by a long train of maceration and visionary reveries, he succeeded in imposing on himself, this, though in a different way, would scarcely less detract from the high stage of eminence upon which the nobler parts of his character would induce us to place him.

Such were some of the main causes that have made his efforts perishable, and the lustre which should have attended his genius in a great degree transitory and fugitive. He was probably much under the influence of a contemptible jealousy, and must be considered as desirous that none of his contemporaries or followers should eclipse their master. All was oracular and dogmatic in the school of Pythagoras. He prized and justly prized the greatness of his attainments and discoveries, and had no conception that any thing could go beyond them. He did not encourage, nay, he resolutely opposed, all true independence of mind, and that undaunted spirit of enterprise which is the atmosphere in which the sublimest thoughts are most naturally generated. He therefore did not throw open the gates of science and wisdom, and invite every comer; but on the contrary narrowed the entrance, and carefully reduced the number of aspirants. He thought not of the most likely methods to give strength and permanence and an extensive sphere to the progress of the human mind. For these reasons he wrote nothing; but consigned all to the frail and uncertain custody of tradition. And distant posterity has amply avenged itself upon the narrowness of his policy; and the name of Pythagoras, which would otherwise have been ranked with the first luminaries of mankind, and consigned to everlasting gratitude, has in consequence of a few radical and fatal mistakes, been often loaded with obloquy, and the hero who bore it been indiscriminately classed among the votaries of imposture and artifice.

EPIMENIDES.

Epimenides has been mentioned among the disciples of Pythagoras; but he probably lived at an earlier period. He was a native of Crete. The first extraordinary circumstance that is recorded of him is, that, being very young, he was sent by his father in search of a stray sheep, when, being overcome by the heat of the weather, he retired into a cave, and slept fifty-seven years.

Supposing that he had slept only a few hours, he repaired first to his father's country-house, which he found in possession of a new tenant, and then to the city, where he encountered his younger brother, now grown an old man, who with difficulty was brought to acknowledge him[a]. It was probably this circumstance that originally brought Epimenides into repute as a prophet, and a favourite of the Gods.

Epimenides appears to have been one of those persons, who make it their whole study to delude their fellow-men, and to obtain for themselves the reputation of possessing supernatural gifts. Such persons, almost universally, and particularly in ages of ignorance and wonder, become themselves the dupes of their own pretensions. He gave out that he was secretly subsisted by food brought to him by the nymphs; and he is said to have taken nourishment in so small quantities, as to be exempted from the ordinary necessities of nature[b]. He boasted that he could send his soul out of his body, and recal it, when he pleased; and alternately appeared an inanimate corpse, and then again his life would return to him, and he appear capable of every human function as before[c]. He is said to have practised the ceremony of exorcising houses and fields, and thus rendering them fruitful and blessed[d]. He frequently uttered prophecies

[a] Laertius, Lib. I, c. 109. Plinius, Lib. VII, c. 52.
[b] Laertius, c. 113.   [c] Ibid.   [d] Ibid. c. 111.

of events with such forms of ceremony and such sagacious judgment, that they seemed to come to pass as he predicted.

One of the most memorable acts of his life happened in this manner. Cylon, the head of one of the principal families in Athens, set on foot a rebellion against the government, and surprised the citadel. His power however was of short duration. Siege was laid to the place, and Cylon found his safety in flight. His partisans forsook their arms, and took refuge at the altars. Seduced from this security by fallacious promises, they were brought to judgment and all of them put to death. The Gods were said to be offended with this violation of the sanctions of religion, and sent a plague upon the city. All things were in confusion, and sadness possessed the whole community. Prodigies were perpetually seen; the spectres of the dead walked the streets; and terror universally prevailed. The sacrifices offered to the gods exhibited the most unfavourable symptoms[e]. In this emergency the Athenian senate resolved to send for Epimenides to come to their relief. His reputation was great. He was held for a holy and devout man, and wise in celestial things by inspiration from above. A vessel was fitted out under the command of one of the first citizens of the state to fetch Epimenides from Crete. He performed various rites and purifications. He took a

[e] Plutarch, Vita Solonis. Laertius, Lib. I, c. 109.

certain number of sheep, black and white, and led them to the Areopagus, where he caused them to be let loose to go wherever they would. He directed certain persons to follow them, and mark the place where they lay down. He enquired to what particular deity the spot was consecrated, and sacrificed the sheep to that deity; and in the result of these ceremonies the plague was stayed. According to others he put an end to the plague by the sacrifice of two human victims. The Athenian senate, full of gratitude to their benefactor, tendered him the gift of a talent. But Epimenides refused all compensation, and only required, as an acknowledgment of what he had done, that there should be perpetual peace between the Athenians and the people of Gnossus, his native city[f]. He is said to have died shortly after his return to his country, being of the age of one hundred and fifty-seven years[g].

EMPEDOCLES.

Empedocles has also been mentioned as a disciple of Pythagoras. But he probably lived too late for that to have been the case. His principles were in a great degree similar to those of that illustrious personage; and he might have studied under one of the immediate successors of Pythagoras. He was a citizen of Agrigentum in Sicily;

[f] Plutarch, Vita Solonis. Laertius, Lib. I. c. 110. [g] Ibid.

and, having inherited considerable wealth, exercised great authority in his native place[a]. He was a distinguished orator and poet. He was greatly conversant in the study of nature, and was eminent for his skill in medicine[b]. In addition to these accomplishments, he appears to have been a devoted adherent to the principles of liberty. He effected the dissolution of the ruling council of Agrigentum, and substituted in their room a triennial magistracy, by means of which the public authority became not solely in the hands of the rich as before, but was shared by them with expert and intelligent men of an inferior class[c]. He opposed all arbitrary exercises of rule. He gave dowries from his own stores to many young maidens of impoverished families, and settled them in eligible marriages[d]. He performed many cures upon his fellow-citizens; and is especially celebrated for having restored a woman to life, who had been apparently dead, according to one account for seven days, but according to others for thirty[e].

But the most memorable things known of Empedocles, are contained in the fragments of his verses that have been preserved to us. In one of them he says of himself, "I well remember the time before I was Empedocles, that I once was a boy, then a girl, a plant, a glittering fish, a bird

[a] Laertius, Lib. VIII, c. 51, 64.   [b] Ibid, c. 57.
[c] Ibid, c. 66.   [d] Ibid, c. 73.
[e] Plinius, Lib. VII, c. 52. Laertius, c. 61.

that cut the air[f]." Addressing those who resorted to him for improvement and wisdom, he says, "By my instructions you shall learn medicines that are powerful to cure disease, and re-animate old age; you shall be able to calm the savage winds which lay waste the labours of the husbandman, and, when you will, shall send forth the tempest again; you shall cause the skies to be fair and serene, or once more shall draw down refreshing showers, re-animating the fruits of the earth; nay, you shall recal the strength of the dead man, when he has already become the victim of Pluto[g]." Further, speaking of himself, Empedocles exclaims: "Friends, who inhabit the great city laved by the yellow Acragas, all hail! I mix with you a God, no longer a mortal, and am every where honoured by you, as is just; crowned with fillets, and fragrant garlands, adorned with which when I visit populous cities, I am revered by both men and women, who follow me by ten thousands, enquiring the road to boundless wealth, seeking the gift of prophecy, and who would learn the marvellous skill to cure all kinds of diseases[h]."

The best known account of the death of Empedocles may reasonably be considered as fabulous. From what has been said it sufficiently appears, that he was a man of extraordinary intellectual endowments, and the most philanthropical dispositions; at the same time that he was immoderately

---

[f] Laertius, c. 77.   [g] Ibid, c. 59.   [h] Ibid, c. 62.

vain, aspiring by every means in his power to acquire to himself a deathless remembrance. Working on these hints, a story has been invented that he aspired to a miraculous way of disappearing from among men; and for this purpose repaired, when alone, to the top of Mount Ætna, then in a state of eruption, and threw himself down the burning crater: but it is added, that in the result of this perverse ambition he was baffled, the volcano having thrown up one of his brazen sandals, by means of which the mode of his death became known[i].

ARISTEAS.

Herodotus tells a marvellous story of one Aristeas, a poet of Proconnesus, an island of the Propontis. This man, coming by chance into a fuller's workshop in his native place, suddenly fell down dead. As the man was of considerable rank, the fuller immediately, quitting and locking up his shop, proceeded to inform his family of what had happened. The relations went accordingly, having procured what was requisite to give the deceased the rites of sepulture, to the shop; but, when it was opened, they could discover no vestige of Aristeas, either dead or alive. A traveller however from the neighbouring town of Cyzicus on the continent, protested that he had just left that place, and, as he set foot in the wherry

[i] Laertius, c. 69. Horat. De Arte Poetica, v. 463.

which had brought him over, had met Aristeas, and held a particular conversation with him. Seven years after, Aristeas reappeared at Proconnesus, resided there a considerable time, and during this abode wrote his poem of the wars of the one-eyed Arimaspians and the Gryphons. He then again disappeared in an unaccountable manner. But, what is more than all extraordinary, three hundred and forty years after this disappearance, he shewed himself again at Metapontum, in Magna Græcia, and commanded the citizens to erect a statue in his honour near the temple of Apollo in the forum; which being done, he raised himself in the air; and flew away in the form of a crow[a].

HERMOTIMUS.

Hermotimus, or, as Plutarch names him, Hermodorus of Clazomene, is said to have possessed, like Epimenides, the marvellous power of quitting his body, and returning to it again, as often, and for as long a time as he pleased. In these absences his unembodied spirit would visit what places he thought proper, observe every thing that was going on, and, when he returned to his fleshy tabernacle, make a minute relation of what he had seen. Hermotimus had enemies, who, one time when his body had lain unanimated unusually long, beguiled his wife, made her believe that he was cer-

[a] Herodotus, Lib. III, c. 14, 15. Plinius, Lib. VII, c. 52.

tainly dead, and that it was disrespectful and indecent to keep him so long in that state. The woman therefore placed her husband on the funeral pyre, and consumed him to ashes; so that, continues the philosopher, when the soul of Hermotimus came back again, it no longer found its customary receptacle to retire into[a]. Certainly this kind of treatment appeared to furnish an infallible criterion, whether the seeming absences of the soul of this miraculous man were pretended or real.

THE MOTHER OF DEMARATUS, KING OF SPARTA.

Herodotus[b] tells a story of the mother of Demaratus, king of Sparta, which bears a striking resemblance to the fairy tales of modern times. This lady, afterward queen of Sparta, was sprung from opulent parents, but, when she was born, was so extravagantly ugly, that her parents hid her from all human observation. According to the mode of the times however, they sent the babe daily in its nurse's arms to the shrine of Helen, now metamorphosed into a Goddess, to pray that the child might be delivered from its present preternatural deformity. On these occasions the

---

[a] Plutarch, De Genio Socratis. Lucian, Muscæ Encomium. Plinius, Lib. VII, c. 52.
[b] Plinius, Lib. III, c. 61, 62.

child was shrouded in many coverings, that it might escape being seen. One day as the nurse came out of the temple, a strange woman met her, and asked her what she carried so carefully concealed. The nurse said it was a female child, but of opulent parents, and she was strictly enjoined that it should be seen by no one. The stranger was importunate, and by dint of perseverance overcame the nurse's reluctance. The woman took the babe in her arms, stroked down its hair, kissed it, and then returning it to the nurse, said that it should grow up the most perfect beauty in Sparta. So accordingly it proved: and the king of the country, having seen her, became so enamoured of her, that, though he already had a wife, and she a husband, he overcame all obstacles, and made her his queen.

ORACLES.

One of the most extraordinary things to be met with in the history of ancient times is the oracles. They maintained their reputation for many successive centuries. The most famous perhaps were that of Delphi in Greece, and that of Jupiter Ammon in the deserts of Lybia. But they were scattered through many cities, many plains, and many islands. They were consulted by the foolish and the wise; and scarcely anything considerable was undertaken, especially about the time of the Persian invasion into Greece, without the parties having first had recourse to these; and they in most cases modified the conduct of princes and armies accordingly. To render the delusion more successful, every kind of artifice was put in practice. The oracle could only be consulted on fixed days; and the persons who resorted to it, prefaced their application with costly offerings to the presiding God. Their questions passed through the hands of certain priests, residing in and about the temple. These priests received the embassy with all due solemnity, and retired. A priestess, or Pythia, who was seldom or never seen by any of the profane vulgar, was the immediate vehicle of communication with the God. She was cut off from all intercourse with the world, and was carefully trained by the attendant priests. Spending almost the whole of her time in solitude, and taught to consider her office as ineffably sacred, she saw visions, and was for the most part in a state of great excitement. The Pythia, at least of the Delphian God, was led on with much ceremony to the performance of her office, and placed upon the sacred tripod. The tripod, we are told, stood over a chasm in the rock, from which issued fumes of an inebriating quality. The Pythia became gradually penetrated through every limb with these fumes, till her bosom swelled, her features enlarged, her mouth foamed, her voice seemed supernatural, and she uttered words that could sometimes scarcely be called articulate. She could with difficulty contain herself, and seemed to be possessed, and wholly overpowered, with the God. After a prelude of many unintelligible sounds, uttered with fervour and a sort of frenzy, she became by degrees more distinct. She uttered incoherent sentences, with breaks and pauses, that were filled up with preternatural efforts and distorted gestures; while the priests stood by, carefully recording her words, and then reducing them into a sort of obscure signification. They finally digested them for the most part into a species of hexameter verse. We may suppose the supplicants during this ceremony placed at a proper distance, so as to observe these things imperfectly, while the less they understood, they were ordinarily the more impressed with religious awe, and prepared implicitly to receive what was communicated to them. Sometimes the priestess found herself in a frame, not entirely equal to her function, and refused for the present to proceed with the ceremony.

The priests of the oracle doubtless conducted them in a certain degree like the gipsies and fortune-tellers of modern times, cunningly procuring to themselves intelligence in whatever way they could, and ingeniously worming out the secrets of their suitors, at the same time contriving that their drift should least of all be suspected. But their main resource probably was in the obscurity, almost amounting to unintelligibleness, of their responses. Their prophecies in most cases required the comment of the event to make them understood; and it not seldom happened, that the meaning in the sequel was found to be the diametrically opposite of that which the pious votaries had originally conceived.

In the mean time the obscurity of the oracles was of inexpressible service to the cause of superstition. If the event turned out to be such as could in no way be twisted to come within the scope of the response, the pious suitor only concluded that the failure was owing to the grossness and carnality of his own apprehension, and not to any deficiency in the institution. Thus the oracle by no means lost credit, even when its meaning remained for ever in its original obscurity. But, when, by any fortunate chance, its predictions seemed to be verified, then the unerringness of the oracle was lauded from nation to nation; and the omniscience of the God was admitted with astonishment and adoration.

It would be a vulgar and absurd mistake however, to suppose that all this was merely the affair of craft, the multitude only being the dupes, while the priests in cold blood carried on the deception, and secretly laughed at the juggle they were palming on the world. They felt their own importance; and they cherished it. They felt that they were regarded by their countrymen as something more than human; and the opinion entertained of them by the world around them, did not fail to excite a responsive sentiment in their own bosoms. If their contemporaries willingly ascribed to them an exclusive sacredness, by how much stronger an impulse were they led fully to receive so flattering a suggestion! Their minds were in a perpetual state of exaltation; and they believed themselves specially favoured by the God whose temple constituted their residence. A small matter is found sufficient to place a creed which flatters all the passions of its votaries, on the most indubitable basis. Modern philosophers think that by their doctrine of gases they can explain all the appearances of the Pythia; but the ancients, to whom this doctrine was unknown, admitted these appearances as the undoubted evidence of an interposition from heaven.

It is certainly a matter of the extremest difficulty, for us in imagination to place ourselves in the situation of those who believed in the ancient polytheistical creed. And yet these believers nearly constituted the whole of the population of the kingdoms of antiquity. Even those who professed to have shaken off the prejudices of their education, and to rise above the absurdities of paganism, had still some of the old leaven adhering to them. One of the last acts of the life of Socrates, was to order the sacrifice of a cock to be made to Æsculapius.

Now the creed of paganism is said to have made up to the number of thirty thousand deities. Every kingdom, every city, every street, nay, in a manner every house, had its protecting God. These Gods were rivals to each other; and were each jealous of his own particular province, and watchful against the intrusion of any neighbour deity upon ground where he had a superior right. The province of each of these deities was of small extent; and therefore their watchfulness and jealousy of their appropriate honours do not enter into the slightest comparison with the Providence of the God who directs the concerns of the universe. They had ample leisure to employ in vindicating their prerogatives. Prophecy was of all means the plainest and most obvious for each deity to assert his existence, and to inforce the reverence and submission of his votaries. Prophecy was that species of interference which was least liable to the being confuted and exposed. The oracles, as we have said, were delivered in terms and phrases that were nearly unintelligible. If therefore they met with no intelligible fulfilment, this lost them nothing; and, if it gained them no additional credit, neither did it expose them to any disgrace. Whereas every example, where the obscure prediction seemed to tally with, and be illustrated by any subsequent event, was hailed with wonder and applause, confirmed the faith of the true believers, and was held forth as a victorious confutation of the doubts of the infidel.

INVASION OF XERXES INTO GREECE.

It is particularly suitable in this place to notice the events which took place at Delphi upon occasion of the memorable invasion of Xerxes into Greece. This was indeed a critical moment for the heathen mythology. The Persians were pointed and express in their hostility against the altars and the temples of the Greeks. It was no sooner known that the straits of Thermopylæ had been forced, than the priests consulted the God, as to whether they should bury the treasures of the temple, so to secure them against the sacrilege of the invader. The answer of the oracle was: "Let nothing be moved; the God is sufficient for the protection of his rights." The inhabitants therefore of the neighbourhood withdrew: only sixty men and the priest remained. The Persians in the mean time approached. Previously to this however, the sacred arms which were placed in the temple, were seen to be moved by invisible hands, and deposited on the declivity which was on the outside of the building. The invaders no sooner shewed themselves, than a miraculous storm of thunder and lightning rebounded and flashed among the multiplied hills which surrounded the sacred area, and struck terror into all hearts. Two vast fragments were detached from the top of mount Parnassus, and crushed hundreds in their fall. A voice of warlike acclamation issued from within the walls. Dismay seized the Persian troops. The Delphians then, rushing from their caverns, and descending from the summits, attacked them with great slaughter. Two persons, exceeding all human stature, and that were said to be the demigods whose fanes were erected near the temple of Apollo, joined in the pursuit, and extended the slaughter. It has been said that the situation of the place was particularly adapted to this mode of defence. Surrounded and almost overhung with lofty mountain-summits, the area of the city was inclosed within crags and precipices. No way led to it but through defiles, narrow and steep, shadowed with wood, and commanded at every step by fastnesses from above. In such a position artificial fires and explosion might imitate a thunder storm. Great pains had been taken, to represent the place as altogether abandoned; and therefore the detachment of rocks from the top of mount Parnassus, though effected by human hands, might appear altogether supernatural.

Nothing can more forcibly illustrate the strength of the religious feeling among the Greeks, than the language of the Athenian government at the

* Herodotus, Lib. VIII, c. 36, 37, 38, 39.

time of the second descent of the Persian armament upon their territory, when they were again compelled to abandon their houses and land to the invader. Mardonius said to them: "I am thus commissioned by the king of Persia, he will release and give back to you your country; he invites you to choose a further territory, whatever you may think desirable, which he will guarantee to you to govern as you shall judge fit. He will rebuild for you, without its costing you either money or labour, the temples which in his former incursion he destroyed with fire. It is in vain for you to oppose him by force, for his armies are innumerable." To which the Athenians replied, "As long as the sun pursues his course in the heavens, so long will we resist the Persian invader." Then turning to the Spartan ambassadors who were sent to encourage and animate them to persist, they added, "It is but natural that your employers should apprehend that we might give way and be discouraged. But there is no sum of money so vast, and no region so inviting and fertile, that could buy us to concur in the enslaving of Greece. Many and resistless are the causes which induce us to this resolve. First and chiefest, the temples and images of the Gods, which Xerxes has burned and laid in ruins, and which we are called upon to avenge to the utmost, instead of forming a league with him who made this devastation. Secondly, the consideration of the Grecian race, the same with us in blood and in speech, the same in religion and manners, and whose cause we will never betray. Know therefore now, if you knew not before, that, as long as a single Athenian survives, we will never swerve from the hostility to Persia to which we have devoted ourselves."

Contemplating this magnanimous resolution, it is in vain for us to reflect on the absurdity, incongruity and frivolousness, as we apprehend it, of the pagan worship, inasmuch as we find, whatever we may think of its demerits, that the most heroic people that ever existed on earth, in the hour of their direst calamity, regarded a zealous and fervent adherence to that religion as the most sacred of all duties[b].

DEMOCRITUS.

The fame of Democritus has sustained a singular fortune. He is represented by Pliny as one of the most superstitious of mortals. This character is founded on certain books which appeared in his name. In these books he is made to say, that, if the blood of certain birds be mingled together, the combination will produce a serpent, of which whoever eats will become endowed with the gift of understanding the language of birds[c]. He attributes a multitude of virtues to the limbs of a dead

[b] Herodotus, Lib. VIII, c. 140, *et seqq.*
[c] Historia Naturalis, Lib. X, c. 49.

camelion: among others that, if the left foot of this animal be grilled, and there be added certain herbs, and a particular unctuous preparation, it will have the quality to render the person who carries it about him invisible[b]. But all this is wholly irreconcileable with the known character of Democritus, who distinguished himself by the hypothesis that the world was framed from the fortuitous concourse of atoms, and that the soul died with the body. And accordingly Lucian[c], a more judicious author than Pliny, expressly cites Democritus as the strenuous opposer of all the pretenders to miracles. "Such juggling tricks," he says, "call for a Democritus, an Epicurus, a Metrodorus, or some one of that temper, who should endeavour to detect the illusion, and would hold it for certain, even if he could not fully lay open the deceit, that the whole was a lying pretence, and had not a spark of reality in it."

Democritus was in reality one of the most disinterested characters on record in the pursuit of truth. He has been styled the father of experimental philosophy. When his father died, and the estate came to be divided between him and two brothers, he chose the part which was in money, though the smallest, that he might indulge him in travelling in pursuit of knowledge. He visited Egypt and Persia, and turned aside into

[b] Plinius, Lib. XXVIII. c. 8.
[c] Pseudomantis, c. 17. See also Philopseudes, c. 32.

Ethiopia and India. He is reported to have said, that he had rather be the possessor of one of the cardinal secrets of nature, than of the diadem of Persia.

SOCRATES.

Socrates is the most eminent of the ancient philosophers. He lived in the most enlightened age of Greece, and in Athens, the most illustrious of her cities. He was born in the middle ranks of life, the son of a sculptor. He was of a mean countenance, with a snub nose, projecting eyes, and otherwise of an appearance so unpromising, that a physiognomist, his contemporary, pronounced him to be given to the grossest vices. But he was of a penetrating understanding, the simplest manners, and a mind wholly bent on the study of moral excellence. He at once abjured all the lofty pretensions, and the dark and recondite pursuits of the most applauded teachers of his time, and led those to whom he addressed his instructions from obvious and irresistible data to the most unexpected and useful conclusions. There was something in his manner of teaching that drew to him the noblest youth of Athens. Plato and Xenophon, two of the most admirable of the Greek writers, were among his pupils. He reconciled in his own person in a surprising degree poverty with the loftiest principles of independence. He taught an unreserved submission to the laws of our country. He several times unequivocally displayed his valour in the field of battle, while at the same time he kept aloof from public offices and trusts. The serenity of his mind never forsook him. He was at all times ready to teach, and never found it difficult to detach himself from his own concerns, to attend to the wants and wishes of others. He was uniformly courteous and unpretending; and, if at any time he indulged in a vein of playful ridicule, it was only against the presumptuously ignorant, and those who were without foundation wise in their own conceit.

Yet, with all these advantages and perfections, the name of Socrates would not have been handed down with such lustre to posterity but for the manner of his death. He made himself many enemies. The plainness of his manner and the simplicity of his instructions were inexpressibly wounding to those (and they were many), who, setting up for professors, had hitherto endeavoured to dazzle their hearers by the loftiness of their claims, and to command from them implicit submission by the arrogance with which they dictated. It must be surprising to us, that a man like Socrates should be arraigned in a country like Athens upon a capital accusation. He was charged with instilling into the youth a disobedience to their duties, and propagating impiety to the Gods, faults of which he was notoriously innocent. But the plot against him was deeply laid, and is said to have been twenty years in the concoction. And he greatly assisted the machinations of his adversaries, by the wonderful firmness of his conduct upon his trial, and his spirited resolution not to submit to any thing indirect and pusillanimous. He defended himself with a serene countenance and the most cogent arguments, but would not stoop to deprecation and intreaty. When sentence was pronounced against him, this did not induce the least alteration of his conduct. He did not think that a life which he had passed for seventy years with a clear conscience, was worth preserving by the sacrifice of honour. He refused to escape from prison, when one of his rich friends had already purchased of the jailor the means of his freedom. And, during the last days of his life, and when he was waiting the signal of death, which was to be the return of a ship that had been sent with sacrifices to Delos, he uttered those admirable discourses, which have been recorded by Xenophon and Plato to the latest posterity.

But the question which introduces his name into this volume, is that of what is called the demon of Socrates. He said that he repeatedly received a divine premonition of dangers impending over himself and others; and considerable pains have been taken to ascertain the cause and author of these premonitions. Several persons, among whom we may include Plato, have conceived that Socrates regarded himself as attended by a supernatural guardian who at all times watched over his welfare and concerns.

But the solution is probably of a simpler nature. Socrates, with all his incomparable excellencies and perfections, was not exempt from the superstitions of his age and country. He had been bred up among the absurdities of polytheism. In them were included, as we have seen, a profound deference for the responses of oracles, and a vigilant attention to portents and omens. Socrates appears to have been exceedingly regardful of omens. Plato tells us that this intimation, which he spoke of as his demon, never prompted him to any act, but occasionally interfered to prevent him or his friends from proceeding in any thing that would have been attended with injurious consequences[a]. Sometimes he described it as a voice, which no one however heard but himself; and sometimes it shewed itself in the act of sneezing. If the sneezing came, when he was in doubt to do a thing or not to do it, it confirmed him; but if, being already engaged in any act, he sneezed, this he considered as a warning to desist. If any of his friends sneezed on his right hand, he interpreted this as a favourable omen; but, if on his left, he immediately relinquished his purpose[b]. Socrates vindicated his mode of expressing himself on the sub-

[a] Theages.
[b] Plutarch, De Genio Socratis.

ject, by saying that others, when they spoke of omens, for example, by the voice of a bird, said the bird told me this, but that he, knowing that the omen was purely instrumental to a higher power, deemed it more religious and respectful to have regard only to the higher power, and to say that God had graciously warned him[c]. One of the examples of this presage was, that, going along a narrow street with several companions in earnest discourse, he suddenly stopped, and turned another way, warning his friends to do the same. Some yielded to him, and others went on, who were encountered by the rushing forward of a multitude of hogs, and did not escape without considerable inconvenience and injury[d]. In another instance one of a company among whom was Socrates, had confederated to commit an act of assassination. Accordingly he rose to quit the place, saying to Socrates, " I will be back presently." Socrates, unaware of his purpose, but having received the intimation of his demon, said to him earnestly, " Go not." The conspirator sat down. Again however he rose, and again Socrates stopped him. At length he escaped, without the observation of the philosopher, and committed the act, for which he was afterwards brought to trial. When led to execution, he exclaimed, " This would never have happened to me, if I had yielded to the inti-

[c] Xenophon, Memorabilia, Lib. I, c. 1.
[d] Plutarch, *ubi supra*.

mation of Socrates[e]." In the same manner, and by a similar suggestion, the philosopher predicted the miscarriage of the Athenian expedition to Sicily under Nicias, which terminated with such signal disaster[f]. This feature in the character of Socrates is remarkable, and may shew the prevalence of superstitious observances, even in persons whom we might think the most likely to be exempt from this weakness.

[e] Plato, Theages.   [f] Ibid.

ROME.

VIRGIL.

FROM the Greeks let us turn to the Romans The earliest examples to our purpose occur in the Æneid. And, though Virgil is a poet, yet is he so correct a writer, that we may well take for granted, that he either records facts which had been handed down by tradition, or that, when he feigns, he feigns things strikingly in accord with the manners and belief of the age of which he speaks.

POLYDORUS.

One of the first passages that occur, is of the ghost of the deceased Polydorus on the coast of Thrace. Polydorus, the son of Priam, was murdered by the king of that country, his host, for the sake of the treasures he had brought with him from Troy. He was struck through with darts made of the wood of the myrtle. The body was cast into a pit, and earth thrown upon it. The stems of myrtle grew and flourished. Æneas, after the burning of Troy, first attempted a settlement in this place. Near the spot where he landed he found a hillock thickly set with myrtle. He attempted to gather some, thinking it might form a suitable screen to an altar which he had just raised. To his astonishment and horror he found the branches he had plucked, dropping with blood. He tried the experiment again and again. At length a voice from the mound was heard, exclaiming, " Spare me! I am Polydorus;" and warning him to fly the blood-stained and treacherous shore.

DIDO.

We have a more detailed tale of necromancy, when Dido, deserted by Æneas, resolves on self-destruction. To delude her sister as to her secret purpose, she sends for a priestess from the gardens of the Hesperides, pretending that her object is by magical incantations again to relumine the passion of love in the breast of Æneas. This priestess is endowed with the power, by potent verse to free the oppressed soul from care, and by similar means to agitate the bosom with passion which is free from its empire. She can arrest the headlong stream, and cause the stars to return back in their orbits. She can call up the ghosts of the dead. She is able to compel the solid earth to rock, and the trees of the forest to descend from their mountains. To give effect to the infernal spell, Dido commands that a funeral pyre shall be set up in the interior court of her palace, and that the arms of Æneas, what remained of his attire, and the marriage-bed in which Dido had received him, shall be heaped upon it. The pyre is hung round with garlands, and adorned with branches of cypress. The sword of Æneas and his picture are added. Altars are placed round the pyre; and the priestess, with dishevelled hair, calls with terrific charms upon her three hundred Gods, upon Erebus, chaos, and the three-faced Hecate. She sprinkles around the waters of Avernus, and adds certain herbs that had been cropped by moonlight with a sickle of brass. She brings with her the excrescence which is found upon the forehead of a new-cast foal, of the size of a dried fig, and which unless first eaten by the mare, the mother never admits her young to the nourishment of her milk. After these preparations, Dido, with garments tucked up, and with one foot bare, approached the altars, breaking over them a consecrated cake, and embracing them successively in her arms. The pyre was then to be set on fire; and, as the different objects placed upon it were gradually consumed, the charm became complete, and the ends proposed to the ceremony were expected to follow. Dido assures her sister, that she well knew the unlawfulness of her proceeding, and protests that nothing but irresistible necessity should have compelled her to have recourse to these unhallowed arts. She finally stabs herself, and expires.

ROMULUS.

The early history of Rome is, as might be expected, interspersed with prodigies. Romulus himself, the founder, after a prosperous reign of many years, disappeared at last by a miracle. The king assembled his army to a general review, when suddenly, in the midst of the ceremony, a tempest arose, with vivid lightnings and tremendous crashes of thunder. Romulus became enveloped in a cloud, and, when, shortly after, a clear sky and serene heavens succeeded, the king was no more seen, and the throne upon which he had sat appeared vacant. The people were somewhat dissatisfied with the event, and appear to have suspected foul play. But the next day Julius Proculus, a senator of the highest character, shewed himself in the general assembly, and assured them, that, with the first dawn of the morning, Romulus had stood before him, and certified to him that the Gods had taken him up to their celestial abodes, authorising him withal to declare to his citizens, that their arms should be for ever successful against all their enemies[a].

NUMA.

Numa was the second king of Rome: and, the object of Romulus having been to render his people soldiers and invincible in war, Numa, an old

[a] Livius, Lib. I, c. 16.

man and a philosopher, made it his purpose to civilise them, and deeply to imbue them with sentiments of religion. He appears to have imagined the thing best calculated to accomplish this purpose, was to lead them by prodigies and the persuasion of an intercourse with the invisible world. A shield fell from heaven in his time, which he caused to be carefully kept and consecrated to the Gods; and he conceived no means so likely to be effectual to this end, as to make eleven other shields exactly like the one which had descended by miracle, so that, if an accident happened to any one, the Romans might believe that the one given to them by the divinity was still in their possession[b].

Numa gave to his people civil statutes, and a code of observances in matters of religion; and these also were inforced with a divine sanction. Numa met the goddess Egeria from time to time in a cave; and by her was instructed in the institutions he should give to the Romans: and this barbarous people, awed by the venerable appearance of their king, by the sanctity of his manners, and still more by the divine favour which was so signally imparted to him, received his mandates with exemplary reverence, and ever after implicitly conformed themselves to all that he had suggested[c].

[b] Dionysius Halicarnassensis.
[c] Livius, Lib. I, c. 19, 21.

TULLUS HOSTILIUS.

Tullus Hostilius, the third king of Rome, restored again the policy of Romulus. In his time, Alba, the parent state, was subdued and united to its more flourishing colony. In the mean time Tullus, who during the greater part of his reign had been distinguished by martial achievements, in the latter part became the victim of superstitions. A shower of stones fell from heaven, in the manner, as Livy tells us, of a hail-storm. A plague speedily succeeded to this prodigy[a]. Tullus, awed by these events, gave his whole attention to the rites of religion. Among other things he found in the sacred books of Numa an account of a certain ceremony, by which, if rightly performed, the appearance of a God, named Jupiter Elicius, would be conjured up. But Tullus, who had spent his best days in the ensanguined field, proved inadequate to this new undertaking. Some defects having occurred in his performance of the magical ceremony, not only no God appeared at his bidding, but, the anger of heaven being awakened, a thunderbolt fell on the palace, and the king, and the place of his abode were consumed together[b].

ACCIUS NAVIUS.

In the reign of Tarquinius Priscus, the fifth

[a] Livius, Lib. 1, c. 31.   [b] Ibid.

king of Rome, another famous prodigy is recorded. The king had resolved to increase the number of the Roman cavalry. Romulus had raised the first body with the customary ceremony of augury. Tarquinius proposed to proceed in the present case, omitting this ceremony. Accius Navius, the chief augur, protested against the innovation. Tarquin, in contempt of his interference, addressed Accius, saying, "Come, augur, consult your birds, and tell me, whether the thing I have now in my mind can be done, or cannot be done." Accius proceeded according to the rules of his art, and told the king it could be done. "What I was thinking of," replied Tarquinius, "was whether you could cut this whetstone in two with this razor." Accius immediately took the one instrument and the other, and performed the prodigy in the face of the assembled people*.

SERVIUS TULLIUS.

Servius Tullius, the sixth king of Rome, was the model of a disinterested and liberal politician, and gave to his subjects those institutions to which, more than to any other cause, they were indebted for their subsequent greatness. Tarquinius subjected nearly the whole people of Latium to his rule, capturing one town of this district after another. In Corniculum, one of these places, Ser-

* Livius, Lib. I, c. 36.

vius Tullius, being in extreme youth, was made a prisoner of war, and subsequently dwelt as a slave in the king's palace. One day as he lay asleep in the sight of many, his head was observed to be on fire. The bystanders, terrified at the spectacle, hastened to bring water that they might extinguish the flames. The queen forbade their assiduity, regarding the event as a token from the Gods. By and by the boy awoke of his own accord, and the flames at the same instant disappeared. The queen, impressed with the prodigy, became persuaded that the youth was reserved for high fortunes, and directed that he should be instructed accordingly in all liberal knowledge. In due time he was married to the daughter of Tarquinius, and was destined in all men's minds to succeed in the throne, which took place in the sequel[b].

In the year of Rome two hundred and ninety one, forty-seven years after the expulsion of Tarquin, a dreadful plague broke out in the city, and carried off both the consuls, the augurs, and a vast multitude of the people. The following year was distinguished by numerous prodigies; fires were seen in the heavens, and the earth shook, spectres appeared, and supernatural voices were heard, an ox spoke, and a shower of raw flesh fell in the fields. Most of these prodigies were not preternatural; the speaking ox was probably received on the report of a single hearer; and the

[b] Livius, Lib. I, c. 39.

whole was invested with exaggerated terror by means of the desolation of the preceding year[c].

THE SORCERESS OF VIRGIL.

Prodigies are plentifully distributed through the earlier parts of the Roman history; but it is not our purpose to enter into a chronological detail on the subject. And in reality those already given, except in the instance of Tullus Hostilius, do not entirely fall within the scope of the present volume. The Roman poets, Virgil, Horace, Ovid and Lucan, give a fuller insight than the Latin prose-writers, into the conceptions of their countrymen upon the subject of incantations and magic.

The eighth eclogue of Virgil, entitled Pharmaceutria, is particularly to our purpose in this point. There is an Idyll of Theocritus under the same name; but it is of an obscurer character; and the enchantress is not, like that of Virgil, triumphant in the success of her arts.

The sorceress is introduced by Virgil, giving direction to her female attendant as to the due administration of her charms. Her object is to recal Daphnis, whom she styles her husband, to his former love for her. At the same time, she says, she will endeavour by magic to turn him away from his wholesome sense. She directs her attendant to burn vervain and frankincense; and

[c] Livius, Lib. III, c. 6, *et seqq.*

she ascribes the highest efficacy to the solemn chant, which, she says, can call down the moon from its sphere, can make the cold-blooded snake burst in the field, and was the means by which Circe turned the companions of Ulysses into beasts. She orders his image to be thrice bound round with fillets of three colours, and then that it be paraded about a prepared altar, while in binding the knots the attendant shall still say, "Thus do I bind the fillets of Venus." One image of clay and one of wax are placed before the same fire; and as the image of clay hardens, so does the heart of Daphnis harden towards his new mistress; and as the image of wax softens, so is the heart of Daphnis made tender towards the sorceress. She commands a consecrated cake to be broken over the image, and crackling laurels to be burned before it, that as Daphnis had tormented her by his infidelity, so he in his turn may be agitated with a returning constancy. She prays that as the wanton heifer pursues the steer through woods and glens, till at length, worn out with fatigue, she lies down on the oozy reeds by the banks of the stream, and the night-dew is unable to induce her to withdraw, so Daphnis may be led on after her for ever with inextinguishable love. She buries the relics of what had belonged to Daphnis beneath her threshold. She bruises poisonous herbs of resistless virtue which had been gathered in the kingdom of Pontus, herbs, which enabled him who gave them to turn himself into a hungry wolf prowling amidst the forests, to call up ghosts from the grave, and to translate the ripened harvest from the field where it grew to the lands of another. She orders her attendant to bring out to the face of heaven the ashes of these herbs, and to cast them over her head into the running stream, and at the same time taking care not to look behind her. After all her efforts the sorceress begins to despair. She says, " Daphnis heeds not my incantations, heeds not the Gods." She looks again; she perceives the ashes on the altar emit sparkles of fire; she hears her faithful house-dog bark before the door; she says, " Can these things be; or do lovers dream what they desire? It is not so! The real Daphnis comes; I hear his steps; he has left the deluding town; he hastens to my longing arms!"

CANIDIA.

In the works of Horace occurs a frightful and repulsive, but a curious detail of a scene of incantation[a]. Four sorceresses are represented as assembled, Canidia, the principal, to perform, the other three to assist in, the concoction of a charm, by means of which a certain youth, named Varus, for whom Canidia had conceived a passion, but who regards the hag with the utmost contempt, may

[a] Epod. V.

be made obsequious to her desires. Canidia appears first, the locks of her dishevelled hair twined round with venomous and deadly serpents, ordering the wild fig-tree and the funereal cypress to be rooted up from the sepulchres on which they grew, and these, together with the egg of a toad smeared with blood, the plumage of the screech-owl, various herbs brought from Thessaly and Georgia, and bones torn from the jaws of a famished dog, to be burned in flames fed with perfumes from Colchis. Of the assistant witches, one traces with hurried steps the edifice, sprinkling it, as she goes, with drops from the Avernus, her hair on her head stiff and erect, like the quills of the sea-hedge-hog, or the bristles of a hunted boar; and another, who is believed by all the neighbourhood to have the faculty of conjuring the stars and the moon down from heaven, contributes her aid.

But, which is most horrible, the last of the assistant witches is seen, armed with a spade, and, with earnest and incessant labour, throwing up earth, that she may dig a trench, in which is to be plunged up to his chin a beardless youth, stripped of his purple robe, the emblem of his noble descent, and naked, that, from his marrow already dry and his liver (when at length his eye-balls, long fixed on the still renovated food which is withheld from his famished jaws, have no more the power to discern), may be concocted the love-potion, from which these hags promise themselves the most marvellous results.

Horace presents before us the helpless victim of their malice, already inclosed in the fatal trench, first viewing their orgies with affright, asking, by the Gods who rule the earth and all the race of mortals, what means the tumult around him? He then intreats Canidia, by her children if ever she had offspring, by the visible evidences of his high rank, and by the never-failing vengeance of Jupiter upon such misdeeds, to say why she casts on him glances, befitting the fury of a stepmother, or suited to a beast already made desperate by the wounds of the hunter.

At length, no longer exhausting himself in fruitless intreaties, the victim has recourse in his agonies to curses on his executioners. He says, his ghost shall haunt them for ever, for no vengeance can expiate such cruelty. He will tear their cheeks with his fangs, for that power is given to the shades below. He will sit, a night-mare, on their bosoms, driving away sleep from their eyes; while the enraged populace shall pursue them with stones, and the wolves shall gnaw and howl over their unburied members. The unhappy youth winds up all with the remark, that his parents who will survive him, shall themselves witness this requital of the sorceresses' infernal deeds.

Canidia, unmoved by these menaces and execrations, complains of the slow progress of her charms. She gnaws her fingers with rage. She invokes the night and the moon, beneath whose rays these preparations are carried on, now, while the wild beasts lie asleep in the forests, and while the dogs alone bay the superanuated letcher, who relies singly on the rich scents with which he is perfumed for success, to speed her incantations, and signalise their power beneath the roof of him whose love she seeks. She impatiently demands why her drugs should be of less avail than those of Medea, with which she poisoned a garment, that, once put on, caused Creusa, daughter of the king of Corinth, to expire in intolerable torments? She discovers that Varus had hitherto baffled her power by means of some magical antidote; and she resolves to prepare a mightier charm, that nothing from earth or hell shall resist. "Sooner," she says, "shall the sky be swallowed up in the sea, and the earth be stretched a covering over both, than thou, my enemy, shalt not be wrapped in the flames of love, as subtle and tenacious as those of burning pitch."

It is not a little curious to remark the operation of the antagonist principles of superstition and scepticism among the Romans in this enlightened period, as it comes illustrated to us in the compositions of Horace on this subject. In the piece, the contents of which have just been given, things are painted in all the solemnity and terror which is characteristic of the darkest ages. But, a few pages further on, we find the poet in a mock Palinodia deprecating the vengeance of the sorceress, who, he says, has already sufficiently punished him by turning through her charms his flaxen hair to hoary white, and overwhelming him by day and night with ceaseless anxieties. He feels himself through her powerful magic tortured, like Hercules in the envenomed shirt of Nessus, or as if he were cast down into the flames of Ætna; nor does he hope that she will cease compounding a thousand deadly ingredients against him, till his very ashes shall have been scattered by the resistless winds. He offers therefore to expiate his offence at her pleasure either by a sacrifice of an hundred oxen, or by a lying ode, in which her chastity and spotless manners shall be applauded to the skies.

What Ovid gives is only a new version of the charms and philtres of Medea[b].

ERICHTHO.

Lucan, in his Pharsalia[a], takes occasion, immediately before the battle which was to decide the fate of the Roman world, to introduce Sextus, the younger son of Pompey, as impatient to enquire, even by the most sacrilegious means, into the important events which are immediately impending. He is encouraged in the attempt by the reflection, that the soil upon which they are now standing, Thessaly, had been notorious for ages as the

[b] Metamorphoses, Lib. VII.   [a] Lib. VI.

noxious and unwholesome seat of sorcery and witchcraft. The poet therefore embraces this occasion to expatiate on the various modes in which this detested art was considered as displaying itself. And, however he may have been ambitious to seize this opportunity to display the wealth of his imagination, the whole does not fail to be curious, as an exhibition of the system of magical power so far as the matter in hand is concerned.

The soil of Thessaly, says the poet, is in the utmost degree fertile in poisonous herbs, and her rocks confess the power of the sepulchral song of the magician. There a vegetation springs up of virtue to compel the Gods; and Colchis itself imports from Thessaly treasures of this sort which she cannot boast as her own. The chaunt of the Thessalian witch penetrates the furthest seat of the Gods, and contains words so powerful, that not the care of the skies, or of the revolving spheres, can avail as an excuse to the deities to decline its force. Babylon and Memphis yield to the superior might; and the Gods of foreign climes fly to fulfil the dread behests of the magician.

Prompted by Thessalian song, love glides into the hardest hearts; and even the severity of age is taught to burn with youthful fires. The ingredients of the poisoned cup, nor the excrescence found on the forehead of the new-cast foal, can rival in efficacy the witching incantation. The soul is melted by its single force. The heart which not all the attractions of the genial bed could fire, nor the influence of the most beautiful form, the wheel of the sorceress shall force from its bent.

But the effects are perhaps still more marvellous that are produced on inanimate and unintellectual nature. The eternal succession of the world is suspended; day delays to rise on the earth; the skies no longer obey their ruler. Nature becomes still at the incantation: and Jove, accustomed to guide the machine, is astonished to find the poles disobedient to his impulse. Now the sorceress deluges the plains with rain, hides the face of heaven with murky clouds, and the thunders roll, unbidden by the thunderer. Anon she shakes her hair, and the darkness is dispersed, and the whole horizon is cleared. At one time the sea rages, urged by no storm; and at another is smooth as glass, in defiance of the tempestuous North. The breath of the enchanter carries along the bark in the teeth of the wind; the headlong torrent is suspended, and rivers run back to their source. The Nile overflows not in the summer; the crooked Meander shapes to itself a direct course; the sluggish Arar gives new swiftness to the rapid Rhone; and the mountains bow their heads to their foundations. Clouds shroud the peaks of the cloudless Olympus; and the Scythian snows dissolve, unurged by the sun. The sea, though impelled by the tempestuous constellations, is counteracted by witchcraft, and no longer beats along the shore.

Earthquakes shake the solid globe; and the affrighted inhabitants behold both hemispheres at once. The animals most dreaded for their fury, and whose rage is mortal, become tame; the hungry tiger and the lordly lion fawn at the sorceress's feet; the snake untwines all her folds amidst the snow; the viper, divided by wounds, unites again its severed parts; and the envenomed serpent pines and dies under the power of a breath more fatal than his own.

What, exclaims the poet, is the nature of the compulsion thus exercised on the Gods, this obedience to song and to potent herbs, this fear to disobey and scorn the enchanter? Do they yield from necessity, or is it a voluntary subjection? Is it the piety of these hags that obtains the reward, or by menaces do they secure their purpose? Are all the Gods subject to this control, or, is there one God upon whom it has power, who, himself compelled, compels the elements? The stars fall from heaven at their command. The silver moon yields to their execrations, and burns with a smouldering flame, even as when the earth comes between her and the sun, and by its shadow intercepts its rays; thus is the moon brought lower and more low, till she covers with her froth the herbs destined to receive her malignant influence.

But Erichtho, the witch of the poet, flouts all these arts, as too poor and timid for her purposes.

She never allows a roof to cover her horrid head, or confesses the influence of the Houshold Gods. She inhabits the deserted tomb, and dwells in a grave from which the ghost of the dead has been previously expelled. She knows the Stygian abodes, and the counsels of the infernals. Her countenance is lean; and her complexion overspread with deadly paleness. Her hair is neglected and matted. But when clouds and tempests obscure the stars, then she comes forth, and defies the midnight lightning. Wherever she treads, the fruits of the earth become withered, and the wholesome air is poisoned with her breath. She offers no prayers, and pours forth no supplications; she has recourse to no divination. She delights to profane the sacred altar with a funereal flame, and pollutes the incense with a torch from the pyre. The Gods yield at once to her voice, nor dare to provoke her to a second mandate. She incloses the living man within the confines of the grave; she subjects to sudden death those who were destined to a protracted age; and she brings back to life the corses of the dead. She snatches the smoaking cinders, and the bones whitened with flame, from the midst of the pile, and wrests the torch from the hand of the mourning parent. She seizes the fragments of the burning shroud, and the embers yet moistened with blood. But, where the sad remains are already hearsed in marble, it is there that she most delights to exercise her sacrilegious power. She tears the limbs of the dead, and digs out their eyes. She gnaws their fingers. She separates with her teeth the rope on the gibbet, and tears away the murderer from the cross on which he hung suspended. She applies to her purposes the entrails withered with the wind, and the marrow that had been dried by the sun. She bears away the nails which had pierced the hands and feet of the criminal, the clotted blood which had distilled from his wounds, and the sinews that had held him suspended. She pounces upon the body of the dead in the battle-field, anticipating the vulture and the beast of prey; but she does not divide the limbs with a knife, nor tear them asunder with her hands: she watches the approach of the wolf, that she may wrench the morsels from his hungry jaws. Nor does the thought of murder deter her, if her rites require the living blood, first spurting from the lacerated throat. She drags forth the foetus from its pregnant mother, by a passage which violence has opened. Wherever there is occasion for a bolder and more remorseless ghost, with her own hand she dismisses him from life; man at every period of existence furnishes her with materials. She drags away the first down from the cheek of the stripling, and with her left hand cuts the favourite lock from the head of the young man. Often she watches with seemingly pious care the dying hours of a relative, and seizes the occasion to bite his lips, to compress his windpipe, and whisper in his expiring organ some message to the infernal shades.

Sextus, guided by the general fame of this woman, sought her in her haunts. He chose his time, in the depth of the night, when the sun is at its lowermost distance from the upper sky. He took his way through the desert fields. He took for companions the associates, the accustomed ministers of his crimes. Wandering among broken graves and crumbling sepulchres, they discovered her, sitting sublime on a ragged rock, where mount Hæmus stretches its roots to the Pharsalic field. She was mumbling charms of the Magi and the magical Gods. For she feared that the war might yet be transferred to other than the Emathian fields. The sorceress was busy therefore enchanting the soil of Philippi, and scattering on its surface the juice of potent herbs, that it might be heaped with carcasses of the dead, and saturated with their blood, that Macedon, and not Italy, might receive the bodies of departed kings and the bones of the noble, and might be amply peopled with the shades of men. Her choicest labour was as to the earth where should be deposited the prostrate Pompey, or the limbs of the mighty Cæsar.

Sextus approached, and bespoke her thus: "Oh, glory of Hæmonia, that hast the power to divulge the fates of men, or canst turn aside fate itself from its prescribed course, I pray thee to exercise thy gift in disclosing events to come. Not the meanest of the Roman race am I, the offspring of an illustrious chieftain, lord of the world in the one case, or in the other the destined heir to my father's calamity. I stand on a tremendous and giddy height: snatch me from this posture of doubt; let me not blindly rush on, and blindly fall; extort this secret from the Gods, or force the dead to confess what they know."

To whom the Thessalian crone replied: "If you asked to change the fate of an individual, though it were to restore an old man, decrepid with age, to vigorous youth, I could comply; but to break the eternal chain of causes and consequences exceeds even our power. You seek however only a foreknowledge of events to come, and you shall be gratified. Meanwhile it were best, where slaughter has afforded so ample a field, to select the body of one newly deceased, and whose flexible organs shall be yet capable of speech, not with lineaments already hardened in the sun."

Saying thus, Erichtho proceeded (having first with her art made the night itself more dark, and involved her head in a pitchy cloud), to explore the field, and examine one by one the bodies of the unburied dead. As she approached, the wolves fled before her, and the birds of prey, unwillingly sheathing their talons, abandoned their repast, while the Thessalian witch, searching into the vital parts of the frames before her, at length fixed on one whose lungs were uninjured, and whose organs of speech had sustained no wound. The fate of many hung in doubt, till she had made her selection. Had the revival of whole armies been her will, armies would have stood up obedient to her bidding. She passed a hook beneath the jaw of the selected one, and, fastening it to a cord, dragged him along over rocks and stones, till she reached a cave, overhung by a projecting ridge. A gloomy fissure in the ground was there, of a depth almost reaching to the Infernal Gods, where the yew-tree spread thick its horizontal branches, at all times excluding the light of the sun. Fearful and withering shade was there, and noisome slime cherished by the livelong night. The air was heavy and flagging as that of the Tænarian promontory; and hither the God of hell permits his ghosts to extend their wanderings. It is doubtful whether the sorceress called up the dead to attend her here, or herself descended to the abodes of Pluto. She put on a fearful and variegated robe; she covered her face with her dishevelled hair, and bound her brow with a wreath of vipers.

Meanwhile she observed Sextus afraid, with his eyes fixed on the ground, and his companions trembling; and thus she reproached them. "Lay aside," she said, "your vainly-conceived terrors! You shall behold only a living and a human figure, whose accents you may listen to with perfect security. If this alarms you, what would you say, if you should have seen the Stygian lakes, and the shores burning with sulphur unconsumed, if the furies stood before you, and Cerberus with his mane of vipers, and the giants chained in eternal adamant? Yet all these you might have witnessed unharmed; for all these would quail at the terror of my brow."

She spoke, and next plied the dead body with her arts. She supples his wounds, and infuses fresh blood into his veins: she frees his scars from the clotted gore, and penetrates them with froth from the moon. She mixes whatever nature has engendered in its most fearful caprices, foam from the jaws of a mad dog, the entrails of the lynx, the backbone of the hyena, and the marrow of a stag that had dieted on serpents, the sinews of the remora, and the eyes of a dragon, the eggs of the eagle, the flying serpent of Arabia, the viper that guards the pearl in the Red Sea, the slough of the hooded snake, and the ashes that remain when the phoenix has been consumed. To these she adds all venom that has a name, the foliage of herbs over which she has sung her charms, and on which she had voided her rheum as they grew.

At length she chaunts her incantation to the Stygian Gods, in a voice compounded of all discords, and altogether alien to human organs. It resembles at once the barking of a dog, and the howl of a wolf; it consists of the hooting of the screech-owl, the yelling of a ravenous wild beast, and the fearful hiss of a serpent. It borrows somewhat from the roar of tempestuous waves, the hollow rushing of the winds among the branches of the forest, and the tremendous crash of deafening thunder.

"Ye Furies," she cries, "and dreadful Styx, ye sufferings of the damned, and Chaos, for ever eager to destroy the fair harmony of worlds, and thou, Pluto, condemned to an eternity of ungrateful existence, Hell, and Elysium, of which no Thessalian witch shall partake, Proserpine, for ever cut off from thy health-giving mother, and horrid Hecate, Cerebrus curst with incessant hunger, ye Destinies, and Charon endlessly murmuring at the task I impose of bringing back the dead again to the land of the living, hear me!—if I call on you with a voice sufficiently impious and abominable, if I have never sung this chaunt, unsated with human gore, if I have frequently laid on your altars the fruit of the pregnant mother, bathing its contents with the reeking brain, if I have placed on a dish before you the head and entrails of an infant on the point to be born—

"I ask not of you a ghost, already a tenant of the Tartarean abodes, and long familiarised to the shades below, but one who has recently quitted the light of day, and who yet hovers over the mouth of hell: let him hear these incantations, and immediately after descend to his destined place! Let him articulate suitable omens to the son of his general, having so late been himself a soldier of the great Pompey! Do this, as you love the very sound and rumour of a civil war!"

Saying this, behold, the ghost of the dead man stood erect before her, trembling at the view of his own unanimated limbs, and loth to enter again the confines of his wonted prison. He shrinks to invest himself with the gored bosom, and the fibres from which death had separated him. Unhappy wretch, to whom death had not given the privilege to die! Erichtho, impatient at the unlooked for delay, lashes the unmoving corpse with one of her serpents. She calls anew on the powers of hell, and threatens to pronounce the dreadful name, which cannot be articulated without consequences never to be thought of, nor without the direst necessity to be ventured upon.

At length the congealed blood becomes liquid and warm; it oozes from the wounds, and creeps steadily along the veins and the members; the fibres are called into action beneath the gelid breast, and the nerves once more become instinct with life. Life and death are there at once. The arteries beat; the muscles are braced; the body raises itself, not by degrees, but at a single impulse, and stands erect. The eyelids unclose. The countenance is not that of a living subject, but of the dead. The paleness of the complexion, the rigidity of the lines, remain; and he looks about with an unmeaning stare, but utters no sound. He waits on the potent enchantress.

"Speak!" said she; "and ample shall be your reward. You shall not again be subject to the art of the magician. I will commit your members to such a sepulchre; I will burn your form with such wood, and will chaunt such a charm over your funeral pyre, that all incantations shall thereafter assail you in vain. Be it enough, that you have once been brought back to life! Tripods, and the voice of oracles deal in ambiguous responses; but the voice of the dead is perspicuous and certain to him who receives it with an unshrinking spirit. Spare not! Give names to things; give places a clear designation; speak with a full and articulate voice."

Saying this, she added a further spell, qualified to give to him who was to answer, a distinct knowledge of that respecting which he was about to be consulted. He accordingly delivers the responses demanded of him; and, that done, earnestly requires of the witch to be dismissed. Herbs and magic rites are necessary, that the corpse may be again unanimated, and the spirit never more be liable to be recalled to the realms of day. The sorceress constructs the funeral pile; the dead man places himself thereon; Erichtho applies the torch; and the charm is for ever at an end.

Lucan in this passage is infinitely too precise, and exhausts his muse in a number of particulars, where he had better have been more succinct and select. He displays the prolific exuberance of a young poet, who had not yet taught himself the multiplied advantages of compression. He had not learned the principle, *Relinquere quæ desperat tractata nitescere posse.*[b] But, as this is the fullest enumeration of the forms of witchcraft that occurs in the writers of antiquity, it seemed proper to give it to the reader entire.

SERTORIUS.

The story of Sertorius and his hind, which occurred about thirty years before, may not be improperly introduced here. It is told by Plutarch in the spirit of a philosopher, and as a mere deception played by that general, to render the barbarous people of Spain more devoted to his service. But we must suppose that it had, at least for the time, the full effect of something preternatural. Sertorius was one of the most highly gifted and well balanced characters that is to be found in Roman story. He considered with the soundest discernment the nature of the persons among whom he was to act, and conducted himself accordingly. The story in Plutarch is this.

"So soone as Sertorius arriued from Africa, he straight leauied men of warre, and with them subdued the people of Spaine fronting upon his

[b] Horat., de Arte Poetica, v. 150.

marches, of which the more part did willingly submit themselues, upon the bruit that ran of him to be mercifull and courteous, and a valiant man besides in present danger. Furthermore, he lacked no fine deuises and subtilties to win their goodwils: as among others, the policy, and deuise of the hind. There was a poore man of the countrey called Spanus, who meeting by chance one day with a hind in his way that had newly calued, flying from the hunters, he let the damme go, not being able to take her; and running after her calfe tooke it, which was a young hind, and of a strange haire, for she was all milk-white. It chanced so, that Sertorius was at that time in those parts. So, this poore man presented Sertorius with his young hind, which he gladly receiued, and which with time he made so tame, that she would come to him when he called her, and follow him whereeuer he went, being nothing the wilder for the daily sight of such a number of armed souldiers together as they were, nor yet afraid of the noise and tumult of the campe. Insomuch as Sertorius by little and little made it a miracle, making the simple barbarous people beleeue that it was a gift that Diana had sent him, by the which she made him understand of many and sundrie things to come: knowing well inough of himselfe, that the barbarous people were men easily deceiued, and quickly caught by any subtill superstition, besides that by art also he brought them to beleeue it as a thing verie true. For when he had any secret intelligence giuen him, that the enemies would inuade some part of the countries and prouinces subject vnto him, or that they had taken any of his forts from him by any intelligence or sudden attempt, he straight told them that his hind spake to him as he slept, and had warned him both to arme his men, and put himselfe in strength. In like manner if he had heard any newes that one of his lieutenants had wonne a battell, or that he had any aduantage of his enemies, he would hide the messenger, and bring his hind abroad with a garland and coller of nosegayes: and then say, it was a token of some good newes comming towards him, perswading them withall to be of good cheare; and so did sacrifice to the Gods, to giue them thankes for the good tidings he should heare before it were long. Thus by putting this superstition into their heades, he made them the more tractable and obedient to his will, in so much as they thought they were not now gouerned any more by a stranger wiser than themselues, but were steadfastly perswaded that they were rather led by some certaine God."———

"Now was Sertorius very heauie, that no man could tell him what was become of his white hind: for thereby all his subtilltie and finenesse to keepe the barbarous people in obedience was taken away, and then specially when they stood in need of most comfort. But by good hap, certaine of his souldiers that had lost themselues in the night, met with the hind in their way, and knowing her by her colour, tooke her and brought her backe againe. Sertorius hearing of her, promised them a good reward, so that they would tell no liuing creature that they brought her againe, and thereupon made her to be secretly kept. Then within a few dayes after, he came abroad among them, and with a pleasant countenance told the noble men and chiefe captaines of these barbarous people, how the Gods had reuealed it to him in his dreame, that he should shortly haue a maruellous good thing happen to him: and with these words sate downe in his chaire to giue audience. Whereupon they that kept the hind not farre from thence, did secretly let her go. The hind being loose, when she had spied Sertorius, ranne straight to his chaire with great joy, and put her head betwixt his legges, and layed her mouth in his right hand, as she before was wont to do. Sertorius also made very much of her, and of purpose appeared maruellous glad, shewing such tender affection to the hind, as it seemed the water stood in his eyes for joy. The barbarous people that stood there by and beheld the same, at the first were much amazed therewith, but afterwards when they had better bethought themselues, for ioy they clapped their hands together, and waited upon Sertorius to his lodging with great and ioyfull shouts, saying, and steadfastly beleeuing, that he he was a heavenly creature, and beloued of the Gods[a]."

CASTING OUT DEVILS.

We are now brought down to the era of the Christian religion; and there is repeated mention of sorcery in the books of the New Testament.

One of the most frequent miracles recorded of Jesus Christ is called the "casting out devils." The Pharisees in the Evangelist, for the purpose of depreciating this evidence of his divine mission, are recorded to have said, " this fellow doth not cast out devils, but by Beelzebub, the prince of devils." Jesus, among other remarks in refutation of this opprobrium, rejoins upon them, " If I by Beelzebub cast out devils, by whom do your children cast them out[b]?" Here then we have a plain insinuation of sorcery from the lips of Christ himself, at the same time that he appears to admit that his adversaries produced supernatural achievements similar to his own.

SIMON MAGUS.

But the most remarkable passage in the New Testament on the subject of sorcery, is one which describes the proceedings of Simon Magus, as follows.

[a] Plutarch, North's Translation. [b] Matt. c. xii, v. 24, 27.

"Then Philip went down to the city of Samaria, and preached Christ unto them. But there was a certain man, called Simon, which before time in the same city used sorcery, and bewitched the people of Samaria, giving out that himself was some great one. To whom they all gave heed, from the least to the greatest, saying, This man is the great power of God. And to him they had regard, because that of long time he had bewitched them with sorceries. But, when they believed Philip, preaching the things concerning the kingdom of God and the name of Jesus Christ, they were baptized both men and women. Then Simon himself believed also. And, when he was baptized, he continued with Philip, and wondered, beholding the miracles and signs which were done.

"Now, when the apostles which were at Jerusalem heard that Samaria had received the word of God, they sent unto them Peter and John. Who, when they were come down, prayed for them, that they might receive the Holy Ghost. For as yet he was fallen upon none of them: only they were baptized in the name of the Lord Jesus. Then laid they their hands on them, and they received the Holy Ghost.

"And, when Simon saw that, through the laying on of the apostles' hands, the Holy Ghost was given, he offered them money, saying, Give me also this power, that on whomsoever I lay hands he may receive the Holy Ghost. But Peter said unto him, Thy money perish with thee! because thou hast thought that the gift of God might be purchased with money. Thou hast neither part nor lot in this matter: for thy heart is not right in the sight of God. Repent therefore of this thy wickedness, and pray God, if perhaps the thought of thy heart may be forgiven thee: for I perceive that thou art in the gall of bitterness, and in the bond of iniquity. Then answered Simon, and said, Pray ye to the Lord for me, that none of these things which ye have spoken come upon me[b]."

This passage of the New Testament leaves us in considerable uncertainty as to the nature of the sorceries, by which "of a long time Simon had bewitched the people of Samaria." But the fathers of the church, Clemens Romanus and Anastasius Sinaita, have presented us with a detail of the wonders he actually performed. When and to whom he pleased he made himself invisible; he created a man out of air; he passed through rocks and mountains without encountering an obstacle; he threw himself from a precipice uninjured; he flew along in the air; he flung himself in the fire without being burned. Bolts and chains were impotent to detain him. He animated statues, so that they appeared to every beholder to be men and women; he made all the furniture

[b] Acts, c. viii.

of the house and the table to change places as required, without a visible mover; he metamorphosed his countenance and visage into that of another person; he could make himself into a sheep, or a goat, or a serpent; he walked through the streets attended with a multitude of strange figures, which he affirmed to be the souls of the departed; he made trees and branches of trees suddenly to spring up where he pleased; he set up and deposed kings at will; he caused a sickle to go into a field of corn, which unassisted would mow twice as fast as the most industrious reaper[c].

Thus endowed, it is difficult to imagine what he thought he would have gained by purchasing from the apostles their gift of working miracles. But Clemens Romanus informs us that he complained that, in his sorceries, he was obliged to employ tedious ceremonies and incantations; whereas the apostles appeared to effect their wonders without difficulty and effort, by barely speaking a word[d].

ELYMAS, THE SORCERER.

But Simon Magus is not the only magician spoken of in the New Testament. When the apostle Paul came to Paphos in the isle of Cyprus,

[c] Clemens Romanus, Recognitiones, Lib. II, cap. 9. Anastasius Sinaita, Quæstiones; Quæstio 20.

[d] Clemens Romanus, Constitutiones Apostolici, Lib. VI, cap. 7.

he found the Roman governor divided in his preference between Paul and Elymas, the sorcerer, who before the governor withstood Paul to his face. Then Paul, prompted by his indignation, said, "Oh, full of all subtlety and mischief, child of the devil, enemy of all righteousness, wilt thou not cease to pervert the right ways of the Lord? And now, behold, the hand of the Lord is upon thee, and thou shalt be blind, not seeing the sun for a season." What wonders Elymas effected to deceive the Roman governor we are not told: but " immediately there fell on him a mist and a darkness; and he went about, seeking some to lead him by the hand*."

In another instance we find certain vagabond Jews, exorcists, who pretended to cast out devils from the possessed. But they came to the apostle, and " confessed, and shewed their deeds. Many of them also which used curious arts, brought their books together, and burned them before all. And they counted the price of them, and found it fifty thousand pieces of silver^f."

It is easy to see however on which side the victory lay. The apostles by their devotion and the integrity of their proceedings triumphed; while those whose only motive was selfishness, the applause of the vulgar, or the admiration of the superficial, gained the honours of a day, and were then swept away into the gulf of general oblivion.

^e Acts, c. xiii.   ^f Ibid, c. xix.

NERO.

The arts of the magician are said to have been called into action by Nero upon occasion of the assassination of his mother, Agrippina. He was visited with occasional fits of the deepest remorse in the recollection of his enormity. Notwithstanding all the ostentatious applauses and congratulations which he obtained from the senate, the army and the people, he complained that he was perpetually haunted with the ghost of his mother, and pursued by the furies with flaming torches and whips. He therefore caused himself to be attended by magicians, who employed their arts to conjure up the shade of Agrippina, and to endeavour to obtain her forgiveness for the crime perpetrated by her son[g]. We are not informed of the success of their evocations.

VESPASIAN.

In the reign of Vespasian we meet with a remarkable record of supernatural power, though it does not strictly fall under the head of magic. It is related by both Tacitus and Suetonius. Vespasian having taken up his abode for some months at Alexandria, a blind man, of the common people, came to him, earnestly intreating the emperor to assist in curing his infirmity, alleging that he was prompted to apply by the admonition of the God

[g] Suetonius, Lib. VI, cap. 14.

Serapis, and importuning the prince to anoint his cheeks and the balls of his eyes with the royal spittle. Vespasian at first treated the supplication with disdain; but at length, moved by the fervour of the petitioner, inforced as it was by the flattery of his courtiers, the emperor began to think that every thing would give way to his prosperous fortune, and yielded to the poor man's desire. With a confident carriage therefore, the multitude of those who stood by being full of expectation, he did as he was requested, and the desired success immediately followed. Another supplicant appeared at the same time, who had lost the use of his hands, and intreated Vespasian to touch the diseased members with his foot; and he also was cured[a].

Hume has remarked that many circumstances contribute to give authenticity to this miracle, "if," as he says, "any evidence could avail to establish so palpable a falsehood. The gravity, solidity, age and probity of so great an emperor, who, through the whole course of his life, conversed in a familiar manner with his friends and courtiers, and never affected any airs of divinity: the historian, a contemporary writer, noted for candour and veracity, and perhaps the greatest and most penetrating genius of all antiquity: and lastly, the persons from whose authority he related the miracle, who we may presume to have been of

[a] Tacitus, Historiæ, Lib. IV, cap. 81. Suetonius, Lib. VIII, cap. 7.

established character for judgment and honour; eye-witnesses of the fact, and confirming their testimony, as Tacitus goes on to say, after the Flavian family ceased to be in power, and could no longer give any reward as the price of a lie[b]."

APOLLONIUS OF TYANA.

Apollonius of Tyana in Asia Minor was born nearly at the same time as Jesus Christ, and acquired great reputation while he lived, and for a considerable time after. He was born of wealthy parents, and seems early to have betrayed a passion for philosophy. His father, perceiving this, placed him at fourteen years of age under Euthydemus, a rhetorician of Tarsus; but the youth speedily became dissatisfied with the indolence and luxury of the citizens, and removed himself to Ægas, a neighbouring town, where was a temple of Æsculapius, and where the God was supposed sometimes to appear in person. Here he became professedly a disciple of the sect of Pythagoras. He refrained from animal food, and subsisted entirely on fruits and herbs. He went barefoot, and wore no article of clothing made from the skins of animals[a]. He further imposed on himself a noviciate of five years silence. At the death of his father, he divided his patrimony equally with his

[b] Hume, Essays, Part III, Section X.
[a] Philostratus, Vita Apollonii, Lib. I, cap. 5, 6.

brother; and, that brother having wasted his estate by prodigality, he again made an equal division with him of what remained[b]. He travelled to Babylon and Susa in pursuit of knowledge, and even among the Brachmans of India, and appears particularly to have addicted himself to the study of magic[c]. He was of a beautiful countenance and a commanding figure, and, by means of these things, combined with great knowledge, a composed and striking carriage, and much natural eloquence, appears to have won universal favour wherever he went. He is said to have professed the understanding of all languages without learning them, to read the thoughts of men, and to be able to interpret the language of animals. A power of working miracles attended him in all places[d].

On one occasion he announced to the people of Ephesus the approach of a terrible pestilence; but the citizens paid no attention to his prophecy. The calamity however having overtaken them, they sent to Apollonius who was then at Smyrna, to implore his assistance. He obeyed the summons. Having assembled the inhabitants, there was seen among them a poor, old and decrepid beggar, clothed in rags, hideous of visage, and with a peculiarly fearful and tremendous expression in his eyes. Apollonius called out to the

[b] Philostratus, Vita Apollonii, Lib. I, c. 10.
[c] Ibid, c. 13. [d] Ibid, c. 13, 14.

Ephesians, " This is an enemy to the Gods; turn all your animosity against him, and stone him to death!" The old man in the most piteous tones besought their mercy. The citizens were shocked with the inhumanity of the prophet. Some however of the more thoughtless flung a few stones, without any determined purpose. The old man, who had stood hitherto crouching, and with his eyes half-closed, now erected his figure, and cast on the crowd glances, fearful, and indeed diabolical. The Ephesians understood at once that this was the genius of the plague. They showered upon him stones without mercy, so as not only to cover him, but to produce a considerable mound where he had stood. After a time Apollonius commanded them to take away the stones, that they might discover what sort of an enemy they had destroyed. Instead of a man they now saw an enormous black dog, of the size of a lion, and whose mouth and jaws were covered with a thick envenomed froth[e].

Another miracle was performed by Apollonius in favour of a young man, named Menippus of Corinth, five and twenty years of age, for whom the prophet entertained a singular favour. This man conceived himself to be beloved by a rich and beautiful woman, who made advances to him, and to whom he was on the point of being contracted in marriage. Apollonius warned his young friend

[e] Philostratus, Lib. IV, c. 10.

against the match in an enigmatical way, telling him that he nursed a serpent in his bosom. This however did not deter Menippus. All things were prepared; and the wedding table was spread. Apollonius meanwhile came among them, and prevented the calamity. He told the young man that the dishes before him, the wine he was drinking, the vessels of gold and silver that appeared around him, and the very guests themselves were unreal and illusory; and to prove his words, he caused them immediately to vanish. The bride alone was refractory. She prayed the philosopher not to torment her, and not to compel her to confess what she was. He was however inexorable. She at length owned that she was an empuse (a sort of vampire), and that she had determined to cherish and pamper Menippus, that she might in the conclusion eat his flesh, and lap up his blood[f].

One of the miracles of Apollonius consisted in raising the dead. A young woman of beautiful person was laid out upon a bier, and was in the act of being conveyed to the tomb. She was followed by a multitude of friends, weeping and lamenting, and among others by a young man, to whom she had been on the point to be married. Apollonius met the procession, and commanded those who bore it, to set down the bier. He exhorted the proposed bridegroom to dry up his tears. He enquired the name of the deceased,

[f] Philostratus, Lib. IV, c. 25.

and, saluting her accordingly, took hold of her hand, and murmured over her certain mystical words. At this act the maiden raised herself on her seat, and presently returned home, whole and sound, to the house of her father[g].

Towards the end of his life Apollonius was accused before Domitian of having conspired with Nerva to put an end to the reign of the tyrant. He appears to have proved that he was at another place, and therefore could not have engaged in the conspiracy that was charged upon him. Domitian publicly cleared him from the accusation, but at the same time required him not to withdraw from Rome, till the emperor had first had a private conference with him. To this requisition Apollonius replied in the most spirited terms. " I thank your majesty," said he, " for the justice you have rendered me. But I cannot submit to what you require. How can I be secure from the false accusations of the unprincipled informers who infest your court? It is by their means that whole towns of your empire are unpeopled, that provinces are involved in mourning and tears, your armies are in mutiny, your senate full of suspicion and alarms, and the islands are crowded with exiles. It is not for myself that I speak, my soul is invulnerable to your enmity; and it is not given to you by the Gods to become master of my body." And, having thus given utterance to the virtuous an-

[g] Philostratus, Lib. IV, c. 45.

guish of his spirit, he suddenly became invisible in the midst of a full assembly, and was immediately after seen at Puteoli in the neighbourhood of Mount Vesuvius[b].

Domitian pursued the prophet no further; and he passed shortly after to Greece, to Ionia, and finally to Ephesus. He every where delivered lectures as he went, and was attended with crowds of the most distinguished auditors, and with the utmost popularity. At length at Ephesus, when he was in the midst of an eloquent harangue, he suddenly became silent. He seemed as if he saw a spectacle which engrossed all his attention. His countenance expressed fervour and the most determined purpose. He exclaimed, " Strike the tyrant; strike him!" and immediately after, raising himself, and addressing the assembly, he said, " Domitian is no more; the world is delivered of its bitterest oppressor."—The next post brought the news that the emperor was killed at Rome, exactly on the day and at the hour when Apollonius had thus made known the event at Ephesus[i].

Nerva succeeded Domitian, between whom and Apollonius there subsisted the sincerest friendship. The prophet however did not long survive this event. He was already nearly one hundred years old. But what is most extraordinary, no one could tell precisely when or where he died. No tomb bore the record of his memory; and his biogra-

[b] Philostratus, Lib. VIII, c. 5.   [i] Ibid, c. 26.

pher inclines to the opinion that he was taken up into heaven[k].

Divine honours were paid to this philosopher, both during his life, and after his death. The inhabitants of Tyana built a temple to him, and his image was to be found in many other temples[l]. The emperor Adrian collected his letters, and treated them as an invaluable relic. Alexander Severus placed his statue in his oratory, together with those of Jesus Christ, Abraham and Orpheus, to whom he was accustomed daily to perform the ceremonies of religion[m]. Vopiscus, in his Life of Aurelian[n], relates that this emperor had determined to rase the city of Tyana, but that Apollonius, whom he knew from his statues, appeared to him, and said, "Aurelian, if you would conquer, do not think of the destruction of my citizens: Aurelian, if you would reign, abstain from the blood of the innocent: Aurelian, if you would conquer, distinguish yourself by acts of clemency." It was at the desire of Julia, the mother of Severus, that Philostratus composed the life of Apollonius, to which he is now principally indebted for his fame[o].

The publicity of Apollonius and his miracles has become considerably greater, from the circumstance of the early enemies of the Christian reli-

---

[k] Philostratus, Lib. VIII, c. 29, 30.   [l] Ibid, c. 29.
[m] Lampridius, in Vita Alex. Severi, c. 29.   [n] C. 24.
[o] Philostratus, Lib. I, c. 3.

gion having instituted a comparison between the miracles of Christ and of this celebrated philosopher, for the obvious purpose of undermining one of the most considerable evidences of the truth of divine revelation. It was probably with an indirect view of this sort that Philostratus was incited by the empress Julia to compose his life of this philosopher; and Hierocles, a writer of the time of Dioclesian, appears to have penned an express treatise in the way of a parallel between the two, attempting to shew a decisive superiority in the miracles of Apollonius.

APULEIUS.

Apuleius of Madaura in Africa, who lived in the time of the Antonines, appears to have been more remarkable as an author, than for any thing that occurs in the history of his life. St. Augustine and Lactantius however have coupled him with Apollonius of Tyana, as one of those who for their pretended miracles were brought into competition with the author of the Christian religion. But this seems to have arisen from their misapprehension respecting his principal work, the Golden Ass, which is a romance detailing certain wonderful transformations, and which they appear to have thought was intended as an actual history of the life of the author.

The work however deserves to be cited in this

place, as giving a curious representation of the ideas which were then prevalent on the subjects of magic and witchcraft. The author in the course of his narrative says: "When the day began to dawn, I chanced to awake, and became desirous to know and see some marvellous and strange things, remembering that I was now in the midst of Thessaly, where, by the common report of the world, sorceries and enchantments are most frequent. I viewed the situation of the place in which I was; nor was there any thing I saw, that I believed to be the same thing which it appeared. Insomuch that the very stones in the street I thought were men bewitched and turned into that figure, and the birds I heard chirping, the trees without the walls, and the running waters, were changed from human creatures into the appearances they wore. I persuaded myself that the statues and buildings could move, that the oxen and other brute beasts could speak and tell strange tidings, and that I should see and hear oracles from heaven, conveyed on the beams of the sun."

ALEXANDER THE PAPHLAGONIAN.

At the same time with Apuleius lived Alexander the Paphlagonian, of whom so extraordinary an account is transmitted to us by Lucian. He was the native of an obscure town, called Abonotica, but was endowed with all that ingenuity and cunning which enables men most effectually to impose upon their fellow-creatures. He was tall of stature, of an impressive aspect, a fair complexion, eyes that sparkled with an awe-commanding fire as if informed by some divinity, and a voice to the last degree powerful and melodious. To these he added the graces of carriage and attire. Being born to none of the goods of fortune, he considered with himself how to turn these advantages to the greatest account; and the plan he fixed upon was that of instituting an oracle entirely under his own direction. He began at Chalcedon on the Thracian Bosphorus; but, continuing but a short time there, he used it principally as an opportunity for publishing that Æsculapius, with Apollo, his father, would in no long time fix his residence at Abonotica. This rumour reached the fellow-citizens of the prophet, who immediately began to lay the foundations of a temple for the reception of the God. In due time Alexander made his appearance; and he so well managed his scheme, that, by means of spies and emissaries whom he scattered in all directions, he not only collected applications to his prophetic skill from the different towns of Ionia, Cilicia and Galatia, but presently extended his fame to Italy and Rome. For twenty years scarcely any oracle of the known world could vie with that of Abonotica; and the emperor Aurelius himself is said to have relied for the success of a military expedition upon the predictions of Alexander the Paphlagonian.

Lucian gives, or pretends to give, an account of the manner in which Alexander gained so extraordinary a success. He says, that this young man in his preliminary travels, coming to Pella in Macedon, found that the environs of this city were distinguished from perhaps all other parts of the world, by a breed of serpents of extraordinary size and beauty. Our author adds that these serpents were so tame, that they inhabited the houses of the province, and slept in bed with the children. If you trod upon them, they did not turn again, or show tokens of anger, and they sucked the breasts of the women to whom it might be of service to draw off their milk. Lucian says, it was probably one of these serpents, that was found in the bed of Olympias, and gave occasion to the tale that Alexander the Great was begotten by Jupiter under the form of a serpent. The prophet bought the largest and finest serpent he could find, and conveyed it secretly with him into Asia. When he came to Abonotica, he found the temple that was built surrounded with a moat; and he took an opportunity privately of sinking a goose-egg, which he had first emptied of its contents, inserting instead a young serpent just hatched, and closing it again with great care. He then told his fellow-citizens that the God was arrived, and hastening to the moat, scooped up the egg in an egg-cup in presence of the whole assembly. He next broke the shell, and shewed the young serpent that twisted about his fingers in presence of the admiring multitude. After this he suffered several days to elapse, and then, collecting crowds from every part of Paphlagonia, he exhibited himself, as he had previously announced he should do, with the fine serpent he had brought from Macedon twisted in coils about the prophet's neck, and its head hid under his arm-pit, while a head artfully formed with linen, and bearing some resemblance to a human face, protruded itself, and passed for the head of the reptile. The spectators were beyond measure astonished to see a little embryo serpent, grown in a few days to so magnificent a size, and exhibiting the features of a human countenance.

Having thus far succeeded, Alexander did not stop here. He contrived a pipe which passed seemingly into the mouth of the animal, while the other end terminated in an adjoining room, where a man was placed unseen, and delivered the replies which appeared to come from the mouth of the serpent. This immediate communication with the God was reserved for a few favoured suitors, who bought at a high price the envied distinction.

The method with ordinary enquirers was for them to communicate their requests in writing, which they were enjoined to roll up and carefully seal; and these scrolls were returned to them in a few days, with the seals apparently unbroken, but with an answer written within, strikingly appropriate to the demand that was preferred.—It is further to be observed, that the mouth of the serpent was occasionally opened by means of a horsehair skilfully adjusted for the purpose, at the same time that by similar means the animal darted out its biforked tongue to the terror of the amazed bystanders.

REVOLUTION PRODUCED IN THE HISTORY OF NECROMANCY AND WITCHCRAFT UPON THE ESTABLISHMENT OF CHRISTIANITY.

IT is necessary here to take notice of the great revolution that took place under Constantine, nearly three hundred years after the death of Christ, when Christianity became the established religion of the Roman empire. This was a period which produced a new era in the history of necromancy and witchcraft. Under the reign of polytheism, devotion was wholly unrestrained in every direction it might chance to assume. Gods known and unknown, the spirits of departed heroes, the Gods of heaven and hell, abstractions of virtue or vice, might unblamed be made the objects of religious worship. Witchcraft therefore, and the invocation of the spirits of the dead, might be practised with toleration; or at all events were not regarded otherwise than as venial deviations from the religion of the state.

It is true, there must always have been a horror of secret arts, especially of such as were of a maleficent nature. At all times men dreaded the mysterious power of spells and incantations, of potent herbs and nameless rites, which were able to control the eternal order of the planets, and the voluntary operations of mind, which could extinguish or recal life, inflame the passions of the soul, blast the works of creation, and extort from invisible beings and the dead the secrets of futurity. But under the creed of the unity of the divine nature the case was exceedingly different. Idolatry, and the worship of other Gods than one, were held to be crimes worthy of the utmost abhorrence and the severest punishment. There was no medium between the worship of heaven and hell. All adoration was to be directed to God the Creator through the mediation of his only begotten Son; or, if prayers were addressed to inferior beings, and the glorified spirits of his saints, at least they terminated in the Most High, were a deprecation of his wrath, a soliciting his favour, and a homage to his omnipotence. On the other hand sorcery and witchcraft were sins of the blackest dye. In opposition to the one only God, the creator of heaven and earth, was the "prince of darkness," the "prince of the power of the air," who contended perpetually against the Almighty, and sought to seduce his creatures and his subjects from their due allegiance. Sorcerers and witches were supposed to do homage and sell themselves to the devil, than which it was not in the mind of man to conceive a greater enormity, or a crime more worthy to cause its perpetrators to be exterminated from the face of the earth. The thought of it was of power to cause the flesh of man to creep and tingle with horror: and such as were prone to indulge their imaginations to the utmost extent of the terrible, found a perverse delight in conceiving this depravity, and were but too much disposed to fasten it upon their fellow-creatures.

MAGICAL CONSULTATIONS RESPECTING THE LIFE OF THE EMPEROR.

It was not within the range of possibility, that such a change should take place in the established religion of the empire as that from Paganism to Christianity, without convulsions and vehement struggle. The prejudices of mankind on a subject so nearly concerned with their dearest interests and affections must inevitably be powerful and obstinate; and the lucre of the priesthood, together with the strong hold they must necessarily have had on the weakness and superstition of their flocks, would tend to give force and perpetuity to the contention. Julian, a man of great ability and unquestionable patriotism, succeeded to the empire only twenty-four years after the death of Constantine; and he employed the most vigorous measures for the restoration of the ancient religion. But the reign of Julian was scarcely more than eighteen months in duration: and that of Jovian, his successor, who again unfurled the standard of Christianity, lasted hardly more than half a year.

The state of things bore a striking similarity to that of England at the time of the Protestant Reformation, where the opposite faiths of Edward the Sixth and his sister Mary, and the shortness of their reigns, gave preternatural keenness to the feelings of the parties, and instigated them to hang with the most restless anticipation upon the chances of the demise of the sovereign, and the consequences, favourable or unfavourable, that might arise from a new accession.

The joint reign of Valentinian and Valens, Christian emperors, had now lasted several years, when information was conveyed to these princes, and particularly to the latter, who had the rule of Asia, that numerous private consultations were held, as to the duration of their authority, and the person of the individual who should come after them. The succession of the Roman empire was elective; and consequently there was almost an unlimited scope for conjecture in this question. Among the various modes of enquiry that were employed we are told, that the twenty-four letters of the alphabet were artificially disposed in a circle, and that a magic ring, being suspended over the centre, was conceived to point to the initial letters of the name of him who should be the future emperor. Theodorus, a man of most eminent qualifications, and high popularity, was put to death by the jealousy of Valens, on the vague evidence that this kind of trial had indicated the early letters of his name[a]. It may easily be imagined, that, where so restless and secret an investigation was employed as to the successor that fate might provide, conspiracy would not always be absent. Charges of this sort were perpetually multiplied; informers were eager to obtain favour or rewards by the disclosures they pretended to communicate; and the Christians, who swayed the sceptre of the state, did not fail to aggravate the guilt of those who had recourse to these means for satisfying their curiosity, by alleging that demons were called up from hell to aid in the magic solution. The historians of these times no doubt greatly exaggerate the terror and the danger, when they say, that the persons apprehended on such charges in the great cities outnumbered the peaceable citizens who were left unsuspected, and that the military who had charge of the prisoners, complained that they were wholly without the power to restrain the flight of the captives, or to control the multitude of partisans who insisted on their immediate release[b]. The punishments were barbarous and indiscriminate; to be accused was almost the same thing as to be convicted; and those were obliged to hold themselves fortunate, who escaped with a fine that in a manner swallowed up their estates.

[a] Zosimus, Lib. IV, cap. 13. Gibbon observes, that the name of Theodosius, who actually succeeded, begins with the same letters which were indicated in this magic trial.
[b] Zosimus, Lib. IV, cap. 14.

HISTORY OF NECROMANCY IN THE EAST.

FROM the countries best known in what is usually styled ancient history, in other words from Greece and Rome, and the regions into which the spirit of conquest led the people of Rome and Greece, it is time we should turn to the East, and those remoter divisions of the world, which to them were comparatively unknown.

With what has been called the religion of the Magi, of Egypt, Persia and Chaldea, they were indeed superficially acquainted; but for a more familiar and accurate knowledge of the East we are chiefly indebted to certain events of modern history; to the conquests of the Saracens, when they possessed themselves of the North of Africa, made themselves masters of Spain, and threatened in their victorious career to subject France to their standard; to the crusades; to the spirit of nautical discovery which broke out in the close of the fifteenth century; and more recently to the extensive conquests and mighty augmentation of territory which have been realised by the English East India Company.

The religion of Persia was that of Zoroaster and the Magi. When Ardshir, or Artaxerxes, the founder of the race of the Sassanides, restored the throne of Persia in the year of Christ 226, he called together an assembly of the Magi from all parts of his dominions, and they are said to have met to the number of eighty thousand[a]. These priests, from a remote antiquity, had to a great degree preserved their popularity, and had remarkably adhered to their ancient institutions.

They seem at all times to have laid claim to the power of suspending the course of nature, and producing miraculous phenomena. But in so numerous a body there must have been some whose pretensions were of a more moderate nature, and others who displayed a loftier aspiration. The more ambitious we find designated in their native language by the name of *Jogees*[b], of the same signification as the Latin *juncti*.

Their notions of the Supreme Being are said to have been of the highest and abstrusest character, as comprehending every possible perfection of power, wisdom and goodness, as purely spiritual in his essence, and incapable of the smallest variation and change, the same yesterday, to-day, and for ever. Such as they apprehended him to be, such the most perfect of their priests aspired to make themselves. They were to put off all human weakness and frailty; and, in proportion as they *assimilated*, or rather *became one* with the Deity, they supposed themselves to partake of his attributes, to become infinitely wise and powerful and

[a] Gibbon, Chap. VIII.   [b] This word is of Sanscrit original.

good. Hence their claim to suspend the course of nature, and to produce miraculous phenomena. For this purpose it was necessary that they should abstract themselves from every thing mortal, have no human passions or partialities, and divest themselves as much as possible of all the wants and demands of our material frame. Zoroaster appears indeed to have preferred morality to devotion, to have condemned celibacy and fasting, and to have pronounced, that "he who sows the ground with diligence and care, acquires a greater stock of religious merit than he who should repeat ten thousand prayers." But his followers at least did not abide by this decision. They found it more practicable to secure to themselves an elevated reputation by severe observances, rigid self-denial, and the practice of the most inconceivable mortifications. This excited wonder and reverence and a sort of worship from the bystander, which industry and benevolence do not so assuredly secure. They therefore in frequent instances lacerated their flesh, and submitted to incredible hardships. They scourged themselves without mercy, wounded their bodies with lancets and nails[c], and condemned themselves to remain for days and years unmoved in the most painful attitudes. It was no unprecedented thing for them to take their station upon the top of a high pillar; and some are said

[c] "They cut themselves with knives and lancets, till the blood gushed out upon them." 1 Kings, xviii, 28.

to have continued in this position, without ever coming down from it, for thirty years. The more they trampled under foot the universal instincts of our nature, and shewed themselves superior to its infirmities, the nearer they approached to the divine essence, and to the becoming one with the Omnipresent. They were of consequence the more sinless and perfect; their will became the will of the Deity, and they were in a sense invested with, and became the mediums of the acts of his power. The result of all this is, that they who exercised the art of magic in its genuine and unadulterated form, at all times applied it to purposes of goodness and benevolence, and that their interference was uniformly the signal of some unequivocal benefit, either to mankind in general, or to those individuals of mankind who were best entitled to their aid. It was theirs to succour virtue in distress, and to interpose the divine assistance in cases that most loudly and unquestionably called for it.

. Such, we are told, was the character of the pure and primitive magic, as it was handed down from the founder of their religion. It was called into action by the Jogees, men who, by an extraordinary merit of whatever sort, had in a certain sense rendered themselves one with the Deity. But the exercise of magical power was too tempting an endowment, not in some cases to be liable to abuse. Even as we read of the angels in heaven, that not all of them stood, and persevered in their original sinlessness and integrity, so of the Jogees some, partaking of the divine power, were also under the direction of a will celestial and divine, while others, having derived, we must suppose, a mighty and miraculous power from the gift of God, afterwards abused it by applying it to capricious, or, as it should seem, to malignant purposes. This appears to have been every where essential to the history of magic. If those who were supposed to possess it in its widest extent and most astonishing degree, had uniformly employed it only in behalf of justice and virtue, they would indeed have been regarded as benefactors, and been entitled to the reverence and love of mankind. But the human mind is always prone to delight in the terrible. No sooner did men entertain the idea of what was supernatural and uncontrolable, than they began to fear it and to deprecate its hostility. They apprehended they knew not what, of the dead returning to life, of invisible beings armed with the power and intention of executing mischief, and of human creatures endowed with the prerogative of bringing down pestilence and slaughter, of dispensing wealth and poverty, prosperity and calamity at their pleasure, of causing health and life to waste away by insensible, but sure degrees, of producing lingering torments, and death in its most fearful form. Accordingly it appears that, as there were certain magicians who were us Gods dispensing benefits to those who best deserved it, so there were others, whose only principle of action was caprice, and against whose malice no innocence and no degree of virtue would prove a defence. As the former sort of magicians were styled *Jogees*, and were held to be the deputies and instruments of infinite goodness, so the other sort were named *Ku-Jogees*, that is, persons who possessing the same species of ascendancy over the powers of nature, employed it only in deeds of malice and wickedness.

In the mean time these magicians appear to have produced the wonderful effects which drew to them the reverence of the vulgar, very frequently by the intervention of certain beings of a nature superior to the human, who should seem, though ordinarily invisible, to have had the faculty of rendering themselves visible when they thought proper, and assuming what shape they pleased. These are principally known by the names of Peris, Dives[d], and Gins, or Genii. Richardson, in the preface to his Persian Dictionary, from which our account will principally be taken, refers us to what he calls a romance, but from which he appears to derive the outline of his Persian mythology. In this romance Kahraman, a mortal, is introduced in conversation with Simurgh, a creature partaking of the nature of a bird and a griffon, who reveals to him the secrets of the past history

---

[d] Otherwise, Deeves.

of the earth. She tells him that she has lived to see the world seven times peopled with inhabitants of so many different natures, and seven times depopulated, the former inhabitants having been so often removed, and giving place to their successors. The beings who occupied the earth previously to man, were distinguished into the Peris and the Dives; and, when they no longer possessed the earth in chief, they were, as it should seem, still permitted, in an airy and unsubstantial form, and for the most part invisibly, to interfere in the affairs of the human race. These beings ruled the earth during seventy-two generations. The last monarch, named Jan bin Jan, conducted himself so ill, that God sent the angel Haris to chastise him. Haris however became intoxicated with power, and employed his prerogative in the most reprehensible manner. God therefore at length created Adam, the first of men, crowning him with glory and honour, and giving him dominion over all other earthly beings. He commanded the angels to obey him; but Haris refused, and the Dives followed his example. The rebels were for the most part sent to hell for their contumacy; but a part of the Dives, whose disobedience had been less flagrant, were reserved, and allowed for a certain term to walk the earth, and by their temptations to put the virtue and constancy of man to trial. Henceforth the human race was secretly surrounded by invisible beings of two species, the Peris, who were friendly to man, and the Dives, who exercised their ingenuity in involving them in error and guilt. The Peris were beautiful and benevolent, but imperfect and offending beings; they are supposed to have borne a considerable resemblance to the Fairies of the western world. The Dives were hideous in form, and of a malignant disposition. The Peris subsist wholly on perfumes, which the Dives, being of a grosser nature, hold in abhorrence. This mythology is said to have been unknown in Arabia till long after Mahomet: the only invisible beings we read of in their early traditions are the Gins, which term, though now used for the most part as synonimous with Dives, originally signified nothing more than certain infernal fiends of stupendous power, whose agency was hostile to man.

There was perpetual war between the Peris and the Dives, whose proper habitation was Kaf, or Caucasus, a line of mountains which was supposed to reach round the globe. In these wars the Peris generally came off with the worst; and in that case they are represented in the traditional tales of the East, as applying to some gallant and heroic mortal to reinforce their exertions. The warriors who figure in these narratives appear all to have been ancient Persian kings. Tahmuras, one of the most celebrated of them, is spoken of as mounting upon Simurgh, surrounded with talismans and enchanted armour, and furnished with a sword the dint of which nothing could resist. He proceeds to Kaf, or Ginnistan, and defeats Arzshank, the chief of the Dives, but is defeated in turn by a more formidable competitor. The war appears to be carried on for successive ages with alternate advantage and disadvantage, till after the lapse of centuries Rustan kills Arzshank, and finally reduces the Dives to a subject and tributary condition. In all this there is a great resemblance to the fables of Scandinavia; and the Northern and the Eastern world seem emulously to have contributed their quota of chivalry and romance, of heroic achievements and miraculous events, of monsters and dragons, of amulets and enchantment, and all those incidents which most rouse the imagination, and are calculated to instil into generous and enterprising youth a courage the most undaunted and invincible.

GENERAL SILENCE OF THE EAST RESPECTING INDIVIDUAL NECROMANCERS.

Asia has been more notorious than perhaps any other division of the globe for the vast multiplicity and variety of its narratives of sorcery and magic. I have however been much disappointed in the thing I looked for in the first place, and that is, in the individual adventures of such persons as might be supposed to have gained a high degree of credit and reputation for their skill in exploits of magic. Where the professors are many (and they have been perhaps no where so numerous as those of magic in the East), it is unavoidable but that some should have been more dextrous than others, more eminently gifted by nature, more enthusiastic and persevering in the prosecution of their purpose, and more fortunate in awakening popularity and admiration among their contemporaries. In the instances of Apollonius Tyanæus and others among the ancients, and of Cornelius Agrippa, Roger Bacon and Faust among the moderns, we are acquainted with many biographical particulars of their lives, and can trace with some degree of accuracy, their peculiarities of disposition, and observe how they were led gradually from one study and one mode of action to another. But the magicians of the East, so to speak, are mere abstractions, not characterised by any of those habits which distinguish one individual of the human race from another, and having those marking traits and petty lineaments which make the person, as it were, start up into life while he passes before our eyes. They are merely reported to us as men prone to the producing great signs and wonders, and nothing more.

Two of the most remarkable exceptions that I have found to this rule, occur in the examples of Rocail, and of Hakem, otherwise called Mocanna.

ROCAIL.

The first of these however is scarcely to be called an exception, as lying beyond the limits of all credible history. Rocail is said to have been the younger brother of Seth, the son of Adam. A Dive, or giant of mount Caucasus, being hard pressed by his enemies, sought as usual among the sons of men for aid that might extricate him out of his difficulties. He at length made an alliance with Rocail, by whose assistance he arrived at the tranquillity he desired, and who in consequence became his grand vizier, or prime minister. He governed the dominions of his principal for many years with great honour and success; but, ultimately perceiving the approaches of old age and death, he conceived a desire to leave behind him a monument worthy of his achievements in policy and war. He according erected, we are not told by what means, a magnificent palace, and a sepulchre equally worthy of admiration. But what was most entitled to notice, he peopled this palace with statues of so extraordinary a quality, that they moved and performed all the functions and offices of living men, so that every one who beheld them would have believed that they were actually informed with souls, whereas in reality all they did was by the power of magic, in consequence of which, though they were in fact no more than inanimate matter, they were enabled to obey the behests, and perform the will, of the persons by whom they were visited[a].

HAKEM, OTHERWISE MOCANNA.

Hakem was a leader in one of the different divisions of the followers of Mahomet. To inspire the greater awe into the minds of his supporters, he pretended that he was the Most High God, the creator of heaven and earth, under one of the different forms by which he has in successive ages become incarnate, and made himself manifest to his creatures. He distinguished himself by the peculiarity of always wearing a thick and impervious veil, by which, according to his followers, he covered the dazzling splendour of his countenance, which was so great that no mortal could behold it and live, but that, according to his enemies, only served to conceal the hideousness of his features, too monstrously deformed to be contemplated without horror. One of his miracles, which seems the most to have been insisted on, was that he nightly, for a considerable space of time, caused an orb, something like the moon, to rise from a sacred well, which gave a light scarcely less splendid than the day, that diffused its beams for many miles around. His followers were enthusiastically devoted to his service, and he supported his authority unquestioned for a number of years. At

[a] D'Herbelot, Bibliothèque Orientale.

length a more formidable opponent appeared, and after several battles he became obliged to shut himself up in a strong fortress. Here however he was so straitly besieged as to be driven to the last despair, and, having administered poison to his whole garrison, he prepared a bath of the most powerful ingredients, which, when he threw himself into it, dissolved his frame, even to the very bones, so that nothing remained of him but a lock of his hair. He acted thus, with the hope that it would be believed that he was miraculously taken up into heaven; nor did this fail to be the effect on the great body of his adherents[b].

ARABIAN NIGHTS' ENTERTAINMENTS.

The most copious record of stories of Asiatic enchantment that we possess, is contained in the Arabian Nights' Entertainments; to which we may add the Persian Tales, and a few other repositories of Oriental adventures. It is true that these are delivered to us in a garb of fiction; but they are known to present so exact a picture of Eastern manners and customs, and so just a delineation of the follies, the weaknesses and credulity of the races of men that figure in them, that, in the absence of materials of a strictly historical sort of which we have to complain, they may not inadequately supply the place, and may furnish us with a pretty full representation of

[b] D'Herbelot, Bibliothèque Orientale.

the ideas of sorcery and magic which for centuries were entertained in this part of the world. They have indeed one obvious defect, which it is proper the reader should keep constantly in mind. The mythology and groundwork of the whole is Persian: but the narrator is for the most part a Mahometan. Of consequence the ancient Fire-worshippers, though they contribute the entire materials, and are therefore solely entitled to our gratitude and deference for the abundant supply they have furnished to our curiosity, are uniformly treated in these books with disdain and contumely as unworthy of toleration, while the comparative upstart race of the believers in the Koran are held out to us as the only enlightened and upright among the sons of men.

Many of the matters most currently related among these supernatural phenomena, are tales of transformation. A lady has two sisters of the most profligate and unprincipled character. They have originally the same share of the paternal inheritance as herself. But they waste it in profusion and folly, while she improves her portion by good judgment and frugality. Driven to the extremity of distress, they humble themselves, and apply to her for assistance. She generously imparts to them the same amount of wealth that they originally possessed, and they are once more reduced to poverty. This happens again and again. At length, finding them incapable of discretion, she prevails on them to come and live with her. By wearisome and ceaseless importunity they induce her to embark in a mercantile enterprise. Here she meets with a prince, who had the misfortune to be born in a region of fire-worshippers, but was providentially educated by a Mahometan nurse. Hence, when his countrymen were by divine vengeance all turned into stones, he alone was saved alive. The lady finds him in this situation, endowed with sense and motion amidst a petrified city, and they immediately fall in love with each other. She brings him away from this melancholy scene, and together they go on board the vessel which had been freighted by herself and her sisters. But the sisters become envious of her good fortune, and conspire, while she and the prince are asleep, to throw them overboard. The prince is drowned; but the lady with great difficulty escapes. She finds herself in a desert island, not far from the place where she had originally embarked on her adventure; and, having slept off the fatigues she had encountered, beholds on her awaking a black woman with an agreeable countenance, a fairy, who leads in her hand two black bitches coupled together with a cord. These black bitches are the lady's sisters, thus metamorphosed, as a punishment for their ingratitude and cruelty. The fairy conveys her through the air to her own house in Bagdad, which she finds well stored with all sorts of commodities, and delivers to her the two animals, with an injunction that she is to whip them every day at a certain hour as a further retribution for their crimes. This was accordingly punctually performed; and, at the end of each day's penance, the lady, having before paid no regard to the animals' gestures and pitiable cries, wept over them, took them in her arms, kissed them, and carefully wiped the moisture from their eyes. Having persevered for a length of time in this discipline, the offenders are finally, by a counter-incantation, restored to their original forms, being by the severities they had suffered entirely cured of the vices which had occasioned their calamitous condition.

Another story is of a calender, a sort of Mahometan monk, with one eye, who had originally been a prince. He had contracted a taste for navigation and naval discoveries; and, in one of his voyages, having been driven by stress of weather into unknown seas, he suddenly finds himself attracted towards a vast mountain of loadstone, which first, by virtue of the iron and nails in the ship, draws the vessel towards itself, and then, by its own intrinsic force, extracts the nails, so that the ship tumbles to pieces, and every one on board is drowned. The mountain, on the side towards the sea, is all covered with nails, which had been drawn from vessels that previously suffered the same calamity; and these nails at once preserve and augment the fatal power of the mountain. The prince only escapes; and he finds himself in a desolate island, with a dome of brass, supported by brazen pillars, and on the top of it a horse of brass, and a rider of the same metal. This rider the prince is fated to throw down, by means of an enchanted arrow, and thus to dissolve the charm which had been fatal to thousands. From the desolate island he embarked on board a boat, with a single rower, a man of metal, and would have been safely conveyed to his native country, had he not inadvertently pronounced the name of God, that he had been warned not to do, and which injunction he had observed many days. On this the boat immediately sunk; but the prince was preserved, who comes into a desolate island, where he finds but one inhabitant, a youth of fifteen. This youth is hid in a cavern, it having been predicted of him that he should be killed after fifty days, by the man that threw down the horse of brass and his rider. A great friendship is struck up between the unsuspecting youth and the prince, who nevertheless fulfils the prediction, having by a pure accident killed the youth on the fiftieth day. He next arrives at a province of the main land, where he visits a castle, inhabited by ten very agreeable young men, each blind of the right eye. He dwells with them for a month, and finds, after a day of pleasant entertainment, that each evening they do penance in squalidness and ashes. His curiosity is greatly excited to obtain an explanation of what he saw, but this they refuse, telling him at the same time, that he may, if he pleases, pass through the same adventure as they have done, and, if he does, wishing it may be attended with a more favourable issue. He determines to make the experiment; and by their direction, after certain preparations, is flown away with through the air by a roc, a stupendous bird, that is capable in the same manner of carrying off an elephant. By this means he is brought to a castle of the most extraordinary magnificence, inhabited by forty ladies of exquisite beauty. With these ladies he lives for eleven months in a perpetual succession of delights. But in the twelfth month they tell him, that they are obliged to leave him till the commencement of the new year. In the mean time they give him for his amusement the keys of one hundred apartments, all but one of which he is permitted to open. He is delighted with the wonders of these apartments till the last day. On that day he opens the forbidden room, where the rarity that most strikes him is a black horse of admirable shape and appearance, with a saddle and bridle of gold. He leads this horse into the open air, and is tempted to mount him. The horse first stands still; but at length, being touched with a switch, spreads a pair of wings which the prince had not before perceived, and mounts to an amazing height in the air. The horse finally descends on the terrace of a castle, where he throws his rider, and leaves him, having first dashed out his right eye with a sudden swing of his tail. The prince goes down into the castle, and to his surprise finds himself in company with the ten young men, blind of one eye, who had passed through the same adventure as he had done, and all been betrayed by means of the same infirmity.

PERSIAN TALES.

These two stories are from the Arabian Nights: the two following are from the Persian Tales.—Fadlallah, king of Mousel, contracted an intimacy with a young dervise, a species of Turkish friar, who makes a vow of perpetual poverty. The dervise, to ingratiate himself the more with the prince, informed him of a secret he possessed, by means of a certain incantation, of projecting his soul into the body of any dead animal he thought proper.

To convince the king that this power was no empty boast, he offered to quit his own body, and animate that of a doe, which Fadlallah had just killed in hunting. He accordingly executed what he proposed, took possession of the body of the doe, displayed the most surprising agility, approached the king, fawning on him with every expression of endearment, and then, after various bounds, deserting the limbs of the animal, and repossessing his own frame, which during the experiment had lain breathless on the ground. Fadlallah became earnest to possess the secret of the dervise; and, after some demurs, it was communicated to him. The king took possession of the body of the doe; but his treacherous confident no sooner saw the limbs of Fadlallah stretched senseless on the ground, than he conveyed his own spirit into them, and, bending his bow, sought to destroy the life of his defenceless victim. The king by his agility escaped; and the dervise, resorting to the palace, took possession of the throne, and of the bed of the queen, Zemroude, with whom Fadlallah was desperately enamoured. The first precaution of the usurper was to issue a decree that all the deer within his dominions should be killed, hoping by this means to destroy the rightful sovereign. But the king, aware of his danger, had deserted the body of the doe, and entered that of a dead nightingale that lay in his path. In this disguise he hastened to the palace, and placed himself in a wide-spreading tree, which grew immediately before the apartment of Zemroude. Here he poured out his complaints and the grief that penetrated his soul in such melodious notes, as did not fail to attract the attention of the queen. She sent out her birdcatchers to make captive the little warbler; and Fadlallah, who desired no better, easily suffered himself to be made their prisoner. In this new position he demonstrated by every gesture of fondness his partiality to the queen; but if any of her women approached him, he pecked at them in anger, and, when the impostor made his appearance, could not contain the vehemence of his rage. It happened one night that the queen's lap-dog died; and the thought struck Fadlallah that he would animate the corpse of this animal. The next morning Zemroude found her favourite bird dead in his cage, and immediately became inconsolable. Never, she said, was so amiable a bird; he distinguished her from all others; he seemed even to entertain a passion for her; and she felt as if she could not survive his loss. The dervise in vain tried every expedient to console her. At length he said, that, if she pleased, he would cause her nightingale to revive every morning, and entertain her with his tunes as long as she thought proper. The dervise accordingly laid himself on a sopha, and by means of certain cabalistic words, transported his soul into the body of the nightingale, and began to sing. Fadlallah watched his time; he lay in a corner of the room unobserved; but no sooner had the dervise deserted his body, than the king proceeded to take possession of it. The first thing he did was to hasten to the cage, to open the door with uncontrolable impatience, and, seizing the bird, to twist off its head. Zemroude, amazed, asked him what he meant by so inhuman an action. Fadlallah in reply related to her all the circumstances that had befallen him; and the queen became so struck with agony and remorse that she had suffered her person, however innocently, to be polluted by so vile an impostor, that she could not get over the recollection, but pined away and died from a sense of the degradation she had endured.

But a much more perplexing and astounding instance of transformation occurs in the history of the Young King of Thibet and the Princess of the Naïmans. The sorcerers in this case are represented as, without any intermediate circumstance to facilitate their witchcraft, having the ability to assume the form of any one they please, and in consequence to take the shape of one actually present, producing a duplication the most confounding that can be imagined.—Mocbel, the son of an artificer of Damascus, but whose father had bequeathed him considerable wealth, contrived to waste his patrimony and his youth together in profligate living with Dilnouaze, a woman of dissolute manners. Finding themselves at once poor and despised, they had recourse to the sage Bedra, the most accomplished magician of the desert, and found means to obtain her favour. In consequence she presented them with two rings, which had the power of enabling them to assume the likeness of any man or woman they please. Thus equipped, Mocbel heard of the death of Mouaffack, prince of the Naïmans, who was supposed to have been slain in a battle, and whose body had never been found. The niece of Mouaffack now filled the throne; and under these circumstances Mocbel conceived the design of personating the absent Mouaffack, exciting a rebellion among his countrymen, and taking possession of the throne. In this project he succeeded; and the princess driven into exile, took refuge in the capital of Thibet. Here the king saw her, fell in love with her, and espoused her. Being made acquainted with her history, he resolved to re-conquer her dominions, and sent a defiance to the usurper. Mocbel, terrified at the thought of so formidable an invader, first pretended to die, and then, with Dilnouaze, who during his brief reign had under the form of a beautiful woman personated his queen, proceeded in his original form to the capital of Thibet. Here his purpose was to interrupt the happiness of those who had disturbed him in his deceitful career. Accordingly one night, when the queen, previously to proceeding to her repose, had shut herself up in her closet to read certain passages of the Alcoran, Dilnouaze, assuming her form with the minutest exactness, hastened to place herself in the royal bed by the side of the king. After a time, the queen shut her book, and went along the gallery to the king's bedchamber. Mocbel watched his time, and placed himself, under the form of a frightful apparition, directly in the queen's path. She started at the sight, and uttered a piercing shriek. The king recognised her voice, and hastened to see what had happened to her. She explained; but the king spoke of something much more extraordinary, and asked her how it could possibly happen that she should be in the gallery, at the same moment that he had left her, undressed and in bed. They proceeded to the chamber to unravel the mystery. Here a contention occurred between the real and the seeming queen, each charging the other with imposture. The king turned from one to the other, and was unable to decide between their pretensions. The courtiers and the ladies of the bedchamber were called, and all were perplexed with uncertainty and doubt. At length they determine in favour of the false queen. It was then proposed that the other should be burned for a sorceress. The king however forbade this. He was not yet altogether decided; and could not resolve to consign his true queen, as it might possibly be, to a cruel death. He was therefore content to strip her of her royal robes, to clothe her in rags, and thrust her ignominiously from his palace.

Treachery however was not destined to be ultimately triumphant. The king one day rode out a hunting; and Mocbel, that he might the better deceive the guards of the palace, seizing the opportunity, assumed his figure, and went to bed to Dilnouaze. The king meanwhile recollected something of importance, that he had forgotten before he went out to hunt, and returning upon his steps, proceeded to the royal chamber. Here to his utter confusion he found a man in bed with his queen, and that man to his greater astonishment the exact counterpart of himself. Furious at the sight, he immediately drew his scymetar. The man contrived to escape down the backstairs. The woman however remained in bed; and, stretching out her hands to intreat for mercy, the king struck off the hand which had the ring on it, and she immediately appeared, as she really was, a frightful hag. She begged for life; and, that she might mollify his rage, explained the mystery, told him that it was by means of a ring that she effected the delusion, and that by a similar enchantment her paramour had assumed the likeness of the king. The king meanwhile was inexorable, and struck off her head. He next turned in pursuit of the adulterer. Mocbel however had had time to mount on horseback. But the king mounted also; and, being the better horseman, in a short time overtook his foe. The impostor did not dare to cope with him, but asked his life; and the king, considering him as the least offender of the two, pardoned him upon condition of his surrendering the ring, in consequence of which he passed the remainder of his life in poverty and decrepitude.

STORY OF A GOULE.

A story in the Arabian Nights, which merits notice for its singularity, and as exhibiting a particular example of the credulity of the people of the East, is that of a man who married a sorceress, without being in any way conscious of her character in that respect. She was sufficiently agreeable in her person, and he found for the most part no reason to be dissatisfied with her. But he became uneasy at the strangeness of her behaviour, whenever they sat together at meals. The husband provided a sufficient variety of dishes, and was anxious that his wife should eat and be refreshed. But she took scarcely any nourishment. He set before her a plate of rice. From this plate she took somewhat, grain by grain; but she would taste of no other dish. The husband remonstrated with her upon her way of eating, but to no purpose; she still went on the same. He knew it was impossible for any one to subsist upon so little as she ate; and his curiosity was roused. One night, as he lay quietly awake, he perceived his wife rise very softly, and put on her clothes. He watched, but made as if he saw nothing. Presently she opened the door, and went out. He followed her unperceived, by moonlight, and tracked her into a place of graves. Here to his astonishment he saw her joined by a Goule, a sort of wandering demon, which is known to infest ruinous buildings, and from time to time suddenly rushes out, seizes children and other defenceless people, strangles, and devours them. Occasionally, for want of other food, this detested race will resort to churchyards, and, digging up the bodies of the newly-buried, gorge their appetites upon the flesh of these. The husband followed his wife and her supernatural companion, and watched their proceedings. He saw them digging in a new-made grave. They extracted the body of the deceased; and, the Goule cutting it up joint by joint, they feasted voraciously, and, having satisfied their appetites, cast the remainder into the grave again, and covered it up as before. The husband now withdrew unobserved to his bed, and the wife followed presently after. He however conceived a horrible loathing of such a wife; and she discovers that he is acquainted with her dreadful secret. They can no longer live together; and a metamorphosis followed. She turned him into a dog, which by ill usage she drove from her door; and he, aided by a benevolent sorceress, first recovers his natural shape, and then, having changed her into a mare, by perpetual hard usage and ill treatment vents his detestation of the character he had discovered in her.

ARABIAN NIGHTS.

A compilation of more vigorous imagination and more exhaustless variety than the Arabian Nights, perhaps never existed. Almost every thing that can be conceived of marvellous and terrific is there to be found. When we should apprehend the author or authors to have come to an end of the rich vein in which they expatiate, still new wonders are presented to us in endless succession. Their power of comic exhibition is not less extraordinary than their power of surprising and terrifying. The splendour of their painting is endless; and the mind of the reader is roused and refreshed by shapes and colours for ever new.

RESEMBLANCE OF THE TALES OF THE EAST AND OF EUROPE.

It is characteristic of this work to exhibit a faithful and particular picture of Eastern manners, customs, and modes of thinking and acting. And yet, now and then, it is curious to observe the coincidence of Oriental imagination with that of antiquity and of the North of Europe, so that it is difficult to conceive the one not to be copied from the other. Perhaps it was so; and perhaps not. Man is every where man, possessed of the same faculties, stimulated by the same passions, deriving pain and pleasure from the same sources, with similar hopes and fears, aspirations and alarms.

In the Third Voyage of Sinbad he arrives at an island were he finds one man, a negro, as tall as a palm-tree, and with a single eye in the middle of his forehead. He takes up the crew, one by one, and selects the fattest as first to be devoured. This is done a second time. At length nine of the boldest seize on a spit, while he lay on his back asleep, and, having heated it red-hot, thrust it into his eye.—This is precisely the story of Ulysses and the Cyclops.

The story of the Little Hunchback, who is choaked with a fish-bone, and, after having brought successive individuals into trouble on the suspicion of murdering him, is restored to life again, is nearly the best known of the Arabian Tales. The merry jest of Dan Hew, Monk of Leicester, who " once was hanged, and four times slain," bears a very striking resemblance to this[a].

A similar resemblance is to be found, only changing the sex of the aggressor, between the well known tale of Patient Grizzel, and that of Cheheristany in the Persian Tales. This lady was a queen of the Gins, who fell in love with the emperor of China, and agrees to marry him upon condition that she shall do what she pleases, and he shall never doubt that what she does is right. She bears him a son, beautiful as the day, and throws him into the fire. She bears him a daughter, and gives her to a white bitch, who runs away with her, and disappears. The emperor goes to war with the Moguls; and the queen utterly destroys the provisions of his army. But the fire was a salamander, and the bitch a fairy, who rear the children in the most admirable manner; and

[a] It is in Selden's Collection of Ballads in the Bodleian Library. See Letters from the Bodleian, Vol. I, p. 120 to 126.

the provisions of the army were poisoned by a traitor, and are in a miraculous manner replaced by such as were wholesome and of the most invigorating qualities.

CAUSES OF HUMAN CREDULITY.

Meanwhile, though the stories above related are extracted from books purely and properly of fiction, they exhibit so just a delineation of Eastern manners and habits of mind, that, in the defect of materials strictly historical, they may to a certain degree supply the place. The principal feature they set before us is credulity and a love of the marvellous. This is ever found characteristic of certain ages of the world; but in Asia it prevails in uninterrupted continuity. Wherever learning and the exercise of the intellectual faculties first shew themselves, there mystery and a knowledge not to be communicated but to the select few must be expected to appear. Wisdom in its natural and genuine form seeks to diffuse itself; but in the East on the contrary it is only valued in proportion to its rarity. Those who devoted themselves to intellectual improvement, looked for it rather in solitary abstraction, than in free communication with the minds of others; and, when they condescended to the use of the organ of speech, they spoke in enigmas and ambiguities, and in phrases better adapted to produce wonder and perplexity, than to enlighten and instruct. When the more consummate instructed the novice, it was by slow degrees only, and through the medium of a long probation. In consequence of this state of things the privileged few conceived of their own attainments with an over-weening pride, and were puffed up with a sense of superiority; while the mass of their fellow-creatures looked to them with astonishment; and, agreeably to the Oriental creed of two independent and contending principles of good and of evil, regarded these select and supernaturally endowed beings anon as a source of the most enviable blessings, and anon as objects of unmingled apprehension and terror, before whom their understandings became prostrate, and every thing that was most appalling and dreadful was most easily believed. In this state superstition unavoidably grew infectious; and the more the seniors inculcated and believed, the more the imagination of the juniors became a pliant and unresisting slave.

The Mantra, or charm, consisting of a few unintelligible words repeated again and again, always accompanied, or rather preceded, the supposed miraculous phenomenon that was imposed on the ignorant. Water was flung over, or in the face of, the thing or person upon whom the miraculous effect was to be produced. Incense was burned; and such chemical substances were set on fire, the dazzling appearance of which might confound the senses of the spectators. The whole consisted in the art of the juggler. The first business was to act on the passions, to excite awe and fear and curiosity in the parties; and next by a sort of slight of hand, and by changes too rapid to be followed by an unpractised eye, to produce phenomena, wholly unanticipated, and that could not be accounted for. Superstition was further an essential ingredient; and this is never perfect, but where the superior and more active party regards himself as something more than human, and the party acted upon beholds in the other an object of religious reverence, or tingles with apprehension of he knows not what of fearful and calamitous. The state of the party acted on, and indeed of either, is never complete, till the senses are confounded, what is imagined is so powerful as in a manner to exclude what is real, in a word, till, as the poet expresses it, " function is smothered in surmise, and nothing is, but what is not."

It is in such a state of the faculties that it is entirely natural and simple, that one should mistake a mere dumb animal for one's relative or near connection in disguise. And, the delusion having once begun, the deluded individual gives to every gesture and motion of limb and eye an explanation that forwards the deception. It is in the same way that in ignorant ages the notion of changeling has been produced. The weak and fascinated mother sees every feature with a turn of expression unknown before, all the habits of the child appear different and strange, till the parent herself denies her offspring, and sees in the object so lately cherished and doated on, a monster uncouth and horrible of aspect.

DARK AGES OF EUROPE.

IN Europe we are slenderly supplied with historians, and with narratives exhibiting the manners and peculiarities of successive races of men, from the time of Theodosius in the close of the fourth century of the Christian era to the end of the tenth. Mankind during that period were in an uncommon degree wrapped up in ignorance and barbarism. We may be morally sure that this was an interval beyond all others, in which superstition and an implicit faith in supernatural phenomena predominated over this portion of the globe. The laws of nature, and the everlasting chain of antecedents and consequents, were little recognised. In proportion as illumination and science have risen on the world, men have become aware that the succession of events is universally operating, and that the frame of men and animals is every where the same, modified only by causes not less unchangeable in their influence than the internal constitution of the frame itself. We have learned to explain much; we are able to predict and investigate the course of things; and the contemplative and the wise are not less intimately and profoundly persuaded that the process of natural events is sure and simple and void of all just occasion for surprise and the lifting up of hands in astonishment, where we are not yet familiarly acquainted with the developement of the elements of things, as where we are. What we have not yet mastered, we feel confidently persuaded that the investigators that come after us will reduce to rules not less obvious, familiar and comprehensible, than is to us the rising of the sun, or the progress of animal and vegetable life from the first bud and seed of existence to the last stage of decrepitude and decay.

But in these ages of ignorance, when but few, and those only the most obvious, laws of nature were acknowledged, every event that was not of almost daily occurrence, was contemplated with more or less of awe and alarm. These men " saw God in clouds, and heard him in the wind." Instead of having regard only to that universal Providence, which acts not by partial impulses, but by general laws, they beheld, as they conceived, the immediate hand of the Creator, or rather, upon most occasions, of some invisible intelligence, sometimes beneficent, but perhaps oftener malignant and capricious, interfering, to baffle the foresight of the sage, to humble the pride of the intelligent, and to place the discernment of the most gifted upon a level with the drivellings of the idiot, and the ravings of the insane.

And, as in events men saw perpetually the supernatural and miraculous, so in their fellow-creatures they continually sought, and therefore frequently imagined that they found, a gifted race, that had command over the elements, held commerce with the invisible world, and could produce the most stupendous and terrific effects. In man, as we now behold him, we can ascertain his nature, the strength and pliability of his limbs, the accuracy of his eye, the extent of his intellectual acquisitions, and the subtlety of his powers of thought, and can therefore in a great measure anticipate what we have to hope or to fear from him. Every thing is regulated by what we call natural means. But, in the times I speak of, all was mysterious: the powers of men were subject to no recognised laws: and therefore nothing that imagination could suggest, exceeded the bounds of credibility. Some men were supposed to be so rarely endowed that " a thousand liveried angels" waited on them invisibly, to execute their behests for the benefit of those they favoured; while, much oftener, the perverse and crookedly disposed, who delighted in mischief, would bring on those to whom, for whatever capricious reason, they were hostile, calamities, which no sagacity could predict, and no merely human power could baffle and resist.

After the tenth century enough of credulity remained, to display in glaring colours the aberrations of the human mind, and to furnish forth tales which will supply abundant matter for the remainder of this volume. But previously to this period, we may be morally sure, reigned most eminently the sabbath of magic and sorcery, when nothing was too wild, and remote from the reality of things, not to meet with an eager welcome, when terror and astonishment united themselves with a nameless delight, and the auditor was alarmed even to a sort of madness, at the same time that he greedily demanded an ever-fresh supply of congenial aliment. The more the known laws of the universe and the natural possibility of things were violated, with the stronger marks of approbation was the tale received: while the dextrous impostor, aware of the temper of his age, and knowing how most completely to blindfold and lead astray his prepared dupes, made a rich harvest of the folly of his contemporaries. But I am wrong to call him an impostor. He imposed upon himself, no less than on the gaping crowd. His discourses, even in the act of being pronounced, won upon his own ear; and the dexterity with which he baffled the observation of others, bewildered his ready sense, and filled him with astonishment at the magnitude of his achievements. The accomplished adventurer was always ready to regard himself rather as a sublime being endowed with great and stupendous attributes, than as a pitiful trickster. He became the God of his own idolatry, and stood astonished, as the witch of Endor in the English Bible is represented to have done, at the success of his incantations.

But all these things are passed away, and are buried in the gulf of oblivion. A thousand tales, each more wonderful than the other, marked the year as it glided away. Every valley had its fairies; and every hill its giants. No solitary dwelling, unpeopled with human inhabitants, was without its ghosts; and no church-yard in the absence of day-light could be crossed with impunity. The gifted enchanter " bedimmed

> The noon-tide sun, called forth the mutinous winds,
> And 'twixt the green sea and the azured vault
> Set roaring war; to the dread, rattling thunder
> He gave forth fire, and rifted Jove's stout oak
> With his own bolt, the strong-based promontory
> He made to shake, and by the spurs plucked up
> The pine and cedar."

It is but a small remnant of these marvellous adventures that has been preserved. The greater part of them are swallowed up in that gulf of oblivion, to which are successively consigned after a brief interval all events as they occur, except so far as their memory is preserved through the medium of writing and records. From the eleventh century commences a stream of historical relation, which since that time never entirely eludes the search of the diligent enquirer. Before this period there occasionally appears an historian or miscellaneous writer: but he seems to start up by chance; the eddy presently closes over him, and all is again impenetrable darkness.

When this succession of writers began, they were unavoidably induced to look back upon the ages that had preceded them, and to collect here and there from tradition any thing that appeared especially worthy of notice. Of course any information they could glean was wild and uncertain, deeply stamped with the credulity and wonder of an ignorant period, and still increasing in marvellousness and absurdity from every hand it passed through, and from every tongue which repeated it.

MERLIN.

One of the most extraordinary personages whose story is thus delivered to us, is Merlin. He appears to have been contemporary with the period of the Saxon invasion of Britain in the latter part of the fifth century; but probably the earliest mention of his name by any writer that has come down to us is not previous to the eleventh. We may the less wonder therefore at the incredible things that are reported of him. He is first mentioned in connection with the fortune of Vortigern, who is represented by Geoffrey of Monmouth as at that time king of England. The Romans having withdrawn their legions from this island, the unwarlike Britons found themselves incompetent to repel the invasions of the uncivilised Scots and Picts, and Vortigern perceived no remedy but in inviting the Saxons from the northern continent to his aid. The Saxons successfully repelled the invader; but, having done this, they refused to return home. They determined to settle here, and, having taken various towns, are represented as at length inviting Vortigern and his principal nobility to a feast near Salisbury under pretence of a peace, where they treacherously slew three hundred of the chief men of the island, and threw Vortigern into chains. Here, by way of purchasing the restoration of his liberty, they induced him to order the surrender of London, York, Winchester, and other principal towns. Having lost all his strong holds, he consulted his magicians as to how he was to secure himself from this terrible foe. They advised him to build an impregnable tower, and pointed out the situation where it was to be erected. But so unfortunately did their advice succeed, that all the work that his engineers did in the building one day, the earth swallowed, so that no vestige was to be found on the next. The magicians were consulted again on this fresh calamity; and they told the king that that there was no remedying this disaster, other than by cementing the walls of his edifice with the blood of a human being, who was born of no human father.

Vortigern sent out his emissaries in every direction in search of this victim; and at length by strange good fortune they lighted on Merlin near the town of Caermarthen, who told them that his mother was the daughter of a king, but that she had been got with child of him by a being of an angelic nature, and not a man. No sooner had they received this information, than they seized him, and hurried him away to Vortigern as the victim required. But in presence of the king he baffled the magicians; he told the king that the ground they had chosen for his tower, had underneath it a lake, which being drained, they would find at the bottom two dragons of inextinguishable hostility, that under that form figured the Britons and Saxons, all of which upon the experiment proved to be true.

Vortigern died shortly after, and was succeeded first by Ambrosius, and then by Uther Pendragon. Merlin was the confident of all these kings. To Uther he exhibited a very criminal sort of compliance. Uther became desperately enamoured of Igerna, wife of the duke of Cornwal, and tried every means to seduce her in vain. Having consulted Merlin, the magician contrived by an extraordinary unguent to metamorphose Uther into the form of the duke. The duke had shut up his wife for safety in a very strong tower; but Uther in his new form gained unsuspected entrance; and the virtuous Igerna received him to her embraces, by means of which he begot Arthur, afterwards the most renowned sovereign of this island. Uther now contrived that the duke, her husband, should be slain in battle, and immediately married the fair Igerna, and made her his queen.

The next exploit of Merlin was with the intent to erect a monument that should last for ever, to the memory of the three hundred British nobles that were massacred by the Saxons. This design produced the extraordinary edifice called Stonehenge. These mighty stones, which by no human power could be placed in the position in which we behold them, had originally been set up in Africa, and afterwards by means unknown were transported to Ireland. Merlin commanded that they should be carried over the sea, and placed where they now are, on Salisbury Plain. The workmen, having received his directions, exerted all their power and skill, but could not move one of them. Merlin, having for some time watched their exertions, at length applied his magic; and to the amazement of every one, the stones spontaneously quitted the situation in which they had been placed, rose to a great height in the air, and then pursued the course which Merlin had prescribed, finally settling themselves in Wiltshire, precisely in the position in which we now find them, and which they will for ever retain.

The last adventure recorded of Merlin proceeded from a project he conceived for surrounding his native town of Caermarthen with a brazen wall. He committed the execution of this project to a multitude of fiends, who laboured upon the plan underground in a neighbouring cavern[a]. In the mean while Merlin had become enamoured of a supernatural being, called the Lady of the Lake. The lady had long resisted his importunities, and in fact had no inclination to yield to his suit. One day however she sent for him in great haste; and Merlin was of course eager to comply with her invitation. Nevertheless, before he set out, he gave it strictly in charge to the fiends, that they should by no means suspend their labours till they saw him return. The design of the lady was to make sport with him, and elude his addresses. Merlin on the contrary, with the hope to melt her severity, undertook to shew her the wonders of his art. Among the rest he exhibited to her observation a tomb, formed to contain two bodies; at the same time teaching her a charm, by means of which the sepulchre would close, and never again be opened. The lady pretended not to believe that the tomb was wide enough for its purpose, and inveigled the credulous Merlin to enter it, and place himself as one dead. No sooner had she so far succeeded, than she closed the lid of the sepulchre, and pronouncing the charm, rendered it impossible that it should ever be opened again till the day of judgment. Thus, according to the story, Merlin was shut in, a corrupted and putrifying body with a living soul, to which still inhered the faculty of

[a] Spenser, Fairy Queen, Book III, Canto III, stanza 9, *et seqq.*

returning in audible sounds a prophetic answer to such as resorted to it as an oracle. Meanwhile the fiends, at work in the cavern near Caermarthen, mindful of the injunction of their taskmaster, not to suspend their labours till his return, proceed for ever in their office; and the traveller who passes that way, if he lays his ear close to the mouth of the cavern, may hear a ghastly noise of iron chains and brazen caldrons, the loud strokes of the hammer, and the ringing sound of the anvil, intermixed with the pants and groans of the workmen, enough to unsettle the brain and confound the faculties of him that for any time shall listen to the din.

As six hundred years elapsed between the time of Merlin and the earliest known records of his achievements, it is impossible to pronounce what he really pretended to perform, and how great were the additions which successive reporters have annexed to the wonders of his art, more than the prophet himself perhaps ever dreamed of. In later times, when the historians were the contemporaries of the persons by whom the supposed wonders were achieved, or the persons who have for these causes been celebrated have bequeathed certain literary productions to posterity, we may be able to form some conjecture as to the degree in which the heroes of the tale were deluding or deluded, and may exercise our sagacity in the question by what strange peculiarity of mind adventures which we now hold to be impossible obtained so general belief. But in a case like this of Merlin, who lived in a time so remote from that in which his history is first known to have been recorded, it is impracticable to determine at what time the fiction which was afterwards generally received began to be reported, or whether the person to whom the miracles were imputed ever heard or dreamed of the extraordinary things he is represented as having achieved.

ST. DUNSTAN.

An individual scarcely less famous in the dark ages, and who, like Merlin, lived in confidence with successive kings, was St. Dunstan. He was born and died in the tenth century. It is not a little instructive to employ our attention upon the recorded adventures, and incidents occurring in the lives, of such men, since, though plentifully interspersed with impossible tales, they serve to discover to us the tastes and prepossessions of the times in which these men lived, and the sort of accomplishments which were necessary to their success.

St. Dunstan is said to have been a man of distinguished birth, and to have spent the early years of his life in much licentiousness. He was however doubtless a person of the most extraordinary endowments of nature. Ambition early lighted its fire in his bosom; and he displayed the greatest facility in acquiring any talent or art on which he fixed his attention. His career of profligacy was speedily arrested by a dangerous illness, in which he was given over by his physicians. While he lay apparently at the point of death, an angel was suddenly seen, bringing a medicine to him which effected his instant cure. The saint immediately rose from his bed, and hastened to the nearest church to give God thanks for his recovery. As he passed along, the devil, surrounded with a pack of black dogs, interposed himself to obstruct his way. Dunstan however intrepidly brandished a rod that he held in his hand, and his opposers took to flight. When he came to the church, he found the doors closed. But the same angel, who effected his cure, was at hand, and, taking him up softly by the hair of his head, placed him before the high altar, where he performed his devotions with suitable fervour.

That he might expiate the irregularities of his past life, St. Dunstan now secluded himself entirely from the world, and constructed for his habitation a cell in the abbey of Glastonbury, so narrow that he could neither stand upright in it, nor stretch out his limbs in repose. He took scarcely so much sustenance as would support life, and mortified his flesh with frequent castigations.

He did not however pass his time during this seclusion in vacuity and indolence. He pursued his studies with the utmost ardour, and made a great proficiency in philosophy, divinity, painting, sculpture and music. Above all, he was an admirable chemist, excelled in manufactures of gold and other metals, and was distinguished by a wonderful skill in the art of magic.

During all these mortifications and the severeness of his industry, he appears to have become a prey to extraordinary visions and imaginations. Among the rest, the devil visited him in his cell, and, thrusting his head in at the window, disturbed the saint with obscene and blasphemous speeches, and the most frightful contortions of the features of his countenance. Dunstan at length, wearied out with his perseverance, seized the red-hot tongs with which he was engaged in some chemical experiment, and, catching the devil by the nose, held him with the utmost firmness, while Satan filled the whole neighbourhood for many miles round with his bellowings. Extraordinary as this may appear, it constitutes one of the most prominent incidents in the life of the saint; and the representations of it were for ever repeated in ancient carvings, and in the illuminations of church-windows.

This was the precise period at which the pope and his adherents were gaining the greatest ascendancy in the Christian world. The doctrine of transubstantiation was now in the highest vogue; and along with it a precept still more essential to the empire of the Catholic church, the celibacy of the clergy. This was not at first established without vehement struggles. The secular clergy, who were required at once to cast off their wives as concubines, and their children as bastards, found every impulse of nature rising in arms against the mandate. The regular clergy, or monks, were in obvious rivalship with the seculars, and engrossed to themselves, as much as possible, all promotions and dignities, as well ecclesiastical as civil. St. Augustine, who first planted Christianity in this island, was a Benedictine monk; and the Benedictines were for a long time in the highest reputation in the Catholic church. St. Dunstan was also a Benedictine. In his time the question of the celibacy of the clergy was most vehemently agitated; and Dunstan was the foremost of the champions of the new institution in England. The contest was carried on with great vehemence. Many of the most powerful nobility, impelled either by pity for the sufferers, or induced by family affinities, supported the cause of the seculars. Three successive synods were held on the subject; and the cause of nature it is said would have prevailed, had not Dunstan and his confederates called in the influence of miracles to their aid. In one instance, a crucifix, fixed in a conspicuous part of the place of assembly, uttered a voice at the critical moment, saying, " Be steady! you have once decreed right; alter not your ordinances." At another time the floor of the place of meeting partially gave way, precipitating the ungodly opposers of celibacy into the place beneath, while Dunstan and his party, who were in another part of the assembly, were miraculously preserved unhurt.

In these instances Dunstan seemed to be engaged in the cause of religion, and might be considered as a zealous, though mistaken, advocate of Christian simplicity and purity. But he was not contented with figuring merely as a saint. He insinuated himself into the favour of Edred, the grandson of Alfred, and who, after two or three short reigns, succeeded to the throne. Edred was an inactive prince, but greatly under the dominion of religious prejudices; and Dunstan, being introduced to him, found him an apt subject for his machinations. Edred first made him abbot of Glastonbury, one of the most powerful ecclesiastical dignities in England, and then treasurer of the kingdom. During the reign of this prince, Dunstan disposed of all ecclesiastical affairs, and even of the treasures of the kingdom, at his pleasure.

But Edred filled the throne only nine years, and was succeeded by Edwy at the early age of seventeen, who is said to have been endowed with every grace of form, and the utmost firmness and intrepidity of spirit. Dunstan immediately conceived a jealousy of these qualities, and took an early opportunity to endeavour to disarm them. Edwy entertained a passion for a princess of the royal house, and even proceeded to marry her, though within the degrees forbidden by the canon law. The rest of the story exhibits a lively picture of the manners of these barbarous times. Odo, archbishop of Canterbury, the obedient tool of Dunstan, on the day of the coronation obtruded himself with his abettor into the private apartment, to which the king had retired with his queen, only accompanied by her mother; and here the ambitious abbot, after loading Edwy with the bitterest reproaches for his shameless sensuality, thrust him back by main force into the hall, where the nobles of the kingdom were still engaged at their banquet.

The spirited young prince conceived a deep resentment of this unworthy treatment, and, seizing an opportunity, called Dunstan to account for malversation in the treasury during the late king's life-time. The priest refused to answer; and the issue was that he was banished the realm.

But he left behind him a faithful and implicit coadjutor in archbishop Odo. This prelate is said actually to have forced his way with a party of soldiers into the palace, and, having seized the queen, barbarously to have seared her cheeks with a red-hot iron, and sent her off a prisoner to Ireland. He then proceeded to institute all the forms of a divorce, to which the unhappy king was obliged to submit. Meanwhile the queen, having recovered her beauty, found means to escape, and, crossing the Channel, hastened to join her husband. But here again the priests manifested the same activity as before. They intercepted the queen in her journey, and by the most cruel means undertook to make her a cripple for life. The princess however sunk under the experiment, and ended her existence and her woes together.

A rebellion was now excited against the sacrilegious Edwy; and the whole north of England, having rebelled, was placed under the dominion of his brother, a boy of thirteen years of age. In the midst of these adventures Dunstan returned from the continent, and fearlessly shewed himself in his native country. His party was every where triumphant; Odo being dead, he was installed archbishop of Canterbury, and Edwy, oppressed with calamity on every side, sunk to an untimely grave.

The rest of the life of Dunstan was passed in comparatively tranquillity. He made and unmade kings as he pleased. Edgar, the successor of Edwy, discovered the happy medium of energy and authority as a sovereign, combined with a disposition to indulge the ambitious policy of the priesthood. He was licentious in his amours, without losing a particle of his ascendancy as a sovereign. He however reigned only a few years; but Dunstan at his death found means to place his eldest son on the throne under his special protection, in defiance of the intrigues of the ambitious

Elfrida, the king's second wife, who moved heaven and earth to cause the crown to descend upon her own son, as yet comparatively an infant.

In this narrative we are presented with a lively picture of the means by which ambition climbed to its purposes in the darkness of the tenth century. Dunstan was enriched with all those endowments which might seem in any age to lead to the highest distinction. Yet it would appear to have been in vain that he was thus qualified, if he had not stooped to arts that fell in with the gross prejudices of his contemporaries. He had continual recourse to the aid of miracles. He gave into practices of the most rigorous mortification. He studied, and excelled in, all the learning and arts that were then known. But his main dependence was on the art of magic. The story of his taking the devil by the nose with a pair of red-hot tongs, seems to have been of greater service to him than any other single adventure of his life. In other times he might have succeeded in the schemes of his political ambition by seemly and specious means. But it was necessary for him in the times in which he lived, to proceed with eclat, and in a way that should confound all opposers. The utmost resolution was required to overwhelm those who might otherwise have been prompted to contend against him. Hence it appears that he took a right measure of the understanding of his contemporaries, when he dragged the young king from the scene of his retirement, and brought him back by force into the assembly of the nobles. And the inconceivable barbarity practised to the queen, which would have rendered his name horrible in a more civilised age, was exactly calculated to overwhelm the feelings and subject the understandings of the men among whom he lived. The great quality by which he was distinguished was confidence, a frame of behaviour which shewed that he acted from the fullest conviction, and never doubted that his proceedings had the immediate approbation of heaven.

COMMUNICATION OF EUROPE AND THE SARACENS.

IT appears to have been about the close of the tenth century that the more curious and inquisitive spirits of Europe first had recourse to the East as a source of such information and art, as they found most glaringly deficient among their countrymen. We have seen that in Persia there was an uninterrupted succession of professors in the art of magic: and, when the followers of Mahomet by their prowess had gained the superiority over the greater part of Asia, over all that was known of Africa, and a considerable tract of Europe, they gradually became awake to the desire of cultivating the sciences, and in particular of making themselves masters of whatever was most liberal and eminent among the disciples of Zoroaster. To this they added a curiosity respecting Greek learning, especially as it related to medicine and the investigation of the powers of physical nature. Bagdad became an eminent seat of learning; and perhaps, next to Bagdad, Spain under the Saracens, or Moors, was a principal abode for the professors of ingenuity and literature.

GERBERT, POPE SILVESTER II.

As a consequence of this state of things the more curious men of Europe by degrees adopted the practice of resorting to Spain for the purpose of enlarging their sphere of observation and knowledge. Among others Gerbert is reported to have been the first of the Christian clergy, who strung themselves up to the resolution of mixing with the followers of Mahomet, that they might learn from thence things, the knowledge of which it was impossible for them to obtain at home. This generous adventurer, prompted by an insatiable thirst for information, is said to have secretly withdrawn himself from his monastery of Fleury in Burgundy, and to have spent several years among the Saracens of Cordova. Here he acquired a knowledge of the language and learning of the Arabians, particularly of their astronomy, geometry and arithmetic; and he is understood to have been the first that imparted to the north and west of Europe a knowledge of the Arabic numerals, a science, which at first sight might be despised for its simplicity, but which in its consequences is no inconsiderable instrument in subtilising the the powers of human intellect. He likewise introduced the use of clocks. He is also represented to have made an extraordinary proficiency in the art of magic; and among other things is said to have constructed a brazen head, which would answer when it was spoken to, and oracularly resolve many difficult questions[a]. The same historian assures us that Gerbert by the art of necro-

[a] William of Malmesbury, Lib. II, c. 10.

mancy made various discoveries of hidden treasures, and relates in all its circumstances the spectacle of a magic palace he visited underground, with the multiplied splendours of an Arabian tale, but distinguished by this feature, that, though its magnificence was dazzling to the sight, it would not abide the test of feeling, but vanished into air, the moment it was attempted to be touched.

It happened with Gerbert, as with St. Dunstan, that he united an aspiring mind and a boundless spirit of ambition, with the intellectual curiosity which has already been described. The first step that he made into public life and the career for which he panted, consisted in his being named preceptor, first to Robert, king of France, the son of Hugh Capet, and next to Otho the Third, emperor of Germany. Hugh Capet appointed him archbishop of Rheims; but, that dignity being disputed with him, he retired into Germany, and, becoming eminently a favourite with Otho the Third, he was by the influence of that prince raised, first to be archbishop of Ravenna, and afterwards to the papacy by the name of Silvester the Second[b].

Cardinal Benno, who was an adherent of the anti-popes, and for that reason is supposed to have calumniated Gerbert and several of his successors, affirms that he was habitually waited on by demons, that by their aid he obtained the papal

---

[b] William of Malmesbury, Lib. II, c. 10.

crown, and that the devil to whom he had sold himself, faithfully promised him that he should live, till he had celebrated high mass at Jerusalem. This however was merely a juggle of the evil spirit; and Gerbert actually died, shortly after having officially dispensed the sacrament at the church of the Holy Cross in Jerusalem, which is one of the seven districts of the city of Rome. This event occurred in the year 1003[c].

BENEDICT THE NINTH.

According to the same authority sorcery was at this time extensively practised by some of the highest dignitaries of the church, and five or six popes in succession were notorious for these sacrilegious practices. About the same period the papal chair was at its lowest state of degradation; this dignity was repeatedly exposed for sale; and the reign of Gerbert, a man of consummate abilities and attainments, is almost the only redeeming feature in the century in which he lived. At length the tiara became the purchase of an ambitious family, which had already furnished two popes, in behalf of a boy of twelve years of age, who reigned by the name of Benedict the Ninth. This youth, as he grew up, contaminated his rule with every kind of profligacy and debauchery.

[c] Naudé, Apologie des Grands Hommes Accusés de Magie. Malmesbury, *ubi supra*.

But even he, according to Benno, was a pupil in the school of Silvester, and became no mean proficient in the arts of sorcery. Among other things he caused the matrons of Rome by his incantations to follow him in troops among woods and mountains, being bewitched and their souls subdued by the irresistible charms of his magic[a].

GREGORY THE SEVENTH.

Benno presents us with a regular catalogue of the ecclesiastical sorcerers of this period: Benedict the Ninth, and Laurence, archbishop of Melfi, (each of whom, he says, learned the art of Silvester), John XX and Gregory VI. But his most vehement accusations are directed against Gregory VII, who, he affirms, was in the early part of his career, the constant companion and assistant of these dignitaries in unlawful practices of this sort.

Gregory VII, whose original name was Hildebrand, is one of the great champions of the Romish church, and did more than any other man to establish the law of the celibacy of the clergy, and to take the patronage of ecclesiastical dignities out of the hands of the laity. He was eminently qualified for this undertaking by the severity of his manners, and the inflexibility of his resolution to accomplish whatever he undertook.

[a] Naudé, Apologie des Grands Hommes Accusés de Magie, chap. 19.

His great adversary was Henry the Fourth, emperor of Germany, a young prince of high spirit, and at that time (1075) twenty-four years of age. Gregory sent to summon him to Rome, to answer an accusation, that he, as all his predecessors had done, being a layman, had conferred ecclesiastical dignities. Henry refused submission, and was immediately declared excommunicated. In retaliation for this offence, the emperor, it is said, gave his orders to a chief of brigands, who, watching his opportunity, seized the pope in the act of saying mass in one of the churches of Rome, and carried him prisoner to a tower in the city which was in the possession of this adventurer. But no sooner was this known, than the citizens of Rome, rose *en masse*, and rescued their spiritual father. Meanwhile Henry, to follow up his blow, assembled a synod at Worms, who pronounced on the pope, that for manifold crimes he was fallen from his supreme dignity, and accordingly fulminated a decree of deposition against him. But Henry had no forces to carry this decree into execution; and Gregory on his side emitted a sentence of degradation against the emperor, commanding the Germans to elect a new emperor in his place. It then became evident that, in this age of ignorance and religious subjugation, the spiritual arm, at least in Germany, was more powerful than the temporal; and Henry, having maturely considered the perils that surrounded him, took the resolution to pass the Alps with a few domestics only, and, repairing to the presence of the pope, submit himself to such penance as the pontiff should impose. Gregory was at this time at Canosa, a fortress beyond Naples, which was surrounded with three walls. Henry, without any attendant, was admitted within the first wall. Here he was required to cast off all the symbols of royalty, to put on a hair-shirt, and to wait barefoot his holiness's pleasure. He stood accordingly, fasting from morn to eve, without receiving the smallest notice from the pontiff. It was in the month of January. He passed through the same trial the second day, and the third. On the fourth day in the morning he was admitted to the presence of the holy father. They parted however more irreconcileable in heart than ever, though each preserved the appearance of good will. The pope insisted that Henry should abide the issue of the congress in Germany, of which he constituted himself president; and the emperor, exasperated at the treatment he had received, resolved to keep no terms with Gregory. Henry proceeded to the election of an anti-pope, Clement the Third, and Gregory patronised a new emperor, Rodolph, duke of Suabia. Henry had however generally been successful in his military enterprises; and he defeated Rodolph in two battles, in the last of which his opponent was slain. In the synod of Brixen, in which Clement the Third was elected, Gregory was sentenced as a magician and a necromancer. The emperor, puffed up with his victories, marched against Rome, and took it, with the exception of the castle of St. Angelo, in which the pope shut himself up; and in the mean time Henry caused the anti-pope, his creature, to be solemnly inaugurated in the church of the Lateran. Gregory however, never dismayed, and never at an end of his expedients, called in the Normans, who had recently distinguished themselves by their victories in Naples and Sicily. Robert Guiscard, a Norman chieftain, drove the Germans out of Rome; but, some altercations ensuing between the pontiff and his deliverer, the city was given up to pillage, and Gregory was glad to take refuge in Salerno, the capital of his Norman ally, where he shortly after expired, an exile and a fugitive.

Gregory was no doubt a man of extraordinary resources and invincible courage. He did not live to witness the triumph of his policy; but his projects for the exaltation of the church finally met with every success his most sanguine wishes could have aspired to. In addition to all the rest it happened, that the countess Matilda, a princess who in her own right possessed extensive sovereignties in Italy, nearly commensurate with what has since been styled the ecclesiastical state, transferred to the pope in her life-time, and confirmed by her testament, all these territories, thus mainly contributing to render him and his successors so considerable as temporal princes, as since that time they have appeared.

It is, however, as a sorcerer, that Gregory VII (Hildebrand) finds a place in this volume. Benno relates that, coming one day from his Alban villa, he found, just as he was entering the church of the Lateran, that he had left behind him his magical book, which he was ascustomed to carry about his person. He immediately sent two trusty servants to fetch it, at the same time threatening them most fearfully if they should attempt to look into the volume. Curiosity however got the better of their fear. They opened the book, and began to read; when presently a number of devils appeared, saying, "We are come to obey your commands, but, if we find ourselves trifled with, we shall certainly fall upon and destroy you." The servants, exceedingly terrified, replied, "Our will is that you should immediately throw down so much of the wall of the city as is now before us." The devils obeyed; and the servants escaped the danger that hung over them.[a] It is further said, that Gregory was so expert in the arts of magic, that he would throw out lightning by shaking his arm, and dart thunder from his sleeve.[b]

But the most conspicuous circumstance in the life of Gregory that has been made the foundation of a charge of necromancy against him, is that,

---

[a] Mornay, Mysterium Iniquitatis, p. 258. Cocffeteau, Reponse à ditto, p. 274.   [b] Ibid.

when Rodolph marched against Henry IV, the pope was so confident of his success, as to venture publicly to prophesy, both in speech and in writing, that his adversary should be conquered and perish in this campaign. " Nay," he added, " this prophecy shall be accomplished before St. Peter's day; nor do I desire any longer to be acknowledged for pope, than on the condition that this comes to pass." It is added, that Rodolph, relying on the prediction, six times renewed the battle, in which finally he perished instead of his competitor. But this does not go far enough to substantiate a charge of necromancy. It is further remarked, that Gregory was deep in the pretended science of judicial astrology; and this, without its being necessary to have recourse to the solution of diabolical aid, may sufficiently account for the undoubting certainty with which he counted on the event.

In the mean time this statement is of great importance, as illustrative of the spirit of the times in general, and the character of Gregory in particular. Rodolph, the competitor for the empire, has his mind wrought up to such a pitch by this prophetic assurance, that, five times repulsed, he yet led on his forces a sixth time, and perished the victim of his faith. Nor were his followers less animated than he, and from the same cause. We see also from the same story, that Gregory was not an artful and crafty impostor, but a man spurred on by a genuine enthusiasm. And this indeed is necessary to account for the whole of his conduct. The audacity with which he opposed the claims of Henry, and the unheard-of severity with which he treated him at the fortress of Canosa, are to be referred to the same feature of character. Invincible perseverance, when united with great resources of intellect and a lofty spirit, will enable a man thoroughly to effect, what a person of inferior endowments would not have dared so much as to dream of. And Gregory, like St. Dunstan, achieved incredible things, by skilfully adapting himself to circumstances, and taking advantage of the temper and weakness of his contemporaries.

DUFF, KING OF SCOTLAND.

It is not to be wondered at, when such things occurred in Italy, the principal seat of all the learning and refinement then existing in Europe, that the extreme northerly and western districts should have been given up to the blindest superstition. Among other instances we have the following account in relation to Duff, king of Scotland, who came to the crown about the year 968. He found his kingdom in the greatest disorder from numerous bands of robbers, many of whom were persons of high descent, but of no competent means of subsistence. Duff resolved to put an end to their depredations, and to secure those who sought a quiet support from cultivating the fruits of the earth from forcible invasion. He executed the law against these disturbers without respect of persons, and hence made himself many and powerful enemies. In the midst of his activity however he suddenly fell sick, and became confined to his bed. His physicians could no way account for his distemper. They found no excess of any humour in his body to which they could attribute his illness; his colour was fresh, and his eyes lively; and he had a moderate and healthful appetite. But with all this he was a total stranger to sleep; he burst out into immoderate perspirations; and there was scarcely any thing that remained of him, but skin and bone. In the meantime secret information was brought that all this evil was the result of witchcraft. And, the house being pointed out in which the sorcerers held their sabbath, a band of soldiers was sent to surprise them. The doors being burst open, they found one woman roasting upon a spit by the fire a waxen image of the king, so like in every feature, that no doubt was entertained that it was modelled by the art of the devil, while another sat by, busily engaged in reciting certain verses of enchantment, by which means, as the wax melted, the king was consumed with perspiration, and, as soon as it was utterly dissolved, his death should immediately follow. The witches were seized, and from their own confession burned alive. The image was broken to pieces, and every fragment of it destroyed. And no sooner was this effected, than Duff had all that night the most refreshing and healthful sleep, and the next day rose without any remains of his infirmity[a].

This reprieve however availed him but for a short time. He was no sooner recovered, than he occupied himself as before with pursuing the outlaws, whom he brought indiscriminately to condign punishment. Among these there chanced to be two young men, near relations of the governor of the castle of Fores, who had hitherto been the king's most faithful adherents. These young men had been deluded by ill company: and the governor most earnestly sued to Duff for their pardon. But the king was inexorable. Meanwhile, as he had always placed the most entire trust in their father, he continued to do so without the smallest suspicion. The night after the execution, the king slept in the castle of Fores, as he had often done before; but the governor, conceiving the utmost rancour at the repulse he had sustained, and moreover instigated by his wife, in the middle of the night murdered Duff in his bed, as he slept. His reign lasted only four years[b].

MACBETH.

The seventh king of Scotland after Duff, with an interval of sixty-eight years, was Macbeth. The

[a] Hollinshed, History of Scotland, p. 206, 207.
[b] Ibid, p. 207, 208.

historian begins his tale of witchcraft, towards the end of the reign of Duncan, his predecessor, with observing, " Shortly after happened a strange and uncouth wonder, which afterward was the cause of much trouble in the realm of Scotland. It fortuned, as Macbeth and Banquo journeyed towards Fores, where the king as then lay, they went sporting by the way together, without other company save only themselves, passing through the woods and fields, when suddenly, in the midst of a laund, there met them three women in strange and ferly apparel, resembling creatures of an elder world, whom when they attentively beheld, wondering much at the sight, the first of them spake and said, All hail, Macbeth, thane of Glamis (for he had lately entered into that dignity and office by the death of his father Synel). The second of them said, Hail, Macbeth, thane of Cawdor. But the third said, All hail, Macbeth, that hereafter shall be king of Scotland. Then Banquo, What sort of women, said he, are you, that seem so little favourable unto me, whereas to my fellow here, besides high offices, ye assign also the kingdom, appointing forth nothing for me at all? Yes, saith the first of them, we promise greater benefits unto thee than unto him, for he shall reign indeed, but with an unlucky end, neither shall he leave any issue behind him to succeed in his place; where contrarily thou indeed shalt not reign at all, but of thee those shall be born, which shall govern the Scottish kingdom by long order of continual descent. Herewith the foresaid women vanished immediately out of their sight.

" This was reputed at the first but some vain fantastical illusion by Macbeth and Banquo, insomuch that Banquo would call Macbeth in jest king of Scotland, and Macbeth again would call him in sport likewise the father of many kings. But afterwards the common opinion was, that these women were either the weird sisters, that is (as you would say) the goddesses of destiny, or else some nymphs or fairies, endued with knowledge of prophecy by their necromantical science, because every thing came to pass as they had spoken.

" For shortly after, the thane of Cawdor, being condemned at Fores of treason against the king committed, his lands, livings and offices were given of the king's liberality unto Macbeth[a]."

Malcolm, the preceding king of Scotland, had two daughters, one of them the mother of Duncan, and the other of Macbeth; and in virtue of this descent Duncan succeeded to the crown. The accession of Macbeth therefore was not very remote, if he survived the present king. Of consequence Macbeth, though he thought much of the prediction of the weird sisters, yet resolved to wait his time, thinking that, as had happened in his former preferment, this might come to pass without his aid. But Duncan had two sons, Malcolm

---

[a] Hollinshed, History of Scotland, p. 243, 244.

Cammore and Donald Bane. The law of succession in Scotland was, that, if at the death of the reigning sovereign he that should succeed were not of sufficient age to take on him the government, he that was next of blood to him should be admitted. Duncan however at this juncture created his eldest son Malcolm prince of Cumberland, a title which was considered as designating him heir to the throne. Macbeth was greatly troubled at this, as cutting off the expectation he thought he had a right to entertain: and, the words of the weird sisters still ringing in his ears, and his wife with ambitious speeches urging him to the deed, he, in conjunction with some trusty friends, among whom was Banquo, came to a resolution to kill the king at Inverness. The deed being perpetrated, Malcolm, the eldest son of Duncan, fled for safety into Cumberland, and Donald, the second, into Ireland[b].

Macbeth, who became king of Scotland in the year 1040, reigned for ten years with great popularity and applause, but at the end of that time changed his manner of government, and became a tyrant. His first action in this character was against Banquo. He remembered that the weird sisters had promised to Banquo that he should be father to a line of kings. Haunted with this recollection, Macbeth invited Banquo and his son Fleance to a supper, and appointed assassins to

[b] Hollinshed, History of Scotland, p. 244, 245.

murder them both on their return. Banquo was slain accordingly; but Fleance, under favour of the darkness of the night, escaped[c].

This murder brought Macbeth into great odium, since every man began to doubt of the security of his life, and Macbeth at the same time to fear the ill will of his subjects. He therefore proceeded to destroy all against whom he entertained any suspicion, and every day more and more to steep his hands in blood. Further to secure himself, he built a castle on the top of a high hill, called Dunsinnan, which was placed on such an elevation, that it seemed impossible to approach it in a hostile manner. This work he carried on by means of requiring the thanes of the kingdom, each one in turn, to come with a set of workmen to help forward the edifice. When it came to the turn of Macduff, thane of Fife, he sent workmen, but did not come himself, as the others had done. Macbeth from that time regarded Macduff with an eye of perpetual suspicion[d].

Meanwhile Macbeth, remembering that the origin of his present greatness consisted in the prophecy of the weird sisters, addicted himself continually to the consulting of wizards. Those he consulted gave him a pointed warning to take heed of Macduff, who in time to come would seek to destroy him. This warning would unquestion-

[c] Hollinshed, History of Scotland, p. 246.
[d] Ibid, p. 248, 249.

ably have proved fatal to Macduff; had not on the other hand Macbeth been buoyed up in security, by the prediction of a certain witch in whom he had great trust, that he should never be vanquished till the wood of Bernane came to the castle of Dunsinnan, and that he should not be slain by any man that was born of a woman; both which he judged to be impossibilities[e].

This vain confidence however urged him to do many outrageous things; at the same time that such was his perpetual uneasiness of mind, that in every nobleman's house he had one servant or another in fee, that he might be acquainted with every thing that was said or meditated against him. About this time Macduff fled to Malcolm, who had now taken refuge in the court of Edward the Confessor; and Macbeth came with a strong party into Fife with the purpose of surprising him. The master being safe, those within Macduff's castle threw open the gates, thinking that no mischief would result from receiving the king. But Macbeth, irritated that he missed of his prey, caused Macduff's wife and children, and all persons who were found within the castle, to be slain.[f]

Shortly after, Malcolm and Macduff, reinforced by ten thousand English under the command of Seyward, earl of Northumberland, marched into Scotland. The subjects of Macbeth stole away daily from him to join the invaders; but he had

[e] Hollinshed, History of Scotland, p. 249.   [f] Ibid.

such confidence in the predictions that had been delivered to him, that he still believed he should never be vanquished. Malcolm meanwhile, as he approached to the castle of Dunsinnan, commanded his men to cut down, each of them, a bough from the wood of Bernane, as large as he could bear, that they might take the tyrant the more by surprise. Macbeth saw, and thought the wood approached him; but he remembered the prophecy, and led forth and marshalled his men. When however the enemy threw down their boughs, and their formidable numbers stood revealed, Macbeth and his forces immediately betook themselves to flight. Macduff pursued him, and was hard at his heels, when the tyrant turned his horse, and exclaimed, "Why dost thou follow me? Know, that it is ordained that no creature born of a woman can ever overcome me." Macduff instantly retorted, "I am the man appointed to slay thee. I was not born of a woman, but was untimely ripped from my mother's womb." And, saying this, he killed him on the spot. Macbeth reigned in the whole seventeen years[g].

VIRGIL.

One of the most curious particulars, and which cannot be omitted in a history of sorcery, is the various achievements in the art of magic which have been related of the poet Virgil. I bring them in

[g] Hollinshed, History of Scotland, p. 251.

here, because they cannot be traced further back than the eleventh or twelfth century. The burial-place of this illustrious man was at Pausilippo, near Naples; the Neapolitans had for many centuries cherished a peculiar reverence for his memory; and it has been supposed that the old ballads, and songs of the minstrels of the north of Italy, first originated this idea respecting him[*]. The vulgar of this city, full of imagination and poetry, conceived the idea of treating him as the guardian genius of the place; and, in bodying forth this conception, they represented him in his life-time as gifted with supernatural powers, which he employed in various ways for the advantage of a city that he so dearly loved. Be this as it will, it appears that Gervais of Tilbury, chancellor to Otho the Fourth, emperor of Germany, Helinandus, a Cisterian monk, and Alexander Neckam, all of whom lived about this time, first recorded these particulars in their works.

They tell us, that Virgil placed a fly of brass over one of the gates of the city, which, as long as it continued there, that is, for a space of eight years, had the virtue of keeping Naples clear from moskitoes and all noxious insects: that he built a set of shambles, the meat in which was at all times free from putrefaction: that he placed two images over the gates of the city, one of which was named Joyful, and the other Sad, one of resplendent beauty, and

[*] Naudé.

the other hideous and deformed, and that whoever entered the town under the former image would succeed in all his undertakings, and under the latter would as certainly miscarry: that he caused a brazen statue to be erected on a mountain near Naples, with a trumpet in his mouth, which when the north wind blew, sounded so shrill as to drive to the sea the fire and smoke which issued from the neighbouring forges of Vulcan: that he built different baths at Naples, specifically prepared for the cure of every disease, which were afterwards demolished by the malice of the physicians: and that he lighted a perpetual fire for the refreshment of all travellers, close to which he placed an archer of brass, with his bow bent, and this inscription, "Whoever strikes me, I will let fly my arrow:" that a fool-hardy fellow notwithstanding struck the statue, when the arrow was immediately shot into the fire, and the fire was extinguished. It is added, that, Naples being infested with a vast multitude of contagious leeches, Virgil made a leech of gold, which he threw into a pit, and so delivered the city from the infection: that he surrounded his garden with a wall of air, within which the rain never fell: that he built a bridge of brass that would transport him wherever he pleased: that he made a set of statues, which were named the salvation of Rome, which had the property that, if any one of the subject nations prepared to revolt, the statue, which bore the name of, and was adored by that nation, rung a bell, and pointed with its finger in the direction of the danger: that he made a head, which had the virtue of predicting things future: and lastly, amidst a world of other wonders, that he cut a subterranean passage through mount Pausilippo, that travellers might pass with perfect safety, the mountain having before been so infested with serpents and dragons, that no one could venture to cross it.

ROBERT OF LINCOLN.

The most eminent person next, after popes Silvester II and Gregory VII, who labours under the imputation of magic, is Robert Grossetête, or Robert of Lincoln, appointed bishop of that see in the year 1235. He was, like those that have previously been mentioned, a man of the most transcendant powers of mind, and extraordinary acquirements. His parents are said to have been so poor, that he was compelled, when a boy, to engage in the meanest offices for bread, and even to beg on the highway. At length the mayor of Lincoln, struck with his appearance, and the quickness of his answers to such questions as were proposed to him, took him into his family, and put him to school. Here his ardent love of learning, and admirable capacity for acquiring it, soon procured him many patrons, by whose assistance he was enabled to prosecute his studies, first at Cambridge, afterwards at Oxford, and finally at Paris. He was master of the Greek and Hebrew languages, then very rare accomplishments; and is pronounced by Roger Bacon, a very competent judge, of whom we shall presently have occasion to speak, to have spent much of his time, for nearly forty years, in the study of geometry, astronomy, optics, and other branches of mathematical learning, in all of which he much excelled. So that, as we are informed from the same authority, this same Robert of Lincoln, and his friend, Friar Adam de Marisco, were the two most learned men in the world, and excelled the rest of mankind in both human and divine knowledge.

This great man especially distinguished himself by his firm and undaunted opposition to the corruptions of the court of Rome. Pope Innocent IV, who filled the papal chair upwards of eleven years, from 1243 to 1254, appears to have exceeded all his predecessors in the shamelessness of his abuses. We are told, that the hierarchy of the church of England was overwhelmed like a flood with an inundation of foreign dignitaries, of whom not a few were mere boys, for the most part without learning, ignorant of the language of the island, and incapable of benefiting the people nominally under their care, the more especially as they continued to dwell in their own countries, and scarcely once in their lives visited the sees to which they had been appointed[a]. Grossetête lifted up his voice against these scandals. He said that it was impossible the genuine apostolic see, which received its authority from the Lord Jesus for edification, and not for destruction, could be guilty of such a crime, for that would forfeit all its glory, and plunge it into the pains of hell. He did not scruple therefore among his most intimate friends to pronounce the reigning pope to be the true Antichrist; and he addressed the pontiff himself in scarcely more measured terms.

Among the other accomplishments of bishop Grossetête he is said to have been profoundly skilled in the art of magic: and the old poet Gower relates of him that he made a head of brass, expressly constructed in such a manner as to be able to answer such questions as were propounded to it, and to foretel future events.

MICHAEL SCOT.

Michael Scot of Balwirie in the county of Fife, was nearly contemporary with bishop Grossetête. He was eminent for his knowledge of the Greek and Arabic languages. He was patronised by the emperor Frederic II, who encouraged him to undertake a translation of the works of Aristotle into Latin. He addicted himself to astrology, che-

[a] Godwin, Præsulibus, art. Gronthead.

mistry, and the still more frivolous sciences of chiromancy and physiognomy. It does not appear that he made any pretences to magic; but the vulgar, we are told, generally regarded him as a sorcerer, and are said to have carried their superstition so far as to have conceived a terror of so much as touching his works.

THE DEAN OF BADAJOZ.

There is a story related by this accomplished scholar, in a collection of aphorisms and anecdotes entitled *Mensa Philosophica*, which deserves to be cited as illustrating the ideas then current on the subject of sorcery. " A certain great necromancer, or nigromancer, had once a pupil of considerable rank, who professed himself extremely desirous for once to have the gratification of believing himself an emperor. The necromancer, tired with his importunities, at length assented to his prayer. He took measures accordingly, and by his potent art caused his scholar to believe that one province and dignity fell to him after another, till at length his utmost desires became satisfied. The magician however appeared to be still at his elbow; and one day, when the scholar was in the highest exultation at his good fortune, the master humbly requested him to bestow upon him some landed possession, as a reward for the extraordinary benefit he had conferred. The imaginary emperor cast upon the necromancer a glance of the utmost disdain and contempt. "Who are you?" said he, "I really have not the smallest acquaintance with you." "I am he," replied the magician, with withering severity of countenance and tone, "that gave you all these things, and will take them away." And, saying this, the illusion with which the poor scholar had been inebriated, immediately vanished; and he became what he had before been, and no more.

The story thus briefly told by Michael Scot, afterwards passed through many hands, and was greatly dilated. In its last form by the abbé Blanchet, it constituted the well known and agreeable tale of the dean of Badajoz. This reverend divine comes to a sorcerer, and intreats a specimen of his art. The magician replies that he had met with so many specimens of ingratitude, that he was resolved to be deluded no more. The dean persists, and at length overcomes the reluctance of the master. He invites his guest into the parlour, and orders his cook to put two partridges to the fire, for that the dean of Badajoz will sup with him. Presently he begins his incantations; and the dean becomes in imagination by turns a bishop, a cardinal, and a pope. The magician then claims his reward. Meanwhile the dean, inflated with his supposed elevation, turns to his benefactor, and says, "I have learned with grief that, under pretence of secret science, you correspond with the prince of darkness. I command you to repent and abjure; and in the mean time I order you to quit the territory of the church in three days, under pain of being delivered to the secular arm, and the rigour of the flames." The sorcerer, having been thus treated, presently dissolves the incantation, and calls aloud to his cook, " Put down but one partridge, the dean of Badajoz does not sup with me to-night."

MIRACLE OF THE TUB OF WATER.

This story affords an additional example of the affinity between the ancient Asiatic and European legends, so as to convince us that it is nearly impossible that the one should not be in some way borrowed from the other. There is, in a compilation called the Turkish Tales, a story of an infidel sultan of Egypt, who took the liberty before a learned Mahometan doctor, of ridiculing some of the miracles ascribed to the prophet, as for example his transportation into the seventh heaven, and having ninety thousand conferences with God, while in the mean time a pitcher of water, which had been thrown down in the first step of his ascent, was found with the water not all spilled at his return.

The doctor, who had the gift of working miracles, told the sultan that, with his consent, he would give him a practical proof of the possibility of the circumstance related of Mahomet. The sultan agreed. The doctor therefore directed that a huge tub of water should be brought in, and, while the prince stood before it with his courtiers around, the holy man bade him plunge his head into the water, and draw it out again. The sultan immersed his head, and had no sooner done so, than he found himself alone at the foot of a mountain on a desert shore. The prince first began to rave against the doctor for this piece of treachery and witchcraft. Perceiving however that all his rage was vain, and submitting himself to the imperiousness of his situation, he began to seek for some habitable tract. By and by he discovered people cutting down wood in a forest, and, having no remedy, he was glad to have recourse to the same employment. In process of time he was brought to a town; and there by great good fortune, after other adventures, he married a woman of beauty and wealth, and lived long enough with her, for her to bear him seven sons and seven daughters. He was afterwards reduced to want, so as to be obliged to 'ply in the streets as a porter for his livelihood. One day, as he walked alone on the sea-shore, ruminating on his hard fate, he was seized with a fit of devotion, and threw off his clothes, that he might wash himself, agreeably to the Mahometan custom, previously to saying his prayers. He had no sooner however plunged into the sea, and raised his head again above water, than he found himself standing by the side of the tub that had been brought in, with all the great persons of his court round him, and the holy man close at his side. He found that the long series of imaginary adventures he had passed through, had in reality occupied but one minute of time.

INSTITUTION OF FRIARS.

About this time a great revolution took place in the state of literature in Europe. The monks, who at one period considerably contributed to preserve the monuments of ancient learning, memorably fell off in reputation and industry. Their communities by the donations of the pious grew wealthy; and the monks themselves inhabited splendid palaces, and became luxurious, dissipated and idle. Upon the ruins of their good fame rose a very extraordinary race of men, called Friars. The monks professed celibacy, and to have no individual property; but the friars abjured all property, both private and in common. They had no place where to lay their heads, and subsisted as mendicants upon the alms of their contemporaries. They did not hide themselves in refectories and dormitories, but lived perpetually before the public. In the sequel indeed they built Friaries for their residence; but these were no less distinguished for the simplicity and humbleness of their appearance, than the monasteries were for their grandeur and almost regal magnificence. The Friars were incessant in preaching and praying, voluntarily exposed themselves to the severest hardships, and were distinguished by a fervour of devotion and charitable activity that knew no bounds. We might figure them to ourselves as swallowed up in these duties. But they added to their merits an incessant earnestness in learning and science. A new era in intellect and subtlety of mind began with them; and a set of the most wonderful men in depth of application, logical acuteness, and discoveries in science distinguished this period. They were few indeed, in comparison of the world of ignorance that every where surrounded them; but they were for that reason only the more conspicuous. They divided themselves principally into two orders, the Dominicans and Franciscans. And all that was most illustrious in intellect at this period belonged either to the one or the other.

ALBERTUS MAGNUS.

Albertus Magnus, a Dominican, was one of the most famous of these. He was born according to some accounts in the year 1193, and according to others in 1205. It is reported of him, that he was naturally very dull, and so incapable of instruction, that he was on the point of quitting the cloister from despair of learning what his vocation required, when the blessed virgin appeared to him in a vision, and enquired of him in which he desired to excel, philosophy or divinity. He chose philosophy; and the virgin assured him that he should become incomparable in that, but, as a punishment for not having chosen divinity, he should sink, before he died, into his former stupidity. It is added that, after this apparition, he had an infinite deal of wit, and advanced in science with so rapid a progress as utterly to astonish the masters. He afterwards became bishop of Ratisbon.

It is related of Albertus, that he made an entire man of brass, putting together its limbs under various constellations, and occupying no less than thirty years in its formation. This man would answer all sorts of questions, and was even employed by its maker as a domestic. But what is more extraordinary, this machine is said to have become at length so garrulous, that Thomas Aquinas, being a pupil of Albertus, and finding himself perpetually disturbed in his abstrusest speculations by its uncontrolable loquacity, in a rage caught up a hammer, and beat it to pieces. According to other accounts the man of Albertus Magnus was composed, not of metal, but of flesh and bones like other men; but this being afterwards judged to be impossible, and the virtue of images, rings, and planetary sigils being in great vogue, it was conceived that this figure was formed of brass, and indebted for its virtue to certain conjunctions and aspects of the planets[*].

A further extraordinary story is told of Albertus Magnus, well calculated to exemplify the ideas of magic with which these ages abounded. William, earl of Holland, and king of the Romans, was expected at a certain time to pass through Cologne. Albertus had set his heart upon obtaining from this prince the cession of a certain tract of land upon which to erect a convent. The better to succeed in his application he conceived the following scheme. He invited the prince on his journey to partake of a magnificent entertainment. To the surprise of every body, when the prince arrived, he found the preparations for the banquet spread in the open air. It was in the depth of winter, when the earth was bound up in frost, and the whole face of things was covered with snow. The attendants of the court were mortified, and began to express their discontent in loud murmurs. No sooner however was the king with Albertus and his courtiers seated at table, than the snow instantly disappeared, the temperature of summer shewed itself, and the sun burst forth with a dazzling splendour. The ground became covered with the richest verdure; the trees were clothed at once with foliage, flowers and fruits: and a vintage of the richest grapes, accompanied with a ravishing odour, invited the spectators to partake.

[*] Naudé, c. 18.

A thousand birds sang on every branch. A train of pages shewed themselves, fresh and graceful in person and attire, and were ready diligently to supply the wants of all, while every one was struck with astonishment as to who they were and from whence they came. The guests were obliged to throw off their upper garments the better to cool themselves. The whole assembly was delighted with their entertainment, and Albertus easily gained his suit of the king. Presently after, the banquet disappeared; all was wintry and solitary as before; the snow lay thick upon the ground; and the guests in all haste snatched up the garments they had laid aside, and hurried into the apartments, that by numerous fires on the blazing hearth they might counteract the dangerous chill which threatened to seize on their limbs[b].

ROGER BACON.

Roger Bacon, of whom extraordinary stories of magic have been told, and who was about twenty years younger than Albertus, was one of the rarest geniuses that have existed on earth. He was a Franciscan friar. He wrote grammars of the Latin, Greek and Hebrew languages. He was profound in the science of optics. He explained the nature of burning-glasses, and of glasses which magnify and diminish, the microscope and the telescope.

[b] Johannes de Becka, *apud* Trithemii Chronica, ann. 1254.

He discovered the composition of gunpowder. He ascertained the true length of the solar year; and his theory was afterwards brought into general use, but upon a narrow scale, by Pope Gregory XIII, nearly three hundred years after his death[a].

But for all these discoveries he underwent a series of the most bitter persecutions. It was imputed to him by the superiors of his order that the improvements he suggested in natural philosophy were the effects of magic, and were suggested to him through an intercourse with infernal spirits. They forbade him to communicate any of his speculations. They wasted his frame with rigorous fasting, often restricting him to a diet of bread and water, and prohibited all strangers to have access to him. Yet he went on indefatigably in pursuit of the secrets of nature[b]. At length Clement IV, to whom he appealed, procured him a considerable degree of liberty. But, after the death of that pontiff, he was again put under confinement, and continued in that state for a further period of ten years. He was liberated but a short time before his death.

Freind says[c], that, among other ingenious contrivances, he put statues in motion, and drew articulate sounds from a brazen head, not however by magic, but by an artificial application of the principles of natural philosophy. This probably fur-

[a] Freind, History of Physick, Vol. II, p. 234 to 239.
[b] Bacon, Epist. ad Clement. IV.   [c] Ubi supra.

nished a foundation for the tale of Friar Bacon and Friar Bungy, which was one of the earliest productions to which the art of printing was applied in England. These two persons are said to have entertained the project of inclosing England with a wall, so as to render it inaccessible to any invader. They accordingly raised the devil, as the person best able to inform them how this was to be done. The devil advised them to make a brazen head, with all the internal structure and organs of a human head. The construction would cost them much time; and they must then wait with patience till the faculty of speech descended upon it. It would finally however become an oracle, and, if the question were propounded to it, would teach them the solution of their problem. The friars spent seven years in bringing the structure to perfection, and then waited day after day, in expectation that it would utter articulate sounds. At length nature became exhausted in them, and they lay down to sleep, having first given it strictly in charge to a servant of theirs, clownish in nature, but of strict fidelity, that he should awaken them the moment the image began to speak. That period arrived. The head uttered sounds, but such as the clown judged unworthy of notice. "Time is!" it said. No notice was taken; and a long pause ensued. "Time was!" A similar pause, and no notice. "Time is passed!" And the moment these words were uttered, a tremendous storm ensued, with thunder and lightning, and the head was shivered into a thousand pieces. Thus the experiment of friar Bacon and friar Bungy came to nothing.

THOMAS AQUINAS.

Thomas Aquinas, who has likewise been brought under the imputation of magic, was one of the profoundest scholars and subtlest logicians of his day. He also furnishes a remarkable instance of the ascendant which the friars at that time obtained over the minds of ingenuous young men smitten with the thirst of knowledge. He was a youth of illustrious birth, and received the rudiments of his education under the monks of Monte Cassino, and in the university of Naples. But, not contented with these advantages, he secretly entered himself into the society of Preaching Friars, or Dominicans, at seventeen years of age. His mother, being indignant that he should thus take the vow of poverty, and sequester himself from the world for life, employed every means in her power to induce him to alter his purpose, but in vain. The friars, to deliver him from her importunities, removed him from Naples to Terracina, from Terracina to Anagnia, and from Anagnia to Rome. His mother followed him in all these changes of residence, but was not permitted so much as to see him. At length she spirited up his two elder brothers to seize him by force. They waylaid him in his road to Paris, whither he was sent to complete his course of instruction, and carried him off to the castle of Aquino where he had been born. Here he was confined for two years; but he found a way to correspond with the superiors of his order, and finally escaped from a window in the castle. St. Thomas Aquinas (for he was canonised after his death) exceeded perhaps all men that ever existed in the severity and strictness of his metaphysical disquisitions, and thus acquired the name of the Seraphic Doctor.

It was to be expected that a man, who thus im: mersed himself in the depths of thought, should be an inexorable enemy to noise and interruption. We have seen that he dashed to pieces the artificial man of brass, that Albertus Magnus, who was his tutor, had spent thirty years in bringing to perfection, being impelled to this violence by its perpetual and unceasing garrulity[a]. It is further said, that his study being placed in a great thoroughfare, where the grooms were all day long exercising their horses, he found it necessary to apply a remedy to this nuisance. He made by the laws of magic a small horse of brass, which he buried two or three feet under ground in the midst of this highway; and, having done so, no horse would any longer pass along the road. It was in vain that the grooms with whip and spur sought to con-

[a] See page 261.

quer their repugnance. They were finally compelled to give up the attempt, and to choose another place for their daily exercise[c].

It has further been sought to fix the imputation of magic upon Thomas Aquinas by imputing to him certain books written on that science; but these are now acknowledged to be spurious[d].

PETER OF APONO.

Peter of Apono, so called from a village of that name in the vicinity of Padua, where he was born in the year 1250, was an eminent philosopher, mathematician and astrologer, but especially excelled in physic. Finding that science at a low ebb in his native country, he resorted to Paris, where it especially flourished; and after a time returning home, exercised his art with extraordinary success, and by this means accumulated great wealth.

But all his fame and attainments were poisoned to him by the accusation of magic. Among other things he was said to possess seven spirits, each of them inclosed in a crystal vessel, from whom he received every information he desired in the seven liberal arts. He was further reported to have had the extraordinary faculty of causing the money he expended in his disbursements, immediately to come back into his own purse. He was besides of a hasty and revengeful temper. In consequence of

[c] Naudé, Cap. 17.   [d] Ibid.

this it happened to him, that, having a neighbour, who had an admirable spring of water in his garden, and who was accustomed to suffer the physician to send for a daily supply, but who for some displeasure or inconvenience withdrew his permission, Peter d'Apono, by the aid of the devil, removed the spring from the garden in which it had flowed, and turned it to waste in the public street. For some of these accusations he was called to account by the tribunal of the inquisition. While he was upon his trial however, the unfortunate man died. But so unfavourable was the judgment of the inquisitors respecting him, that they decreed that his bones should be dug up, and publicly burned. Some of his friends got intimation of this, and saved him from the impending disgrace by removing his remains. Disappointed in this, the inquisitors proceeded to burn him in effigy.

ENGLISH LAW OF HIGH TREASON.

It may seem strange that in a treatise concerning necromancy we should have occasion to speak of the English law of high treason. But on reflection perhaps it may appear not altogether alien to the subject. This crime is ordinarily considered by our lawyers as limited and defined by the statute of 25 Edward III. As Blackstone has observed, " By the ancient common law there was a great latitude left in the breast of the judges, to determine what was treason, or not so: whereby the creatures of tyrannical power had opportunity to create abundance of constructive treasons; that is, to raise, by forced and arbitrary constructions, offences into the crime and punishment of treason, which were never suspected to be such. To prevent these inconveniences, the statute of 25 Edward III was made^a." This statute divides treason into seven distinct branches; and the first and chief of these is, "when a man doth compass or imagine the death of our lord the king."

Now the first circumstance that strikes us in this affair is, why the crime was not expressed in more perspicuous and appropriate language? Why, for example, was it not said, that the first and chief branch of treason was to "kill the king?" Or, if that limitation was not held to be sufficiently ample, could it not have been added, it is treason to "attempt, intend, or contrive to kill the king?" We are apt to make much too large an allowance for what is considered as the vague and obsolete language of our ancestors. Logic was the element in which the scholars of what are called the dark ages were especially at home. It was at that period that the description of human geniuses, called the Schoolmen, principally flourished. The writers who preceded the Christian era, possessed in an extraordinary degree the gift of imagination and invention. But they had little to boast on the

^a Commentaries, Book IV. chap. vi.

score of arrangement, and discovered little skill in the strictness of an accurate deduction. Meanwhile the Schoolmen had a surprising subtlety in weaving the web of an argument, and arriving by a close deduction, through a multitude of steps, to a sound and irresistible conclusion. Our lawyers to a certain degree formed themselves on the discipline of the Schoolmen. Nothing can be more forcibly contrasted, than the mode of pleading among the ancients, and that which has characterised the processes of the moderns. The pleadings of the ancients were praxises of the art of oratorical persuasion; the pleadings of the moderns sometimes, though rarely, deviate into oratory, but principally consist in dextrous subtleties upon words, or a nice series of deductions, the whole contexture of which is endeavoured to be woven into one indissoluble substance. Several striking examples have been preserved of the mode of pleading in the reign of Edward II, in which the exceptions taken for the defendant, and the replies supporting the mode of proceeding on behalf of the plaintiff, in no respect fall short of the most admired shifts, quirks and subtleties of the great lawyers of later times[b].

It would be certainly wrong therefore to consider the legal phrase, to " compass or imagine the death of the king," as meaning the same thing as to " kill, or intend to kill" him. At all events we may take it for granted, that to " compass" does not

Life of Chaucer, c. xviii.

mean to accomplish; but rather to "take in hand, to go about to effect." There is therefore no form of words here forbidding to "kill the king." The phrase, to "imagine," does not appear less startling. What is, to a proverb, more lawless than imagination?

> Evil into the mind of God or man
> May come and go, so unapproved, and leave
> No spot or blame behind.

What can be more tyrannical, than an inquisition into the sports and freaks of fancy? What more unsusceptible of detection or evidence? How many imperceptible shades of distinction between the guilt and innocence that characterise them!— Meanwhile the force and propriety of these terms will strikingly appear, if we refer them to the popular ideas of witchcraft. Witches were understood to have the power of destroying life, without the necessity of approaching the person whose life was to be destroyed, or producing any consciousness in him of the crime about to be perpetrated. One method was by exposing an image of wax to the action of fire; while, in proportion as the image wasted away, the life of the individual who was the object contrived against, was undermined and destroyed. Another was by incantations and spells. Either of these might fitly be called the "compassing or imagining the death." Imagination is, beside this, the peculiar province of witchcraft. And in these pretended hags the faculty is no longer desultory and erratic. Conscious of their power, they are supposed to have subjected it to system and discipline. They apply its secret and trackless energy with an intentness and a vigour, which ordinary mortals may in vain attempt to emulate in an application of the force of inert matter, or of the different physical powers by means of which such stupendous effects have often been produced.—How universal and familiar then must we consider the ideas of witchcraft to have been before language which properly describes the secret practices of such persons, and is not appropriate to any other, could have been found to insinuate itself into the structure of the most solemn act of our legislature, that act which beyond all others was intended to narrow or shut out the subtle and dangerous inroads of arbitrary power!

ZIITO.

Very extraordinary things are related of Ziito, a sorcerer, in the court of Wenceslaus, king of Bohemia and afterwards emperor of Germany, in the latter part of the fourteenth century. This is perhaps, all things considered, the most wonderful specimen of magical power any where to be found. It is gravely recorded by Dubravius, bishop of Olmutz, in his History of Bohemia. It was publicly exhibited on occasion of the marriage of Wenceslaus with Sophia, daughter of the elector

Palatine of Bavaria, before a vast assembled multitude.

The father-in-law of the king, well aware of the bridegroom's known predilection for theatrical exhibitions and magical illusions, brought with him to Prague, the capital of Wenceslaus, a whole waggon-load of morrice-dancers and jugglers, who made their appearance among the royal retinue. Meanwhile Ziito, the favourite magician of the king, took his place obscurely among the ordinary spectators. He however immediately arrested the attention of the strangers, being remarked for his extraordinary deformity, and a mouth that stretched completely from ear to ear. Ziito was for some time engaged in quietly observing the tricks and sleights that were exhibited. At length, while the chief magician of the elector Palatine was still busily employed in shewing some of the most admired specimens of his art, the Bohemian, indignant at what appeared to him the bungling exhibitions of his brother-artist, came forward, and reproached him with the unskilfulness of his performances. The two professors presently fell into warm debate. Ziito, provoked at the insolence of his rival, made no more ado but swallowed him whole before the multitude, attired as he was, all but his shoes, which he objected to because they were dirty. He then retired for a short while to a closet, and presently returned, leading the magician along with him.

Having thus disposed of his rival, Ziito proceeded to exhibit the wonders of his art. He shewed himself first in his proper shape, and then in those of different persons successively, with countenances and a stature totally dissimilar to his own; at one time splendidly attired in robes of purple and silk, and then in the twinkling of an eye in coarse linen and a clownish coat of frieze. He would proceed along the field with a smooth and undulating motion without changing the posture of a limb, for all the world as if he were carried along in a ship. He would keep pace with the king's chariot, in a car drawn by barn-door fowls. He also amused the king's guests as they sat at table, by causing, when they stretched out their hands to the different dishes, sometimes their hands to turn into the cloven feet of an ox, and at other times into the hoofs of a horse. He would clap on them the antlers of a deer, so that, when they put their heads out at window to see some sight that was going by, they could by no means draw them back again; while he in the mean time feasted on the savoury cates that had been spread before them, at his leisure.

At one time he pretended to be in want of money, and to task his wits to devise the means to procure it. On such an occasion he took up a handful of grains of corn, and presently gave them the form and appearance of thirty hogs well fatted for the market. He drove these hogs to the residence of one Michael, a rich dealer, but who was remarked for being penurious and thrifty in his bargains. He offered them to Michael for whatever price he should judge reasonable. The bargain was presently struck, Ziito at the same time warning the purchaser, that he should on no account drive them to the river to drink. Michael however paid no attention to this advice; and the hogs no sooner arrived at the river, than they turned into grains of corn as before. The dealer, greatly enraged at this trick, sought high and low for the seller that he might be revenged on him. At length he found him in a vintner's shop seemingly in a gloomy and absent frame of mind, reposing himself, with his legs stretched out on a form. The dealer called out to him, but he seemed not to hear. Finally he seized Ziito by one foot, plucking at it with all his might. The foot came away with the leg and thigh; and Ziito screamed out, apparently in great agony. He seized Michael by the nape of the neck, and dragged him before a judge. Here the two set up their separate complaints, Michael for the fraud that had been committed on him, and Ziito for the irreparable injury he had suffered in his person. From this adventure came the proverb, frequent in the days of the historian, speaking of a person who had made an improvident bargain, "He has made just such a purchase as Michael did with his hogs."

TRANSMUTATION OF METALS.

Among the different pursuits, which engaged the curiosity of active minds in these unenlightened ages, was that of the transmutation of the more ordinary metals into gold and silver. This art, though not properly of necromantic nature, was however elevated by its professors, by means of an imaginary connection between it and astrology, and even between it and an intercourse with invisible spirits. They believed, that their investigations could not be successfully prosecuted but under favourable aspects of the planets, and that it was even indispensible to them to obtain supernatural aid.

In proportion as the pursuit of transmutation, and the search after the elixir of immortality grew into vogue, the adepts became desirous of investing them with the venerable garb of antiquity. They endeavoured to carry up the study to the time of Solomon; and there were not wanting some who imputed it to the first father of mankind. They were desirous to track its footsteps in Ancient Egypt; and they found a mythological representation of it in the expedition of Jason after the golden fleece, and in the cauldron by which Medea restored the father of Jason to his original youth[a]. But, as has already been said, the first unquestionable mention of the subject is to be referred to the time of Dioclesian[b]. From that pe-

---

[a] Wotton, Reflections on Learning, Chap. X.
[b] See above, p. 29.

irod traces of the studies of the alchemists from time to time regularly discover themselves.

The study of chemistry and its supposed invaluable results was assiduously cultivated by Geber and the Arabians.

ARTEPHIUS.

Artephius is one of the earliest names that occur among the students who sought the philosopher's stone. Of him extraordinary things are told. He lived about the year 1130, and wrote a book of the Art of Prolonging Human Life, in which he professes to have already attained the age of one thousand and twenty-five years[a]. He must by this account have been born about one hundred years after our Saviour. He professed to have visited the infernal regions, and there to have seen Tantalus seated on a throne of gold. He is also said by some to be the same person, whose life has been written by Philostratus under the name of Apollonius of Tyana[b]. He wrote a book on the philosopher's stone, which was published in Latin and French at Paris in the year 1612.

RAYMOND LULLI.

Among the European students of these interesting secrets a foremost place is to be assigned to Raymond Lulli and Arnold of Villeneuve.

[a] Biographie Universelle. [b] Naudé.

Lulli was undoubtedly a man endowed in a very eminent degree with the powers of intellect. He was a native of the island of Majorca, and was born in the year 1234. He is said to have passed his early years in profligacy and dissipation, but to have been reclaimed by the accident of falling in love with a young woman afflicted with a cancer. This circumstance induced him to apply himself intently to the study of chemistry and medicine, with a view to discover a cure for her complaint, in which he succeeded. He afterwards entered into the community of Franciscan friars.

Edward the First was one of the most extraordinary princes that ever sat on a throne. He revived the study of the Roman civil law with such success as to have merited the title of the English Justinian. He was no less distinguished as the patron of arts and letters. He invited to England Guido dalla Colonna, the author of the Troy Book, and Raymond Lulli. This latter was believed in his time to have prosecuted his studies with such success as to have discovered the *elixir vitæ*, by means of which he could keep off the assaults of old age, at least for centuries, and the philosopher's stone. He is affirmed by these means to have supplied to Edward the First six millions of money, to enable him to carry on war against the Turks.

But he was not only indefatigable in the pursuit of natural science. He was also seized with an invincible desire to convert the Mahometans to the Christian faith. For this purpose he entered earnestly upon the study of the Oriental languages. He endeavoured to prevail on different princes of Europe to concur in his plan, and to erect colleges for the purpose, but without success. He at length set out alone upon his enterprise, but met with small encouragement. He penetrated into Africa and Asia. He made few converts, and was with difficulty suffered to depart, under a solemn injunction that he should not return. But Lulli chose to obey God rather than man, and ventured a second time. The Mahometans became exasperated with his obstinacy, and are said to have stoned him to death at the age of eighty years. His body was however transported to his native place; and miracles are reported to have been worked at his tomb[a].

Raymond Lulli is beside famous for what he was pleased to style his Great Art. The ordinary accounts however that are given of this art assume a style of burlesque, rather than of philosophy. He is said to have boasted that by means of it he could enable any one to argue logically on any subject for a whole day together, independently of any previous study of the subject in debate. To the details of the process Swift seems to have been indebted for one of the humorous projects described by him in his voyage to Laputa. Lulli recom-

[a] Moreri.

mended that certain general terms of logic, metaphysics, ethics or theology should first be collected. These were to be inscribed separately upon square pieces of parchment. They were then to be placed on a frame so constructed that by turning a handle they might revolve freely, and form endless combinations. One term would stand for a subject, and another for a predicate. The student was then diligently to inspect the different combinations that fortuitously arose, and exercising the subtlety of his faculties to select such as he should find best calculated for his purposes. He would thus carry on the process of his debate; and an extraordinary felicity would occasionally arise, suggesting the most ingenious hints, and leading on to the most important discoveries[b].—If a man with the eminent faculties which Lulli otherwise appeared to have possessed really laid down the rules of such an art, all he intended by it must have been to satirize the gravity with which the learned doctors of his time carried on their grave disputations in mood and figure, having regard only to the severity of the rule by which they debated, and holding themselves totally indifferent whether they made any real advances in the discovery of truth.

ARNOLD OF VILLENEUVE.

Arnold of Villeneuve, who lived about the same time, was a man of eminent attainments. He

[b] Enfield, History of Philosophy, Book VIII, chapter i.

made a great proficiency in Greek, Hebrew, and Arabic. He devoted himself in a high degree to astrology, and was so confident in his art, as to venture to predict that the end of the world would occur in a few years; but he lived to witness the fallaciousness of his prophecy. He had much reputation as a physician. He appears to have been a bold thinker. He maintained that deeds of charity were of more avail than the sacrifice of the mass, and that no one would be damned hereafter, but such as were proved to afford an example of immoral conduct. Like all the men of these times who were distinguished by the profoundness of their studies, he was accused of magic. For this, or upon a charge of heresy, he was brought under the prosecution of the inquisition. But he was alarmed by the fate of Peter of Apono, and by recantation or some other mode of prudent contrivance was fortunate enough to escape. He is one of the persons to whom the writing of the book, *De Tribus Impostoribus*, Of the Three Impostors (Moses, Jesus Christ and Mahomet) was imputed![a]

ENGLISH LAWS RESPECTING TRANSMUTATION.

So great an alarm was conceived about this time respecting the art of transmutation, that an act of parliament was passed in the fifth year of Henry IV, 1404, which lord Coke states as the shortest

[a] Moreri.

of our statutes, determining that the making of gold or silver shall be deemed felony. This law is said to have resulted from the fear at that time entertained by the houses of lords and commons, lest the executive power, finding itself by these means enabled to increase the revenue of the crown to any degree it pleased, should disdain to ask aid from the legislature; and in consequence should degenerate into tyranny and arbitrary power[a].

George Ripley, of Ripley in the county of York, is mentioned, towards the latter part of the fifteenth century, as having discovered the philosopher's stone, and by its means contributed one hundred thousand pounds to the knights of Rhodes, the better to enable them to carry on their war against the Turks[b].

About this time however the tide appears to have turned, and the alarm respecting the multiplication of the precious metals so greatly to have abated, that patents were issued in the thirty-fifth year of Henry VI, for the encouragement of such as were disposed to seek the universal medicine, and to endeavour the transmutation of inferior metals into gold[c].

[a] Watson, Chemical Essays, Vol. I.
[b] Fuller, Worthies of England.
[c] Watson, *ubi supra*.

REVIVAL OF LETTERS.

WHILE these things were going on in Europe, the period was gradually approaching, when the energies of the human mind were to loosen its shackles, and its independence was ultimately to extinguish those delusions and that superstition which had so long enslaved it. Petrarch, born in the year 1304, was deeply impregnated with a passion for classical lore, was smitten with the love of republican institutions, and especially distinguished himself for an adoration of Homer. Dante, a more sublime and original genius than Petrarch, was his contemporary. About the same time Boccaccio in his Decamerone gave at once to Italian prose that purity and grace, which none of his successors in the career of literature have ever been able to excel. And in our own island Chaucer with a daring hand redeemed his native tongue from the disuse and ignominy into which it had fallen, and poured out the immortal strains that the genuine lovers of the English tongue have ever since perused with delight, while those who are discouraged by its apparent crabbedness, have yet grown familiar with his thoughts in the smoother and more modern versification of Dryden and Pope. From that time the principles of true taste have been more or less cultivated, while with equal career independence of thought and an ardent spirit of discovery have continually proceeded, and made a rapid advance towards the perfect day.

But the dawn of literature and intellectual freedom were still a long time ere they produced their full effect. The remnant of the old woman clung to the heart with a tenacious embrace. Three or four centuries elapsed, while yet the belief in sorcery and witchcraft was alive in certain classes of society. And then, as is apt to occur in such cases, the expiring folly occasionally gave tokens of its existence with a convulsive vehemence, and became only the more picturesque and impressive through the strong contrast of lights and shadows that attended its manifestations.

JOAN OF ARC.

One of the most memorable stories on record is that of Joan of Arc, commonly called the Maid of Orleans. Henry the Fifth of England won the decisive battle of Agincourt in the year 1415, and some time after concluded a treaty with the reigning king of France, by which he was recognised, in case of that king's death, as heir to the throne. Henry V died in the year 1422, and Charles VI of France in less than two months after. Henry VI was only nine months old at the time of his father's death; but such was the deplorable state of France, that he was in the same year proclaimed king in Paris, and for some years seemed to have every prospect of a fortunate reign. John duke of Bedford, the king's uncle, was declared regent of France: the son of Charles VI was reduced to the last extremity; Orleans was the last strong town in the heart of the kingdom which held out in his favour; and that place seemed on the point to surrender to the conqueror.

In this fearful crisis appeared Joan of Arc, and in the most incredible manner turned the whole tide of affairs. She was a servant in a poor inn at Domremi, and was accustomed to perform the coarsest offices, and in particular to ride the horses to a neighbouring stream to water. Of course the situation of France and her hereditary king formed the universal subject of conversation; and Joan became deeply impressed with the lamentable state of her country and the misfortunes of her king. By dint of perpetual meditation, and feeling in her breast the promptings of energy and enterprise, she conceived the idea that she was destined by heaven to be the deliverer of France. Agreeably to the state of intellectual knowledge at that period, she persuaded herself that she saw visions, and held communication with the saints. She had conversations with St. Margaret, and St. Catherine of Fierbois. They told her that she was commissioned by God to raise the siege of Orleans, and to conduct Charles VII to his coronation at Rheims.

St. Catherine commanded her to demand a sword which was in her church at Fierbois, which the Maid described by particular tokens, though she had never seen it. She then presented herself to Baudricourt, governor of the neighbouring town of Vaucouleurs, telling him her commission, and requiring him to send her to the king at Chinon. Baudricourt at first made light of her application; but her importunity and the ardour she expressed at length excited him. He put on her a man's attire, gave her arms, and sent her under an escort of two gentlemen and their attendants to Chinon. Here she immediately addressed the king in person, who had purposely hid himself behind his courtiers that she might not know him. She then delivered her message, and offered in the name of the Most High to raise the siege of Orleans, and conduct king Charles to Rheims to be anointed. As a further confirmation she is said to have revealed to the king before a few select friends, a secret, which nothing but divine inspiration could have discovered to her.

Desperate as was then the state of affairs, Charles and his ministers immediately resolved to seize the occasion that offered, and put forward Joan as an instrument to revive the prostrate courage of his subjects. He had no sooner determined on this, than he pretended to submit the truth of her mission to the most rigorous trial. He called together an assembly of theologians and doctors, who rigorously examined Joan, and pronounced in her favour. He referred the question to the parliament of Poitiers; and they, who met persuaded that she was an impostor, became convinced of her inspiration. She was mounted on a high-bred steed, furnished with a consecrated banner, and marched, escorted by a body of five thousand men, to the relief of Orleans. The French, strongly convinced by so plain an interposition of heaven, resumed the courage to which they had long been strangers. Such a phenomenon was exactly suited to the superstition and credulity of the age. The English were staggered with the rumours that every where went before her, and struck with a degree of apprehension and terror that they could not shake off. The garrison, informed of her approach, made a sally on the other side of the town; and Joan and her convoy entered without opposition. She displayed her standard in the market-place, and was received as a celestial deliverer.

She appears to have been endowed with a prudence, not inferior to her courage and spirit of enterprise. With great docility she caught the hints of the commanders by whom she was surrounded; and, convinced of her own want of experience and skill, delivered them to the forces as the dictates of heaven. Thus the knowledge and discernment of the generals were brought into play, at the same time that their suggestions acquired new weight, when falling from the lips of the heaven-instructed heroine. A second convoy arrived; the waggons and troops passed between the redoubts of the English; while a dead silence and astonishment reigned among the forces, so lately enterprising and resistless. Joan now called on the garrison no longer to stand upon the defensive, but boldly to attack the army of the besiegers. She took one redoubt and then another. The English, overwhelmed with amazement, scarcely dared to lift a hand against her. Their veteran generals became spell-bound and powerless; and their soldiers were driven before the prophetess like a flock of sheep. The siege was raised.

Joan followed the English garrison to a fortified town which they fixed on as their place of retreat. The siege lasted ten days; the place was taken; and all the English within it made prisoners. The late victorious forces now concentred themselves at Patay in the Orleanois; Joan advanced to meet them. The battle lasted not a moment; it was rather a flight than a combat; Fastolfe, one of the bravest of our commanders, threw down his arms, and ran for his life; Talbot and Scales, the other generals, were made prisoners. The siege of Orleans was raised on the eighth of May, 1429; the battle of Patay was fought on the tenth of the following month. Joan was at this time twenty-two years of age.

This extraordinary turn having been given to

the affairs of the kingdom, Joan next insisted that the king should march to Rheims, in order to his being crowned. Rheims lay in a direction expressly through the midst of the enemies' garrisons. But every thing yielded to the marvellous fortune that attended upon the heroine. Troyes opened its gates; Chalons followed the example; Rheims sent a deputation with the keys of the city, which met Charles on his march. The proposed solemnity took place amidst the extacies and enthusiastic shouts of his people. It was no sooner over, than Joan stept forward. She said, she had now performed the whole of what God had commissioned her to do; she was satisfied; she intreated the king to dismiss her to the obscurity from which she had sprung.

The ministers and generals of France however found Joan too useful an instrument, to be willing to part with her thus early; and she yielded to their earnest expostulations. Under her guidance they assailed Laon, Soissons, Chateau Thierry, Provins, and many other places, and took them one after another. She threw herself into Compiegne, which was besieged by the Duke of Burgundy in conjunction with certain English commanders. The day after her arrival she headed a sally against the enemy; twice she repelled them; but, finding their numbers increase every moment with fresh reinforcements, she directed a retreat. Twice she returned upon her pursuers, and made them recoil, the third time she was less fortunate. She found herself alone, surrounded with the enemy; and after having enacted prodigies of valour, she was compelled to surrender a prisoner. This happened on the twenty-fifth of May, 1430.

It remained to be determined what should be the fate of this admirable woman. Both friends and enemies agreed that her career had been attended with a supernatural power. The French, who were so infinitely indebted to her achievements, and who owed the sudden and glorious reverse of their affairs to her alone, were convinced that she was immediately commissioned by God, and vied with each other in reciting the miraculous phenomena which marked every step in her progress. The English, who saw all the victorious acquisitions of Henry V crumbling from their grasp, were equally impressed with the manifest miracle, but imputed all her good-fortune to a league with the prince of darkness. They said that her boasted visions were so many delusions of the devil. They determined to bring her to trial for the tremendous crimes of sorcery and witchcraft. They believed that, if she were once convicted and led out to execution, the prowess and valour which had hitherto marked their progress would return to them, and that they should obtain the same superiority over their disheartened foes. The devil, who had hitherto been her constant ally, terrified at the spectacle of the flames that consumed her, would instantly return to the infernal regions, and leave the field open to English enterprise and energy, and to the interposition of God and his saints.

An accusation was prepared against her, and all the solemnities of a public trial were observed. But the proofs were so weak and unsatisfactory, and Joan, though oppressed and treated with the utmost severity, displayed so much acuteness and presence of mind, that the court, not venturing to proceed to the last extremity, contented themselves with sentencing her to perpetual imprisonment, and to be allowed no other nourishment than bread and water for life. Before they yielded to this mitigation of punishment, they caused her to sign with her mark a recantation of her offences. She acknowledged that the enthusiasm that had guided her was an illusion, and promised never more to listen to its suggestions.

The hatred of her enemies however was not yet appeased. They determined in some way to entrap her. They had clothed her in a female garb; they insidiously laid in her way the habiliments of a man. The fire smothered in the bosom of the maid, revived at the sight; she was alone; she caught up the garments, and one by one adjusted them to her person. Spies were set upon her to watch for this event; they burst into the apartment. What she had done was construed into no less offence than that of a relapsed heretic; there was no more pardon for such confirmed delinquency; she was brought out to be burned alive in the market-place of Rouen, and she died, embracing a crucifix, and in her last moments calling upon the name of Jesus. A few days more than twelve months, had elapsed between the period of her first captivity and her execution.

ELEANOR COBHAM, DUCHESS OF GLOUCESTER.

This was a period in which the ideas of witchcraft had caught fast hold of the minds of mankind; and those accusations, which by the enlightened part of the species would now be regarded as worthy only of contempt, were then considered as charges of the most flatigious nature. While John, duke of Bedford, the eldest uncle of king Henry VI, was regent of France, Humphrey of Gloucester, next brother to Bedford, was lord protector of the realm of England. Though Henry was now nineteen years of age, yet, as he was a prince of slender capacity, Humphrey still continued to discharge the functions of sovereignty. He was eminently endowed with popular qualities, and was a favourite with the majority of the nation. He had however many enemies, one of the chief of whom was Henry Beaufort, great-uncle to the king, and cardinal of Winchester. One of the means employed by this prelate to undermine the power of Humphrey, consisted in a charge of witchcraft brought against Eleanor Cobham, his wife.

This woman had probably yielded to the delusions, which artful persons, who saw into the weakness of her character, sought to practise upon her. She was the second wife of Humphrey, and he was suspected to have indulged in undue familiarity with her, before he was a widower. His present duchess was reported to have had recourse to witchcraft in the first instance, by way of securing his wayward inclinations. The duke of Bedford had died in 1435; and Humphrey now, in addition to the actual exercise of the powers of sovereignty, was next heir to the crown in case of the king's decease. This weak and licentious woman, being now duchess of Gloucester, and wife to the lord protector, directed her ambition to the higher title and prerogatives of a queen, and by way of feeding her evil passions, called to her counsels Margery Jourdain, commonly called the witch of Eye, Roger Bolingbroke, an astrologer and supposed magician, Thomas Southwel, canon of St. Stephen's, and one John Hume, or Hun, a priest. These persons frequently met the duchess in secret cabal. They were accused of calling up spirits from the infernal world; and they made an image of wax, which they slowly consumed before a fire, expecting that, as the image gradually wasted away, so the constitution and life of the poor king would decay and finally perish.

Hume, or Hun, is supposed to have turned informer, and upon his information several of these persons were taken into custody. After previous examination, on the twenty-fifth of July, 1441, Bolingbroke was placed upon a scaffold before the cross of St. Paul's, with a chair curiously painted, which was supposed to be one of his implements of necromancy, and dressed in mystical attire, and there, before the archbishop of Canterbury, the cardinal of Winchester, and several other bishops, made abjuration of all his unlawful arts.

A short time after, the duchess of Gloucester, having fled to the sanctuary at Westminster, her case was referred to the same high persons, and Bolingbroke was brought forth to give evidence against her. She was of consequence committed to custody in the castle of Leeds near Maidstone, to take her trial in the month of October. A commission was directed to the lord treasurer, several noblemen, and certain judges of both benches, to enquire into all manner of treasons, sorceries, and other things that might be hurtful to the king's person, and Bolingbroke and Southwel as principals, and the duchess of Gloucester as accessory, were brought before them. Margery Jourdain was arraigned at the same time; and she, as a witch and relapsed heretic, was condemned to be burned in Smithfield. The duchess of Gloucester was sentenced to do penance on three several days, walking through the streets of London, with a lighted taper in her hand, attended by the lord mayor, the sheriffs, and a select body of the livery, and then to be banished for life to the isle of Man. Thomas Southwel died in prison; and Bolingbroke was hanged at Tyburn on the eighteenth of November.

RICHARD III.

An event occurred not very long after this, which deserves to be mentioned, as being well calculated to shew how deep an impression ideas of witchcraft had made on the public mind even in the gravest affairs and the counsels of a nation. Richard duke of Gloucester, afterwards Richard III, shortly before his usurpation of the crown in 1483, had recourse to this expedient for disarming the power of his enemies, which he feared as an obstacle to his project. Being lord protector, he came abruptly into the assembly of the council that he had left but just before, and suddenly asked, what punishment they deserved who should be found to have plotted against his life, being the person, as nearest akin to the young king, intrusted in chief with the affairs of the nation? And, a suitable answer being returned, he said the persons he accused were the queen-dowager, and Jane Shore, the favourite concubine of the late king, who by witchcraft and forbidden arts had sought to destroy him. And, while he spoke, he laid bare his left arm up to the elbow, which appeared shrivelled and wasted in a pitiable manner. "To this condition," said he, "have these abandoned women reduced me."—The historian adds, that it was well known that his arm had been thus wasted from his birth.

In January 1484 the parliament met which recognised the title of Richard, and pronounced the marriage of Edward IV null, and its issue illegitimate. The same parliament passed an act of attainder against Henry earl of Richmond, afterwards Henry VII, the countess of Richmond, his mother, and a great number of other persons, many of them the most considerable adherents of the house of Lancaster. Among these persons are enumerated Thomas Nandick and William Knivet, necromancers. In the first parliament of Henry VII this attainder was reversed, and Thomas Nandick of Cambridge, conjurer, is specially nominated as an object of free pardon[b].

[a] Sir Thomas More, History of Edward the Fifth.
[b] Buck, Life and Reign of Richard III.

SANGUINARY PROCEEDINGS AGAINST WITCHCRAFT.

I AM now led to the most painful part of my subject, but which does not the less constitute one of its integral members, and which, though painful, is deeply instructive, and constitutes a most essential branch in the science of human nature. Wherever I could, I have endeavoured to render the topics which offered themselves to my examination, entertaining. When men pretended to invert the known laws of nature, " murdering impossibility; to make what cannot be, slight work;" I have been willing to consider the whole as an ingenious fiction, and merely serving as an example how far credulity could go in setting aside the deductions of our reason, and the evidence of sense. The artists in these cases did not fail to excite admiration, and gain some sort of applause from their contemporaries, though still with a tingling feeling that all was not exactly as it should be, and with a confession that the professors were exercising unhallowed arts. It was like what has been known of the art of acting; those who employed it were caressed and made every where welcome, but were not allowed the distinction of Christian burial.

But, particularly in the fifteenth century, things

took a new turn. In the dawn of the day of good sense, and when historical evidence at length began to be weighed in the scales of judgment, men became less careless of truth, and regarded prodigies and miracles with a different temper. And, as it often happens, the crisis, the precise passage from ill to better, shewed itself more calamitous, and more full of enormities and atrocity, than the period when the understanding was completely hood-winked, and men digested absurdities and impossibility with as much ease as their every day food. They would not now forgive the tampering with the axioms of eternal truth; they regarded cheat and imposture with a very different eye; and they had recourse to the stake and the faggot, for the purpose of proving that they would no longer be trifled with. They treated the offenders as the most atrocious of criminals, and thus, though by a very indirect and circuitous method, led the way to the total dispersion of those clouds, which hung, with most uneasy operation, on the human understanding.

The university of Paris in the year 1398 promulgated an edict, in which they complained that the practice of witchcraft was become more frequent and general than at any former period[a].

A stratagem was at this time framed by the ecclesiastical persecutors, of confounding together the crimes of heresy and witchcraft. The first of

[a] Hutchinson on Witchcraft.

these might seem to be enough in the days of bigotry and implicit faith, to excite the horror of the vulgar; but the advocates of religious uniformity held that they should be still more secure of their object, if they could combine the sin of holding cheap the authority of the recognised heads of Christian faith, with that of men's enlisting under the banners of Satan, and becoming the avowed and sworn vassals of his infernal empire. They accordingly seem to have invented the ideas of a sabbath of witches, a numerous assembly of persons who had cast off all sense of shame, and all regard for those things which the rest of the human species held most sacred, where the devil appeared among them in his most forbidding form, and, by rites equally ridiculous and obscene, the persons present acknowledged themselves his subjects. And, having invented this scene, these cunning and mischievous persecutors found means, as we shall presently see, of compelling their unfortunate victims to confess that they had personally assisted at the ceremony, and performed all the degrading offices which should consign them in the world to come to everlasting fire.

While I express myself thus, I by no means intend to encourage the idea that the ecclesiastical authorities of these times were generally hypocrites. They fully partook of the narrowness of thought of the period in which they lived. They believed that the sin of heretical pravity was " as the sin of witchcraft[b];" they regarded them alike with horror, and were persuaded that there was a natural consent and alliance between them. Fully impressed with this conception, they employed means from which our genuine and undebauched nature revolts, to extort from their deluded victims a confession of what their examiners apprehended to be true; they asked them leading questions; they suggested the answers they desired to receive; and led the ignorant and friendless to imagine that, if these answers were adopted, they might expect immediately to be relieved from insupportable tortures. The delusion went round. These unhappy wretches, finding themselves the objects of universal abhorrence, and the hatred of mankind, at length many of them believed that they had entered into a league with the devil, that they had been transported by him through the air to an assembly of souls consigned to everlasting reprobation, that they had bound themselves in acts of fealty to their infernal taskmasters, and had received from him in return the gift of performing superhuman and supernatural feats. This is a tremendous state of degradation of what Milton called the " the faultless proprieties of nature[c]," which cooler thinking and more enlightened times would lead us to regard as impossible, but to which the uncontradicted and authentic voice of history compels us to subscribe.

[b] 1 Samuel, xv, 23.   [c] Doctrine of Divorce, Preface.

The Albigenses and Waldenses were a set of men, who, in the flourishing provinces of Languedoc, in the darkest ages, and when the understandings of human creatures by a force not less memorable than that of Procrustes were reduced to an uniform stature, shook off by some strange and unaccountable freak, the chains that were universally imposed, and arrived at a boldness of thinking similar to that which Luther and Calvin after a lapse of centuries advocated with happier auspices. With these manly and generous sentiments however they combined a considerable portion of wild enthusiasm. They preached the necessity of a community of goods, taught that it was necessary to wear sandals, because sandals only had been worn by the apostles, and devoted themselves to lives of rigorous abstinence and the most severe self-denial.

The Catholic church knew no other way in those days of converting heretics, but by fire and sword; and accordingly pope Innocent the Third published a crusade against them. The inquisition was expressly appointed in its origin to bring back these stray sheep into the flock of Christ; and, to support this institution in its operations, Simon Montfort marched a numerous army for the extermination of the offenders. One hundred thousand are said to have perished. They disappeared from the country which had witnessed their commencement, and dispersed themselves in the vallies of

Piedmont, in Artois, and in various other places. This crusade occurred in the commencement of the thirteenth century; and they do not again attract the notice of history till the middle of the fifteenth.

Monstrelet, in his Chronicle, gives one of the earliest accounts of the proceedings at this time instituted against these unfortunate people, under the date of the year 1459. " In this year," says he, " in the town of Arras, there occurred a miserable and inhuman scene, to which, I know not why, was given the name of *Vaudoisie*. There were taken up and imprisoned a number of considerable persons inhabitants of this town, and others of a very inferior class. These latter were so cruelly put to the torture, that they confessed, that they had been transported by supernatural means to a solitary place among woods, where the devil appeared before them in the form of a man, though they saw not his face. He instructed them in the way in which they should do his bidding, and exacted from them acts of homage and obedience. He feasted them, and after, having put out the lights, they proceeded to acts of the grossest licentiousness." These accounts, according to Monstrelet, were dictated to the victims by their tormentors; and they then added, under the same suggestion, the names of divers lords, prelates, and governors of towns and bailliages, whom they affirmed they had seen at these meetings, and who joined in the same unholy ceremonies. The historian adds, that it cannot be concealed that these accusations were brought by certain malicious persons, either to gratify an ancient hatred, or to extort from the rich sums of money, by means of which they might purchase their escape from further prosecution. The persons apprehended were many of them put to the torture so severely, and for so long a time, and were tortured again and again, that they were obliged to confess what was laid to their charge. Some however shewed so great constancy, that they could by no means be induced to depart from the protestation of their innocence. In fine, many of the poorer victims were inhumanly burned; while the richer with great sums of money procured their discharge, but at the same time were compelled to banish themselves to distant places, remote from the scene of this cruel outrage.—Balduinus of Artois gives a similar account, and adds that the sentence of the judges was brought by appeal under the revision of the parliament of Paris, and was reversed by that judicature in the year 1491[d].

I have not succeeded in tracing to my satisfaction from the original authorities the dates of the following examples, and therefore shall refer them to the periods assigned them in Hutchinson on Witchcraft. The facts themselves rest for the most part on the most unquestionable authority.

[d] Delrio, Disquisitiones Magicæ, p. 746.

Innocent VIII published about the year 1484 a bull, in which he affirms: " It has come to our ears, that numbers of both sexes do not avoid to have intercourse with the infernal fiends, and that by their sorceries they afflict both man and beast; they blight the marriage-bed, destroy the births of women, and the increase of cattle; they blast the corn on the ground, the grapes of the vineyard, the fruits of the trees, and the grass and herbs of the field." For these reasons he arms the inquisitors with apostolic power to " imprison, convict and punish" all such as may be charged with these offences.—The consequences of this edict were dreadful all over the continent, particularly in Italy, Germany and France.

Alciatus, an eminent lawyer of this period, relates, that a certain inquisitor came about this time into the vallies of the Alps, being commissioned to enquire out and proceed against heretical women with whom those parts were infested. He accordingly consigned more than one hundred to the flames, every day, like a new holocaust, sacrificing such persons to Vulcan, as, in the judgment of the historian, were subjects demanding rather hellebore than fire; till at length the peasantry of the vicinity rose in arms, and drove the merciless judge out of the country. The culprits were accused of having dishonoured the crucifix, and denying Christ for their God. They were asserted to have solemnised after a detestable way the devil's sabbath, in which the fiend appeared personally among them, and instructed them in the ceremonies of his worship. Meanwhile a question was raised whether they personally assisted on the occasion, or only saw the solemnities in a vision, credible witnesses having sworn that they were at home in their beds, at the very time that they were accused of having taken part in these blasphemies[e].

In 1515, more than five hundred persons are said to have suffered capitally for the crime of witchcraft in the city of Geneva in the course of three months[f].

In 1524, one thousand persons were burned on this accusation in the territory of Como, and one hundred per annum for several year after[g].

Danæus commences his Dialogue of Witches with this observation. "Within three months of the present time (1575) an almost infinite number of witches have been taken, on whom the parliament of Paris has passed judgment: and the same tribunal fails not to sit daily, as malefactors accused of this crime are continually brought before them out of all the provinces."

In the year 1595 Nicholas Remi, otherwise Remigius, printed a very curious work, entitled Demonolatreia, in which he elaborately expounds the principles of the compact into which the devil en-

[e] Alciatus, Parergon Juris, L. VIII, cap. 22.
[f] Danæus, *apud* Delrio, Proloquium.
[g] Bartholomæus de Spina, De Strigibus, c. 13.

ters with his mortal allies, and the modes of conduct specially observed by both parties. He boasts that his exposition is founded on an exact observation of the judicial proceedings which had taken place under his eye in the duchy of Lorraine, where for the preceding fifteen years nine hundred persons, more or less, had suffered the extreme penalty of the law for the crime of sorcery. Most of the persons tried seem to have been sufficiently communicative as to the different kinds of menace and compulsion by which the devil had brought them into his terms, and the various appearances he had exhibited, and feats he had performed: but others, says the author, had, "by preserving an obstinate silence, shewn themselves invincible to every species of torture that could be inflicted on them."

But the most memorable record that remains to us on the subject of witchcraft, is contained in an ample quarto volume, entitled A Representation (*Tableau*) of the Ill Faith of Evil Spirits and Demons, by Pierre De Lancre, Royal Counsellor in the Parliament of Bordeaux. This man was appointed with one coadjutor, to enquire into certain acts of sorcery, reported to have been committed in the district of Labourt, near the foot of the Pyrenees; and his commission bears date in May, 1609, and by consequence twelve months before the death of Henry the Fourth.

The book is dedicated to M. de Silleri, chancellor of France; and in the dedication the author observes, that formerly those who practised sorcery were well known for persons of obscure station and narrow intellect; but that now the sorcerers who confess their misdemeanours, depose, that there are seen in the customary meetings held by such persons a great number of individuals of quality, whom Satan keeps veiled from ordinary gaze, and who are allowed to approach near to him, while those of a poorer and more vulgar class are thrust back to the furthest part of the assembly. The whole narrative assumes the form of a regular warfare between Satan on the one side, and the royal commissioners on the other.

At first the devil endeavoured to supply the accused with strength to support the tortures by which it was sought to extort confession from them, insomuch that, in an intermission of the torture, the wretches declared that, presently falling asleep, they seemed to be in paradise, and to enjoy the most beautiful visions. The commissioners however, observing this, took care to grant them scarcely any remission, till they had drawn from them, if possible, an ample confession. The devil next proceeded to stop the mouths of the accused that they might not confess. He leaped on their throats, and evidently caused an obstruction of the organs of speech, so that in vain they endeavoured to relieve themselves by disclosing all that was demanded of them.

The historian proceeds to say that, at these sacrilegious assemblings, they now began to murmur against the devil, as wanting power to relieve them in their extremity. The children, the daughters, and other relatives of the victims reproached him, not scrupling to say, "Out upon you! you promised that our mothers who were prisoners should not die; and look how you have kept your word with us! They have been burned, and are a heap of ashes." In answer to this charge the devil stoutly affirmed, that their parents, who seemed to have suffered, were not dead, but were safe in a foreign country, assuring the malcontents that, if they called on them, they would receive an answer. The children called accordingly, and by an infernal illusion an answer came, exactly in the several voices of the deceased, declaring that they were in a state of happiness and security.

Further to satisfy the complainers, the devil produced illusory fires, and encouraged the dissatisfied to walk through them, assuring them that the fires lighted by a judicial decree were as harmless and inoffensive as these. The demon further threatened that he would cause the prosecutors to be burned in their own fire, and even proceeded to make them in semblance hover and alight on the branches of the neighbouring trees. He further caused a swarm of toads to appear like a garland to crown the heads of the sufferers, at which when in one instance the bystanders threw stones to drive them away, one monstrous black toad remained to the last uninjured, and finally mounted aloft, and vanished from sight. De Lancre goes on to describe the ceremonies of the sabbath of the devil; and a plate is inserted, presenting the assembly in the midst of their solemnities. He describes in several chapters the sort of contract entered into between the devil and the sorcerers, the marks by which they may be known, the feast with which the demon regaled them, their distorted and monstrous dance, the copulation between the fiend and the witch, and its issue.—It is easy to imagine with what sort of fairness the trials were conducted, when such is the description the judge affords us of what passed at these assemblies. Six hundred were burned under this prosecution.

The last chapter is devoted to an accurate account of what took place at an *auto da fé* in the month of November 1610 at Logrogno on the Ebro in Spain, the victims being for the greater part the unhappy wretches, who had escaped through the Pyrenees from the merciless prosecution that had been exercised against them by the historian of the whole.

SAVONAROLA.

Jerome Savonarola was one of the most remarkable men of his time, and his fortunes are well adapted to illustrate the peculiarities of that period. He was born in the year 1452 at Ferrara in Italy. He became a Dominican Friar at Bologna without the knowledge of his parents in the twenty-second year of his age. He was first employed by his superiors in elucidating the principles of physics and metaphysics. But, after having occupied some years in this way, he professed to take a lasting leave of these subtleties, and to devote himself exclusively to the study of the Scriptures. In no long time he became an eminent preacher, by the elegance and purity of his style acquiring the applause of hearers of taste, and by the unequalled fervour of his eloquence securing the hearts of the many. It was soon obvious, that, by his power gained in this mode, he could do any thing he pleased with the people of Florence among whom he resided. Possessed of such an ascendancy, he was not contented to be the spiritual guide of the souls of men, but further devoted himself to the temporal prosperity and grandeur of his country. The house of Medici was at this time masters of the state, and the celebrated Lorenzo de Medici possessed the administration of affairs. But the political maxims of Lorenzo were in discord with those of our preacher. Lorenzo sought to concentre all authority in the opulent few; but Savonarola, proceeding on the model of the best times of ancient Rome, endeavoured to vest the sovereign power in the hands of the people.

He had settled at Florence in the thirty-fourth year of his age, being invited to become prior of the convent of St. Mark in that city: and such was his popularity, that, four years after, Lorenzo on his death-bed sent for Savonarola to administer to him spiritual consolation. Meanwhile, so stern did this republican shew himself, that he insisted on Lorenzo's renunciation of his absolute power, before he would administer to him the sacrament and absolution: and Lorenzo complied with these terms.

The prince being dead, Savonarola stepped immediately into the highest authority. He reconstituted the state upon pure republican principles, and enjoined four things especially in all his public preachings, the fear of God, the love of the republic, oblivion of all past injuries, and equal rights to all for the future.

But Savonarola was not contented with the delivery of Florence, where he is said to have produced a total revolution of manners, from libertinism to the most exemplary purity and integrity; he likewise aspired to produce an equal effect on the entire of Italy. Alexander VI, the most profligate of popes, then filled the chair at Rome; and Savonarola thundered against him in the cathedral at Florence the most fearful denunciations. The pope did not hesitate a moment to proceed to extremities against the friar. He cited him to Rome, under pain, if disobeyed, of excommunication to the priest, and an interdict to the republic that harboured him. The Florentines several times succeeded in causing the citation to be revoked, and, making terms with the sovereign pontiff, Jerome again and again suspending his preachings, which were however continued by other friars, his colleagues and confederates. Savonarola meanwhile could not long be silent; he resumed his philippics as fiercely as ever.

At this time faction raged strongly at Florence. Jerome had many partisans; all the Dominicans, and the greater part of the populace. But he had various enemies leagued against him; the adherents of the house of Medici, those of the pope, the libertines, and all orders of monks and friars except the Dominicans. The violence proceeded so far, that the preacher was not unfrequently insulted in his pulpit, and the cathedral echoed with the dissentions of the parties. At length a conspiracy was organized against Savonarola; and, his adherents having got the better, the friar did not dare to trust the punishment of his enemies to the general assembly, where the question would have led to a scene of warfare, but referred it to a more limited tribunal, and finally proceeded to the infliction of death on its sole authority.

This extremity rendered his enemies more furious against him. The pope directed absolution, the communion, and the rites of sepulture, to be refused to his followers. He was now expelled from the cathedral at Florence, and removed his preachings to the chapel of his convent, which was enlarged in its accommodations to adapt itself to his numerous auditors. In this interim a most extraordinary scene took place. One Francis de Pouille offered himself to the trial of fire, in favour of the validity of the excommunication of the pope against the pretended inspiration and miracles of the prophet. He said he did not doubt to perish in the experiment, but that he should have the satisfaction of seeing Savonarola perish along with him. Dominic de Pescia however and another Dominican presented themselves to the flames instead of Jerome, alledging that he was reserved for higher things. De Pouille at first declined the substitution, but was afterwards prevailed on to submit. A vast fire was lighted in the market-place for the trial; and a low and narrow gallery of iron passed over the middle, on which the challenger and the challenged were to attempt to effect their passage. But a furious deluge of rain was said to have occurred at the instant every thing was ready; the fire was extinguished; and the trial for the present was thus rendered impossible.

Savonarola in the earnestness of his preachings pretended to turn prophet, and confidently to predict future events. He spoke of Charles VIII of France as the Cyrus who should deliver Italy, and subdue the nations before him; and even named the spring of the year 1498 as the period that should see all these things performed.

But it was not in prophecy alone that Savonarola laid claim to supernatural aid. He described various contests that he had maintained against a multitude of devils at once in his convent. They tormented in different ways the friars of St. Mark, but ever shrank with awe from his personal interposition. They attempted to call upon him by name; but the spirit of God overruled them, so that they could never pronounce his name aright, but still misplaced syllables and letters in a ludicrous fashion. They uttered terrific threatenings against him, but immediately after shrank away with fear, awed by the holy words and warnings which he denounced against them. Savonarola besides undertook to expel them by night, by sprinkling holy water, and the singing of hymns in a solemn chorus. While however he was engaged in these sacred offices, and pacing the cloister of his convent, the devils would arrest his steps, and suddenly render the air before him so thick, that it was impossible for him to advance further. On another occasion one of his colleagues assured Francis Picus of Mirandola, the writer of his Life, that he had himself seen the Holy Ghost in the form of a dove more than once, sitting on Savonarola's shoulder, fluttering his feathers, which were sprinkled with silver and gold, and, putting his beak to his ear, whispering to him his divine suggestions. The prior besides relates in a book of his own composition at great length a dialogue that he held with the devil, appearing like, and having been mistaken by the writer for, a hermit.

The life of Savonarola however came to a speedy and tragical close. The multitude, who are always fickle in their impulses, conceiving an unfavourable impression in consequence of his personally declining the trial by fire, turned against him. The same evening they besieged the convent where he resided, and in which he had taken refuge. The signory, seeing the urgency of the case, sent to the brotherhood, commanding them to surrender the prior, and the two Dominicans who had presented themselves in his stead to the trial by fire. The pope sent two judges to try them on the spot. They were presently put to the torture. Savonarola, who we are told was of a delicate habit of body, speedily confessed and expressed contrition for what he had done. But no sooner was he delivered from the strappado, than he retracted all that he had before confessed. The experiment was repeated several times, and always with the same success.

At length he and the other two were adjudged to perish in the flames. This sentence was no sooner pronounced than Savonarola resumed all the constancy of a martyr. He advanced to the place of execution with a steady pace and a serene countenance, and in the midst of the flames resignedly commended his soul into the hands of his maker. His adherents regarded him as a witness to the truth, and piously collected his relics; but his judges, to counteract this defiance of authority, commanded his remains and his ashes to be cast into the river[a].

TRITHEMIUS.

A name that has in some way become famous in the annals of magic, is that of John Trithemius, abbot of Spanheim, or Sponheim, in the circle of the Upper Rhine. He was born in the year 1462. He early distinguished himself by his devotion to literature; insomuch that, according to the common chronology, he was chosen in the year 1482, being about twenty years of age, abbot of the Benedictine monastery of St. Martin at Spanheim. He has written a great number of works, and has left some memorials of his life. Learning was at a low ebb when he was chosen to this dignity. The library of the convent consisted of little more than forty volumes. But, shortly after, under his superintendence it amounted to many hundreds. He insisted upon his monks diligently employing themselves in the multiplication of manuscripts. The monks, who had hitherto spent their days in luxurious idleness, were greatly dissatisfied with this revolution, and led their abbot a very uneasy life. He was in consequence removed to preside over the abbey of St. Jacques in Wurtzburg in

[a] Biographie Universelle.

1506, where he died in tranquillity and peace in 1516.

Trithemius has been accused of necromancy and a commerce with demons. The principal ground of this accusation lies in a story that has been told of his intercourse with the emperor Maximilian. Maximilian's first wife was Mary of Burgundy, whom he lost in the prime of her life. The emperor was inconsolable upon the occasion; and Trithemius, who was called in as singularly qualified to comfort him, having tried all other expedients in vain, at length told Maximilian that he would undertake to place his late consort before him precisely in the state in which she had lived. After suitable preparations, Mary of Burgundy accordingly appeared. The emperor was struck with astonishment. He found the figure before him in all respects like the consort he had lost. At length he exclaimed, " There is one mark by which I shall infallibly know whether this is the same person. Mary, my wife, had a wart in the nape of her neck, to the existence of which no one was privy but myself." He examined, and found the wart there, in all respects as it had been during her life. The story goes on to say, that Maximilian was so disgusted and shocked with what he saw, that he banished Trithemius his presence for ever.

This tale has been discredited, partly on the score of the period of the death of Mary of Burgundy, which happened in 1481, when Trithemius was only nineteen years of age. He himself expressly disclaims all imputation of sorcery. One ground of the charge has been placed upon the existence of a work of his, entitled Steganographia, or the art, by means of a secret writing, of communicating our thoughts to a person absent. He says however, that in this work he had merely used the language of magic, without in any degree having had recourse to their modes of proceeding. Trithemius appears to have been the first writer who has made mention of the extraordinary feats of John Faust of Wittenburg, and that in a way that shews he considered these enchantments as the work of a supernatural power[h].

LUTHER.

It is particularly proper to introduce some mention of Luther in this place; not that he is in any way implicated in the question of necromancy, but that there are passages in his writings in which he talks of the devil in what we should now think a very extraordinary way. And it is curious, and not a little instructive, to see how a person of so masculine an intellect, and who in many respects so far outran the illumination of his age, was accustomed to judge respecting the intercourse of mortals with the inhabitants of the infernal world. Luther was born in the year 1483.

[h] Biographie Universelle.

It appears from his Treatise on the Abuses attendant on Private Masses, that he had a conference with the devil on the subject. He says, that this supernatural personage caused him by his visits "many bitter nights and much restless and wearisome repose." Once in particular he came to Luther, "in the dead of the night, when he was just awaked out of sleep. The devil," he goes on to say, "knows well how to construct his arguments, and to urge them with the skill of a master. He delivers himself with a grave, and yet a shrill voice. Nor does he use circumlocutions, and beat about the bush, but excels in forcible statements and quick rejoinders. I no longer wonder," he adds, " that the persons whom he assails in this way, are occasionally found dead in their beds. He is able to compress and throttle, and more than once he has so assaulted me and driven my soul into a corner, that I felt as if the next moment it must leave my body. I am of opinion that Gesner and Oecolampadius and others in that manner came by their deaths. The devil's manner of opening a debate is pleasant enough; but he urges things so peremptorily, that the respondent in a short time knows not how to acquit himself^a." He elsewhere says, "The reasons why the sacramentarians understood so little of the Scriptures, is that they do not encounter the true opponent, that is, the devil, who presently drives

_a Hospinian, Historia Sacramentaria, Part II, fol. 131.

one up in a corner, and thus makes one perceive the just interpretation. For my part I am thoroughly acquainted with him, and have eaten a bushel of salt with him. He sleeps with me more frequently, and lies nearer to me in bed, than my own wife does[b]."

CORNELIUS AGRIPPA.

Henry Cornelius Agrippa was born in the year 1486. He was one of the most celebrated men of his time. His talents were remarkably great; and he had a surprising facility in the acquisition of languages. He is spoken of with the highest commendations by Trithemius, Erasmus, Melancthon, and others, the greatest men of his times. But he was a man of the most violent passions, and of great instability of temper. He was of consequence exposed to memorable vicissitudes. He had great reputation as an astrologer, and was assiduous in the cultivation of chemistry. He had the reputation of possessing the philosopher's stone, and was incessantly experiencing the privations of poverty. He was subject to great persecutions, and was repeatedly imprisoned. He received invitations at the same time from Henry VIII, from the chancellor of the emperor, from a distinguished Italian marquis, and from Margaret of Austria, governess of the Low Countries. He

[b] Bayle.

made his election in favour of the last, and could find no way so obvious of showing his gratitude for her patronage, as composing an elaborate treatise on the Superiority of the Female Sex, which he dedicated to her. Shortly after, he produced a work not less remarkable, to demonstrate the Vanity and Emptiness of Scientifical Acquirements. Margaret of Austria being dead, he was subsequently appointed physician to Louisa of Savoy, mother to Francis I. This lady however having assigned him a task disagreeable to his inclination, a calculation according to the rules of astrology, he made no scruple of turning against her, and affirming that he should henceforth hold her for a cruel and perfidious Jezebel. After a life of storms and perpetual vicissitude, he died in 1534, aged 48 years.

He enters however into the work I am writing, principally on account of the extraordinary stories that have been told of him on the subject of magic. He says of himself, in his Treatise on the Vanity of Sciences, "Being then a very young man, I wrote in three books of a considerable size Disquisitions concerning Magic."

The first of the stories I am about to relate is chiefly interesting, inasmuch as it is connected with the history of one of the most illustrious ornaments of our early English poetry, Henry Howard earl of Surrey, who suffered death at the close of the reign of King Henry VIII. The earl of Surrey, we are told, became acquainted with Cornelius

Agrippa at the court of John George elector of Saxony. On this occasion were present, beside the English nobleman, Erasmus, and many other persons eminent in the republic of letters. These persons shewed themselves enamoured of the reports that had been spread of Agrippa, and desired him before the elector to exhibit something memorable. One intreated him to call up Plautus, and shew him as he appeared in garb and countenance, when he ground corn in the mill. Another before all things desired to see Ovid. But Erasmus earnestly requested to behold Tully in the act of delivering his oration for Roscius. This proposal carried the most votes. And, after marshalling the concourse of spectators, Tully appeared, at the command of Agrippa, and from the rostrum pronounced the oration, precisely in the words in which it has been handed down to us, " with such astonishing animation, so fervent an exaltation of spirit, and such soul-stirring gestures, that all the persons present were ready, like the Romans of old, to pronounce his client innocent of every charge that had been brought against him." The story adds, that, when sir Thomas More was at the same place, Agrippa shewed him the whole destruction of Troy in a dream. To Thomas Lord Cromwel he exhibited in a perspective glass King Henry VIII and all his lords hunting in his forest at Windsor. To Charles V he shewed David, Solomon, Gideon, and the rest, with the Nine Worthies, in their habits and similitude as they had lived.

Lord Surrey, in the mean time having gotten into familiarity with Agrippa, requested him by the way side as they travelled, to set before him his mistress, the fair Geraldine, shewing at the same time what she did, and with whom she talked. Agrippa accordingly exhibited his magic glass, in which the noble poet saw this beautiful dame, sick, weeping upon her bed, and inconsolable for the absence of her admirer.—It is now known, that the sole authority for this tale is Thomas Nash, the dramatist, in his Adventures of Jack Wilton, printed in the year 1593.

Paulus Jovius relates that Agrippa always kept a devil attendant upon him, who accompanied him in all his travels in the shape of a black dog. When he lay on his death-bed, he was earnestly exhorted to repent of his sins. Being in consequence struck with a deep contrition, he took hold of the dog, and removed from him a collar studded with nails, which formed a necromantic inscription, at the same time saying to him, " Begone, wretched animal, which hast been the cause of my entire destruction!"—It is added, that the dog immediately ran away, and plunged itself in the river Soane, after which it was seen no more[a]. It is further related of Agrippa, as of many other magicians, that he was in the habit, when he regaled himself

[a] Paulus Jovius, Elogia Doctorum Virorum, c. 101.

at an inn, of paying his bill in counterfeit money, which at the time of payment appeared of sterling value, but in a few days after became pieces of horn and worthless shells[b].

But the most extraordinary story of Agrippa is told by Delrio, and is as follows. Agrippa had occasion one time to be absent for a few days from his residence at Louvain. During his absence he intrusted his wife with the key of his Museum, but with an earnest injunction that no one on any account should be allowed to enter. Agrippa happened at that time to have a boarder in his house, a young fellow of insatiable curiosity, who would never give over importuning his hostess, till at length he obtained from her the forbidden key. The first thing in the Museum that attracted his attention, was a book of spells and incantations. He spread this book upon a desk, and, thinking no harm, began to read aloud. He had not long continued this occupation, when a knock was heard at the door of the chamber. The youth took no notice, but continued reading. Presently followed a second knock, which somewhat alarmed the reader. The space of a minute having elapsed, and no answer made, the door was opened, and a demon entered. "For what purpose am I called?" said the stranger sternly. "What is it you demand to have done?" The youth was seized with the greatest alarm, and struck speechless. The de-

[b] Delrio, Disquisitiones Magicæ, Lib. II, Quæstio xi, § 18.

mon advanced towards him, seized him by the throat, and strangled him, indignant that his presence should thus be invoked from pure thoughtlessness and presumption.

At the expected time Agrippa came home, and to his great surprise found a number of devils capering and playing strange antics about, and on the roof of his house. By his art he caused them to desist from their sport, and with authority demanded what was the cause of this novel appearance. The chief of them answered. He told how they had been invoked, and insulted, and what revenge they had taken. Agrippa became exceedingly alarmed for the consequences to himself of this unfortunate adventure. He ordered the demon without loss of time to reanimate the body of his victim, then to go forth, and to walk the boarder three or four times up and down the market-place in the sight of the people. The infernal spirit did as he was ordered, shewed the student publicly alive, and having done this, suffered the body to fall down, the marks of conscious existence being plainly no more. For a time it was thought that the student had been killed by a sudden attack of disease. But, presently after, the marks of strangulation were plainly discerned, and the truth came out. Agrippa was then obliged suddenly to withdraw himself, and to take up his residence in a distant province[r].

[r] Delrio, Lib. II, Quæstio xxix. § 7.

Wierus in his well known book, *De Præstigiis Demonum*, informs us that he had lived for years in daily attendance on Cornelius Agrippa, and that the black dog respecting which such strange surmises had been circulated, was a perfectly innocent animal that he had often led in a string. He adds, that the sole foundation for the story lay in the fact, that Agrippa had been much attached to the dog, which he was accustomed to permit to eat off the table with its master, and even to lie of nights in his bed. He further remarks, that Agrippa was accustomed often not to go out of his room for a week together, and that people accordingly wondered that he could have such accurate information of what was going on in all parts of the world, and would have it that his intelligence was communicated to him by his dog. He subjoins however, that Agrippa had in fact correspondents in every quarter of the globe, and received letters from them daily, and that this was the real source of his extraordinary intelligence[d].

Naudé, in his Apology for Great Men accused of Magic, mentions, that Agrippa composed a book of the Rules and Precepts of the Art of Magic, and that, if such a work could entitle a man to the character of a magician, Agrippa indeed well deserved it. But he gives it as his opinion that this was the only ground for fastening the imputation on this illustrious character.

[d] Wierus, Lib. II, c. v, § 11, 12.

Without believing however any of the tales of the magic practices of Cornelius Agrippa, and even perhaps without supposing that he seriously pretended to such arts, we are here presented with a striking picture of the temper and credulity of the times in which he lived. We plainly see from the contemporary evidence of Wierus, that such things were believed of him by his neighbours; and at that period it was sufficiently common for any man of deep study, of recluse habits, and a certain sententious and magisterial air to undergo these imputations. It is more than probable that Agrippa was willing by a general silence and mystery to give encouragement to the wonder of the vulgar mind. He was flattered by the terror and awe which his appearance inspired. He did not wish to come down to the ordinary level. And if to this we add his pursuits of alchemy and astrology, with the formidable and various apparatus supposed to be required in these pursuits, we shall no longer wonder at the results which followed. He loved to wander on the brink of danger, and was contented to take his chance of being molested, rather than not possess that ascendancy over the ordinary race of mankind which was evidently gratifying to his vanity.

FAUSTUS.

Next in respect of time to Cornelius Agrippa comes the celebrated Dr. Faustus. Little in point of fact is known respecting this eminent personage in the annals of necromancy. His pretended history does not seem to have been written till about the year 1587, perhaps half a century after his death. This work is apparently in its principal features altogether fictitious. We have no reason however to deny the early statements as to his life. He is asserted by Camerarius and Wierus to have been born at Cundling near Cracow in the kingdom of Poland, and is understood to have passed the principal part of his life at the university of Wittenberg. He was probably well known to Cornelius Agrippa and Paracelsus. Melancthon mentions him in his Letters; and Conrad Gessner refers to him as a contemporary. The author of his Life cites the opinions entertained respecting him by Luther. Philip Camerarius speaks of him in his Horæ Subsecivæ as a celebrated name among magicians, apparently without reference to the Life that has come down to us[a]; and Wierus does the same thing[b]. He was probably nothing more than an accomplished juggler, who appears to have practised his art with great success in several towns of Germany. He was also no doubt a pretender to necromancy.

[a] Cent. 1, cap. 70.
[b] De Præstigiis Demonum, Lib. II, cap. iv, sect. 8.

On this basis the well known History of his Life has been built. The author has with great art expanded very slender materials, and rendered his work in a striking degree a code and receptacle of all the most approved ideas respecting necromancy and a profane and sacrilegious dealing with the devil. He has woven into it with much skill the pretended arts of the sorcerers, and has transcribed or closely imitated the stories that have been handed down to us of many of the extraordinary feats they were said to have performed. It is therefore suitable to our purpose to dwell at some length upon the successive features of this history.

The life has been said to have been originally written in Spain by Franciscus Schottus of Toledo, in the Latin language[c]. But this biographical work is assigned to the date of 1594, previously to which the Life is known to have existed in German. It is improbable that a Spanish writer should have chosen a German for the hero of his romance, whereas nothing can be more natural than for a German to have conceived the idea of giving fame and notoriety to his countryman. The mistake seems to be the same, though for an opposite reason, as that which appears to have been made in representing the Gil Blas of Le Sage as a translation.

The biographical account professes to have been begun by Faustus himself, though written in the

[c] Durrius, *apud* Schelhorn, Amoenitates Literariæ, Tom. V, p. 50, *et seqq.*

third person, and to have been continued by Wagner, his confidential servant, to whom the doctor is affirmed to have bequeathed his memoirs, letters and manuscripts, together with his house and its furniture.

Faustus then, according to his history, was the son of a peasant, residing on the banks of the Roda in the duchy of Weimar, and was early adopted by an uncle, dwelling in the city of Wittenberg, who had no children. Here he was sent to college, and was soon distinguished by the greatness of his talents, and the rapid progress he made in every species of learning that was put before him. He was destined by his relative to the profession of theology. But singularly enough, considering that he is represented as furnishing materials for his own Memoirs, he is said ungraciously to have set at nought his uncle's pious intentions by deriding God's word, and thus to have resembled Cain, Reuben and Absalom, who, having sprung from godly parents, afflicted their fathers' hearts by their apostasy. He went through his examinations with applause, and carried off all the first prizes among sixteen competitors. He therefore obtained the degree of doctor in divinity; but his success only made him the more proud and headstrong. He disdained his theological eminence, and sighed for distinction as a man of the world. He took his degree as a doctor of medicine, and aspired to celebrity as a practitioner of physic. About the same time he fell in with certain contemporaries, of tastes similar to his own, and associated with them in the study of Chaldean, Greek and Arabic science, of strange incantations and supernatural influences, in short, of all the arts of a sorcerer.

Having made such progress as he could by dint of study and intense application, he at length resolved to prosecute his purposes still further by actually raising the devil. He happened one evening to walk in a thick, dark wood, within a short distance from Wittenberg, when it occurred to him that that was a fit place for executing his design. He stopped at a solitary spot where four roads met, and made use of his wand to mark out a large circle, and then two small ones within the larger. In one of these he fixed himself, appropriating the other for the use of his expected visitor. He went over the precise range of charms and incantations, omitting nothing. It was now dark night between the ninth and tenth hour. The devil manifested himself by the usual signs of his appearance. " Wherefore am I called?" said he, "and what is it that you demand?" " I require," rejoined Faustus, "that you should sedulously attend upon me, answer my enquiries, and fulfil my behests."

Immediately upon Faustus pronouncing these words, there followed a tumult over head, as if heaven and earth were coming together. The trees in their topmost branches bended to their very roots. It seemed as if the whole forest were peopled with devils, making a crash like a thousand waggons, hurrying to the right and the left, before and behind, in every possible direction, with thunder and lightning, and the continual discharge of great cannon. Hell appeared to have emptied itself, to have furnished the din. There succeeded the most charming music from all sorts of instruments, and sounds of hilarity and dancing. Next came a report as of a tournament, and the clashing of innumerable lances. This lasted so long, that Faustus was many times about to rush out of the circle in which he had inclosed himself, and to abandon his preparations. His courage and resolution however got the better; and he remained immoveable. He pursued his incantations without intermission. Then came to the very edge of the circle a griffin first, and next a dragon, which in the midst of his enchantments grinned at him horribly with his teeth, but finally fell down at his feet, and extended his length to many a rood. Faustus persisted. Then succeeded a sort of fireworks, a pillar of fire, and a man on fire at the top, who leaped down; and there immediately appeared a number of globes here and there redhot, while the man on fire went and came to every part of the circle for a quarter of an hour. At length the devil came forward in the shape of a grey monk, and asked Faustus what he wanted. Faustus adjourned their further conference, and appointed the devil to come to him at his lodgings.

He in the mean time busied himself in the necessary preparations. He entered his study at the appointed time, and found the devil waiting for him. Faustus told him that he had prepared certain articles, to which it was necessary that the demon should fully accord,—that he should attend him at all times, when required, for all the days of his life, that he should bring him every thing he wanted, that he should come to him in any shape that Faustus required, or be invisible, and Faustus should be invisible too, whenever he desired it, that he should deny him nothing, and answer him with perfect veracity to every thing he demanded. To some of these requisitions the spirit could not consent, without authority from his master, the chief of devils. At length all these concessions were adjusted. The devil on his part also prescribed his conditions. That Faustus should abjure the Christian religion and all reverence for the supreme God; that he should enjoy the entire command of his attendant demon for a certain term of years, and that at the end of that period the devil should dispose of him body and soul at his pleasure [the term was fixed for twenty-four years]; that he should at all times stedfastly refuse to listen to any one who should desire to convert him, or convince him of the error of his ways, and lead him to repentance; that Faustus should draw up a writing containing these particulars, and sign it with his blood, that he should deliver this writing to the devil, and keep a duplicate of it for himself, that so there might be no misunderstanding. It was further appointed by Faustus that the devil should usually attend him in the habit of cordelier, with a pleasing countenance and an insinuating demeanour. Faustus also asked the devil his name, who answered that he was usually called Mephostophiles (perhaps more accurately Nephostophiles, a lover of clouds).

Previously to this deplorable transaction, in which Faustus sold himself, soul and body, to the devil, he had consumed his inheritance, and was reduced to great poverty. But he was now no longer subjected to any straits. The establishments of the prince of Chutz, the duke of Bavaria, and the archbishop of Saltzburgh were daily put under contribution for his more convenient supply. By the diligence of Mephostophiles provisions of all kinds continually flew in at his windows; and the choicest wines were perpetually found at his board to the annoyance and discredit of the cellarers and butlers of these eminent personages, who were extremely blamed for defalcations in which they had no share. He also brought him a monthly supply of money, sufficient for the support of his establishment. Besides, he supplied him with a succession of mistresses, such as his heart desired, which were in truth nothing but devils disguised under the semblance of beautiful women. He further gave to Faustus a book, in which were amply detailed the processes of sorcery and witchcraft, by means of which the doctor could obtain whatever he desired.

One of the earliest indulgences which Faustus proposed to himself from the command he possessed over his servant-demon, was the gratification of his curiosity in surveying the various nations of the world. Accordingly Mephostophiles converted himself into a horse, with two hunches on his back like a dromedary, between which he conveyed Faustus through the air whereever he desired. They consumed fifteen months in their travels. Among the countries they visited the history mentions Pannonia, Austria, Germany, Bohemia, Silesia, Saxony, Misnia, Thuringia, Franconia, Suabia, Bavaria, Lithuania, Livonia, Prussia, Muscovy, Friseland, Holland, Westphalia, Zealand, Brabant, Flanders, France, Spain, Italy, Poland, and Hungary; and afterwards Turkey, Egypt, England, Sweden, Denmark, India, Africa and Persia. In most of these countries Mephostophiles points out to his fellow-traveller their principal curiosities and antiquities. In Rome they sojourned three days and three nights, and, being themselves invisible, visited the residence of the pope and the other principal palaces.

At Constantinople Faustus visited the emperor of the Turks, assuming to himself the figure of the prophet Mahomet. His approach was preceded by a splendid illumination, not less than that of the sun in all his glory. He said to the emperor, " Happy art thou, oh sultan, who art found worthy to be visited by the great prophet." And the emperor in return fell prostrate before him, thanking Mahomet for his condescension in this visit. The doctor also entered the seraglio, where he remained six days under the same figure, the building and its gardens being all the time environed with a thick darkness, so that no one, not the emperor himself, dared to enter. At the end of this time the doctor, still under the figure of Mahomet, was publicly seen, ascending, as it seemed, to heaven. The sultan afterwards enquired of the women of his seraglio what had occurred to them during the period of the darkness; and they answered, that the God Mahomet had been with them, that he had enjoyed them corporeally, and had told them that from his seed should arise a great people, capable of irresistible exploits.

Faustus had conceived a plan of making his way into the terrestrial paradise, without awakening suspicion in his demon-conductor. For this purpose he ordered him to ascend the highest mountains of Asia. At length they came so near, that they saw the angel with the flaming sword forbidding approach to the garden. Faustus, perceiving this, asked Mephostophiles what it meant.

His conductor told him, but added that it was in vain for them, or any one but the angels of the Lord, to think of entering within.

Having gratified his curiosity in other ways, Faustus was seized with a vehement desire to visit the infernal regions. He proposed the question to Mephostophiles, who told him that this was a matter out of his department, and that on that journey he could have no other conductor than Beelzebub. Accordingly, every thing being previously arranged, one day at midnight Beelzebub appeared, being already equipped with a saddle made of dead men's bones. Faustus speedily mounted. They in a short time came to an abyss, and encountered a multitude of enormous serpents; but a bear with wings came to their aid, and drove the serpents away. A flying bull next came with a hideous roar, so fierce that Beelzebub appeared to give way, and Faustus tumbled at once heels-over-head into the pit. After having fallen to a considerable depth, two dragons with a chariot came to his aid, and an ape helped him to get into the vehicle. Presently however came on a storm with thunder and lightning, so dreadful that the doctor was thrown out, and sunk in a tempestuous sea to a vast depth. He contrived however to lay hold of a rock, and here to secure himself a footing. He looked down, and perceived a great gulph, in which lay floating many of the vulgar, and not a few emperors, kings, princes, and such as had been mighty lords. Faustus with a sudden impulse cast himself into the midst of the flames with which they were surrounded, with the desire to snatch one of the damned souls from the pit. But, just as he thought he had caught him by the hand, the miserable wretch slided from between his fingers, and sank again.

At length the doctor became wholly exhausted with the fatigue he had undergone, with the smoke and the fog, with the stifling, sulphureous air, with the tempestuous blasts, with the alternate extremes of heat and cold, and with the clamours, the lamentations, the agonies, and the howlings of the damned every where around him,—when, just in the nick of time, Beelzebub appeared to him again, and invited him once more to ascend the saddle, which he had occupied during his infernal journey. Here he fell asleep, and, when he awoke, found himself in his own bed in his house. He then set himself seriously to reflect on what had passed. At one time he believed that he had been really in hell, and had witnessed all its secrets. At another he became persuaded that he had been subject to an illusion only, and that the devil had led him through an imaginary scene, which was truly the case; for the devil had taken care not to shew him the real hell, fearing that it might have caused too great a terror, and have induced him to repent him of his misdeeds perhaps before it was too late.

It so happened that, once upon a time, the emperor Charles V was at Inspruck, at a time when Faustus also resided there. His courtiers informed the emperor that Faustus was in the town, and Charles expressed a desire to see him. He was introduced. Charles asked him whether he could really perform such wondrous feats as were reported of him. Faustus modestly replied, inviting the emperor to make trial of his skill. "Then," said Charles, "of all the eminent personages I have ever read of, Alexander the Great is the man who most excites my curiosity, and whom it would most gratify my wishes to see in the very form in which he lived." Faustus rejoined, that it was out of his power truly to raise the dead, but that he had spirits at his command who had often seen that great conqueror, and that Faustus would willingly place him before the emperor as he required. He conditioned that Charles should not speak to him, nor attempt to touch him. The emperor promised compliance. After a few ceremonies therefore, Faustus opened a door, and brought in Alexander exactly in the form in which he had lived, with the same garments, and every circumstance corresponding. Alexander made his obeisance to the emperor, and walked several times round him. The queen of Alexander was then introduced in the same manner. Charles just then recollected, he had read that Alexander had a wart on the nape of his neck; and with proper precautions Faustus allowed the emperor to examine the apparition by this test. Alexander then vanished.

As doctor Faustus waited in court, he perceived a certain knight, who had fallen asleep in a bow-window, with his head out at window. The whim took the doctor, to fasten on his brow the antlers of a stag. Presently the knight was roused from his nap, when with all his efforts he could not draw in his head on account of the antlers which grew upon it. The courtiers laughed exceedingly at the distress of the knight, and, when they had sufficiently diverted themselves, Faustus took off his conjuration, and set the knight at liberty.

Soon after Faustus retired from Inspruck. Meanwhile the knight, having conceived a high resentment against the conjuror, waylaid him with seven horsemen on the road by which he had to pass. Faustus however perceived them, and immediately made himself invisible. Meanwhile the knight spied on every side to discover the conjuror; but, as he was thus employed, he heard a sudden noise of drums and trumpets and cymbals, and saw a regiment of horse advancing against him. He immediately turned off in another direction; but was encountered by a second regiment of horse. This occurred no less than six times; and the knight and his companions were compelled to surrender at discretion. These regiments were so many devils; and Faustus now appeared in a new form as the general of this army. He obliged the knight and his party to dismount, and give up their swords. Then with a seeming generosity he gave them new horses and new swords. But this was all enchantment. The swords presently turned into switches; and the horses, plunging into a river on their road, vanished from beneath their riders, who were thoroughly drenched in the stream, and scarcely escaped with their lives.

Many of Faustus's delusions are rather remarkable as tricks of merry vexation, than as partaking of those serious injuries which we might look for in an implement of hell. In one instance he inquired of a countryman who was driving a load of hay, what compensation he would judge reasonable for the doctor's eating as much of his hay as he should be inclined to. The waggoner replied, that for half a stiver (one farthing) he should be welcome to eat as much as he pleased. The doctor presently fell to, and ate at such a rate, that the peasant was frightened lest his whole load should be consumed. He therefore offered Faustus a gold coin, value twenty-seven shillings, to be off his bargain. The doctor took it; and, when the countryman came to his journey's end, he found his cargo undiminished even by a single blade.

Another time, as Faustus was walking along the road near Brunswick, the whim took him of asking a waggoner who was driving by, to treat him with a ride in his vehicle. "No, I will not," replied the boor; "my horses will have enough to do to drag their proper load." "You churl," said the doctor, "since you will not let your wheels carry me, you shall carry them yourself as far as from the gates of the city." The wheels then detached themselves, and flew through the air, to the gates of the town from which they came. At the same time the horses fell to the ground, and were utterly unable to raise themselves up. The countryman, frightened, fell on his knees to the doctor, and promised, if he would forgive him, never to offend in like manner again. Faustus now, relenting a little, bade the waggoner take a handful of sand from the road, and scatter on his horses, and they would be well. At the same time he directed the man to go to the four gates of Brunswick, and he would find his wheels, one at each gate.

In another instance, Faustus went into a fair, mounted on a noble beast, richly caparisoned, the sight of which presently brought all the horse-fanciers about him. After considerable haggling, he at last disposed of his horse to a dealer for a handsome price, only cautioning him at parting, how he rode the horse to water. The dealer, despising the caution that had been given him, turned his horse the first thing towards the river. He had however no sooner plunged in, than the horse vanished, and the rider found himself seated on a saddle of straw, in the middle of the stream. With difficulty he waded to the shore, and immediately, enquiring out the doctor's inn, went to him to complain of the cheat. He was directed to Faustus's room, and entering found the conjuror on his bed, apparently asleep. He called to him lustily, but the doctor took no notice. Worked up beyond his patience, he next laid hold of Faustus's foot, that he might rouse him the more effectually. What was his surprise, to find the doctor's leg and foot come off in his hand! Faustus screamed, apparently in agony of pain, and the dealer ran out of the room as fast as he could, thinking that he had the devil behind him.

In one instance three young noblemen applied to Faustus, having been very desirous to be present at the marriage of the son of the duke of Bavaria at Mentz, but having overstaid the time, in which it would have been possible by human means to accomplish the journey, Faustus, to oblige them, led them into his garden, and, spreading a large mantle upon a grass-plot, desired them to step on it, and placed himself in the midst. He then recited a certain form of conjuration. At the same time he conditioned with them, that they should on no account speak to any one at the marriage, and, if spoken to, should not answer again. They were carried invisibly through the air, and arrived in excellent time. At a certain moment they became visible, but were still bound to silence. One of them however broke the injunction, and amused himself with the courtiers. The consequence was that, when the other two were summoned by the doctor to return, he was left behind. There was something so extraordinary in their sudden appearance, and the subsequent disappearance of the others, that he who remained was put in prison, and threatened with the torture the next day, if he would not make a full disclosure. Faustus however returned before break of day, opened the gates of the prison, laid all the guards asleep, and carried off the delinquent in triumph.

On one occasion Faustus, having resolved to pass a jovial evening, took some of his old college-companions, and invited them to make free with the archbishop of Saltzburgh's cellar. They took a ladder, and scaled the wall. They seated themselves round, and placed a three-legged stool, with bottles and glasses in the middle. They were in the heart of their mirth, when the butler made his appearance, and began to cry thieves with all his might. The doctor at once conjured him, so that he could neither speak nor move. There he was obliged to sit, while Faustus and his companions tapped every vat in the cellar. They then carried him along with them in triumph. At length they came to a lofty tree, where Faustus ordered them to stop; and the butler was in the greatest fright, apprehending that they would do no less than hang him. The doctor however was contented, by his art to place him on the topmost branch, where he was obliged to remain trembling and almost dead with the cold, till certain peasants came out to their work, whom he hailed, and finally with great difficulty they rescued him from his painful eminence, and placed him safely on the ground.

On another occasion Faustus entertained several of the junior members of the university of Wittenberg at his chambers. One of them, referring to the exhibition the doctor had made of Alexander the Great to the emperor Charles V, said it would gratify him above all things, if he could once behold the famous Helen of Greece, whose beauty was so great as to have roused all the princes of her country to arms, and to have occasioned a ten years' war. Faustus consented to indulge his curiosity, provided all the company would engage to be merely mute spectators of the scene. This being promised, he left the room, and presently brought in Helen. She was precisely as Homer has described her, when she stood by the side of Priam on the walls of Troy, looking on the Grecian chiefs. Her features were irresistibly attractive; and her full, moist lips were redder than the summer cherries. Faustus shortly after obliged his guests with her bust in marble, from which several copies were taken, no one knowing the name of the original artist.

No long time elapsed after this, when the doctor was engaged in delivering a course of lectures on

Homer at Erfurth, one of the principal cities of Germany. It having been suggested to him that it would very much enhance the interest of his lectures, if he would exhibit to the company the heroes of Greece exactly as they appeared to their contemporaries, Faustus obligingly yielded to the proposal. The heroes of the Trojan war walked in procession before the astonished auditors, no less lively in the representation than Helen had been shewn before, and each of them with some characteristic attitude and striking expression of countenance.

When the doctor happened to be at Frankfort, there came there four conjurors, who obtained vast applause by the trick of cutting off one another's heads, and fastening them on again. Faustus was exasperated at this proceeding, and regarded them as laying claim to a skill superior to his own. He went, and was invisibly present at their exhibition. They placed beside them a vessel with liquor which they pretended was the elixir of life, into which at each time they threw a plant resembling the lily, which no sooner touched the liquor than its buds began to unfold, and shortly it appeared in full blossom. The chief conjuror watched his opportunity; and, when the charm was complete, made no more ado but struck off the head of his fellow that was next to him, and dipping it in the liquor, adjusted it to the shoulders, where it became as securely fixed as before the operation. This was repeated a second and a third time. At length it came to the turn of the chief conjuror to have his head smitten off. Faustus stood by invisibly, and at the proper time broke off the flower of the lily without any one being aware of it. The head therefore of the principal conjuror was struck off; but in vain was it steeped in the liquor. The other conjurors were at a loss to account for the disappearance of the lily, and fumbled for a long time with the old sorcerer's head, which would not stick on in any position in which it could be placed.

Faustus was in great favour with the Prince of Anhalt. On one occasion, after residing some days in his court, he said to the prince, "Will your highness do me the favour to partake of a small collation at a castle which belongs to me out at your city-gates?" The prince graciously consented. The prince and princess accompanied the doctor, and found a castle which Faustus had erected by magic during the preceding night. The castle, with five lofty towers, and two great gates, inclosing a spacious court, stood in the midst of a beautiful lake, stocked with all kinds of fish, and every variety of water-fowl. The court exhibited all sorts of animals, beside birds of every colour and song, which flitted from tree to tree. The doctor then ushered his guests into the hall, with an ample suite of apartments, branching off on each side. In one of the largest they found a banquet prepared, with the pope's plate of gold, which Mephostophiles had borrowed for the day. The viands were of the most delicious nature, with the choicest wines in the world. The banquet being over, Faustus conducted the prince and princess back to the palace. But, before they had gone far, happening to turn their heads, they saw the whole castle blown up, and all that had been prepared for the occasion vanish at once in a vast volume of fire.

One Christmas-time Faustus gave a grand entertainment to certain distinguished persons of both sexes at Wittenberg. To render the scene more splendid, he contrived to exhibit a memorable inversion of the seasons. As the company approached the doctor's house, they were surprised to find, though there was a heavy snow through the neighbouring fields, that Faustus's court and garden bore not the least marks of the season, but on the contrary were green and blooming as in the height of summer. There was an appearance of the freshest vegetation, together with a beautiful vineyard, abounding with grapes, figs, raspberries, and an exuberance of the finest fruits. The large, red Provence roses, were as sweet to the scent as the eye, and looked perfectly fresh and sparkling with dew.

As Faustus was now approaching the last year of his term, he seemed to resolve to pamper his appetite with every species of luxury. He carefully accumulated all the materials of voluptuousness and magnificence. He was particularly anxious in the selection of women who should serve for his pleasures. He had one Englishwoman, one Hungarian, one French, two of Germany, and two from different parts of Italy, all of them eminent for the perfections which characterised their different countries.

As Faustus's demeanour was particularly engaging, there were many respectable persons in the city in which he lived, that became interested in his welfare. These applied to a certain monk of exemplary purity of life and devotion, and urged him to do every thing he could to rescue the doctor from impending destruction. The monk began with him with tender and pathetic remonstrances. He then drew a fearful picture of the wrath of God, and the eternal damnation which would certainly ensue. He reminded the doctor of his extraordinary gifts and graces, and told him how different an issue might reasonably have been expected from him. Faustus listened attentively to all the good monk said, but replied mournfully that it was too late, that he had despised and insulted the Lord, that he had deliberately sealed a solemn compact to the devil, and that there was no possibility of going back. The monk answered, "You are mistaken. Cry to the Lord for grace; and it shall still be given. Shew true remorse; confess your sins; abstain for the future from all acts of sorcery and diabolical interference; and you may rely on final salvation." The doctor however felt that all endeavours would be hopeless. He found in himself an incapacity for true repentance. And finally the devil came to him, reproached him for breach of contract in listening to the pious expostulations of a saint, threatened that in case of infidelity he would take him away to hell even before his time, and frightened the doctor into the act of signing a fresh contract in ratification of that which he had signed before.

At length Faustus ultimately arrived at the end of the term for which he had contracted with the devil. For two or three years before it expired, his character gradually altered. He became subject to fits of despondency, was no longer susceptible of mirth and amusement, and reflected with bitter agony on the close in which the whole must terminate. During the last month of his period, he no longer sought the services of his infernal ally, but with the utmost unwillingness saw his arrival. But Mephostophiles now attended him unbidden, and treated him with biting scoffs and reproaches. "You have well studied the Scriptures," he said, "and ought to have known that your safety lay in worshipping God alone. You sinned with your eyes open, and can by no means plead ignorance. You thought that twenty-four years was a term that would have no end; and you now see how rapidly it is flitting away. The term for which you sold yourself to the devil is a very different thing; and, after the lapse of thousands of ages, the prospect before you will be still as unbounded as ever. You were warned; you were earnestly pressed to repent; but now it is too late."

After the demon, Mephostophiles, had long tormented Faustus in this manner, he suddenly disappeared, consigning him over to wretchedness, vexation and despair.

The whole twenty-four years were now expired. The day before, Mephostophiles again made his appearance, holding in his hand the bond which the doctor had signed with his blood, giving him notice that the next day, the devil, his master, would come for him, and advising him to hold himself in readiness. Faustus, it seems, had earned himself much good will among the younger members of the university by his agreeable manners, by his willingness to oblige them, and by the extraordinary spectacles with which he occasionally diverted them. This day he resolved to pass in a friendly farewel. He invited a number of them to meet him at a house of public reception, in a hamlet adjoining to the city. He bespoke a large room in the house for a banqueting room, another apartment overhead for his guests to sleep in, and a smaller chamber at a little distance for himself. He furnished his table with abundance of delicacies and wines. He endeavoured to appear among them in high spirits; but his heart was inwardly sad.

When the entertainment was over, Faustus addressed them, telling them that this was the last day of his life, reminding them of the wonders with which he had frequently astonished them, and informing them of the condition upon which he had held this power. They, one and all, expressed the deepest sorrow at the intelligence. They had had the idea of something unlawful in his proceedings; but their notions had been very far from coming up to the truth. They regretted exceedingly that he had not been unreserved in his communications at an earlier period. They would have had recourse in his behalf to the means of religion, and have applied to pious men, desiring them to employ their power to intercede with heaven in his favour. Prayer and penitence might have done much for him; and the mercy of heaven was unbounded. They advised him still to call upon God, and endeavour to secure an interest in the merits of the Saviour.

Faustus assured them that it was all in vain, and that his tragical fate was inevitable. He led them to their sleeping apartment, and recommended to them to pass the night as they could, but by no means, whatever they might happen to hear, to come out of it; as their interference could in no way be beneficial to him, and might be attended with the most serious injury to themselves.

They lay still therefore, as he had enjoined them; but not one of them could close his eyes.

Between twelve and one in the night they heard first a furious storm of wind round all sides of the house, as if it would have torn away the walls from their foundations. This no sooner somewhat abated, than a noise was heard of discordant and violent hissing, as if the house was full of all sorts of venomous reptiles, but which plainly proceeded from Faustus's chamber. Next they heard the doctor's room-door vehemently burst open, and cries for help uttered with dreadful agony, but a half-suppressed voice, which presently grew fainter and fainter. Then every thing became still, as if the everlasting motion of the world was suspended.

When at length it became broad day, the students went in a body into the doctor's apartment. But he was no where to be seen. Only the walls were found smeared with his blood, and marks as if his brains had been dashed out. His body was finally discovered at some distance from the house, his limbs dismembered, and marks of great violence about the features of his face. The students gathered up the mutilated parts of his body, and afforded them private burial at the temple of Mars in the village where he died.

A ludicrous confusion of ideas has been produced by some persons from the similarity of names of Faustus, the supposed magician of Wittenberg, and Faust or Fust of Mentz, the inventor, or first establisher of the art of printing. It has been alleged that the exact resemblance of the copies of books published by the latter, when no other mode of multiplying copies was known but by the act of transcribing, was found to be such, as could no way be accounted for by natural means, and that therefore it was imputed to the person who presented these copies, that he must necessarily be assisted by the devil. It has further been stated, that Faust, the printer, swore the craftsmen he employed at his press to inviolable secrecy, that he might the more securely keep up the price of his books. But this notion of the identity of the two persons is entirely groundless. Faustus, the magician, is described in the romance as having been born in 1491, twenty-five years after the period at which the printer is understood to have died, and there is no one coincidence between the histories of the two persons, beyond the similarity of names, and a certain mystery (or magical appearance) that inevitably adheres to the practice of an art hitherto unknown. If any secret reference had been intended in the romance to the real character of the illustrious introducer of an art which has been productive of such incalculable benefits to mankind, it would be impossible to account for such a marvellous inconsistence in the chronology.

Others have carried their scepticism so far, as to have started a doubt whether there was ever really such a person as Faustus of Wittenberg, the alleged magician. But the testimony of Wierus, Philip Camerarius, Melancthon and others, his contemporaries, sufficiently refutes this supposition. The fact is, that there was undoubtedly such a man, who, by sleights of dexterity, made himself a reputation as if there was something supernatural in his performances, and that he was probably also regarded with a degree of terror and abhorrence by the superstitious. On this theme was constructed a romance, which once possessed the highest popularity, and furnished a subject to the dramatical genius of Marlow, Lessing, Goethe, and others.—It is sufficiently remarkable, that the notoriety of this romance seems to have suggested to Shakespear the idea of sending the grand conception of his brain, Hamlet, prince of Denmark, to finish his education at the university of Wittenberg.

And here it may not be uninstructive to remark the different tone of the record of the acts of Ziito, the Bohemian, and Faustus of Wittenburg, though little more than half a century elapsed between the periods at which they were written. Dubravius, bishop of Olmutz in Moravia, to whose pen we are indebted for what we know of Ziito, died in the year 1553. He has deemed it not unbecoming to record in his national history of Bohemia, the achievements of this magician, who, he says, exhibited them before Wenceslaus, king of the country, at the celebration of his marriage. A waggon-load of sorcerers arrived at Prague on that occasion for the entertainment of the company. But, at the close of that century, the exploits of Faustus were no longer deemed entitled to a place in national history, but were more appropriately taken for the theme of a romance. Faustus and his performances were certainly contemplated with at least as much horror as the deeds of Ziito. But popular credulity was no longer wound to so high a pitch: the marvels effected by Faustus are not represented as challenging the observation of thousands at a public court, and on the occasion of a royal festival. They "hid their diminished heads," and were performed comparatively in a corner.

SABELLICUS.

A pretended magician is recorded by Naudé, as living about this time, named Georgius Sabellicus, who, he says, if loftiness and arrogance of assumption were enough to establish a claim to the possession of supernatural gifts, would beyond all controversy be recognised for a chief and consummate sorcerer. It was his ambition by the most sounding appellations of this nature to advance his claim to immortal reputation. He called himself, " The most accomplished Georgius Sabellicus, a second Faustus, the spring and centre of necromantic art, an astrologer, a magician, consummate in chiromancy, and in agromancy, pyromancy and hydromancy inferior to none that ever lived." I mention this the rather, as affording an additional proof how highly Faustus was rated at the time in which he is said to have flourished.

It is specially worthy of notice, that Naudé, whose book is a sort of register of all the most distinguished names in the annals of necromancy, drawn up for the purpose of vindicating their honour, now here mentions Faustus, except once in this slight and cursory way.

PARACELSUS.

Paracelsus, or, as he styled himself, Philippus Aureolus Theophrastus Bombastus Paracelsus de Hohenheim, was a man of great notoriety and eminence, about the same time as Dr. Faustus. He was born in the year 1493, and died in 1541. His father is said to have lived in some repute; but the son early became a wanderer in the world, passing his youth in the occupation of foretelling future events by the stars and by chiromancy, invoking the dead, and performing various operations of alchemy and magic. He states Trithemius to have been his instructor in the science of metals. He was superficial in literature, and says of himself that at one time he did not open a book for ten years together. He visited the mines of Bohemia, Sweden and the East to perfect himself in metallic knowledge. He travelled through Prussia,

Lithuania, Poland, Transylvania and Illyria, conversing indifferently with physicians and old women, that he might extract from them the practical secrets of their art. He visited Egypt, Tartary and Constantinople, at which last place, as he says, he learned the transmutation of metals and the philosopher's stone. He boasts also of the elixir of life, by means of which he could prolong the life of man to the age of the antediluvians. He certainly possessed considerable sagacity and a happy spirit of daring, which induced him to have recourse to the application of mercury and opium in the cure of diseases, when the regular physicians did not venture on the use of them. He therefore was successfully employed by certain eminent persons in desperate cases, and was consulted by Erasmus. He gradually increased in fame, and in the year 1526 was chosen professor of natural philosophy and surgery in the university of Bale. Here he delivered lectures in a very bold and presumptuous style. He proclaimed himself the monarch of medicine, and publicly burned the writings of Galen and Avicenna as pretenders and impostors.

This however was the acme of his prosperity. His system was extremely popular for one year; but then he lost himself by brutality and intemperance. He had drunk water only for the first five-and-twenty years of his life; but now indulged himself in beastly crapulence with the dregs of society, and scarcely ever took off his clothes by day or night. After one year therefore spent at Bale, he resumed his former vagabond life, and, having passed through many vicissitudes, some of them of the most abject poverty, he died at the age of forty-eight.

Paracelsus in fact exhibited in his person the union of a quack, a boastful and impudent pretender, with a considerable degree of natural sagacity and shrewdness. Such an union is not uncommon in the present day; but it was more properly in its place, when the cultivation of the faculties of the mind was more restricted than now, and the law of criticism of facts and evidence was nearly unknown. He took advantage of the credulity and love of wonder incident to the generality of our species; and, by dint of imposing on others, succeeded in no small degree in imposing on himself. His intemperance and arrogance of demeanour gave the suitable finish to his character. He therefore carefully cherished in those about him the idea that there was in him a kind of supernatural virtue, and that he had the agents of an invisible world at his command. In particular he gave out that he held conferences with a familiar or demon, whom for the convenience of consulting he was in the habit of carrying about with him in the hilt of his sword.

CARDAN.

Jerome Cardan, who was only a few years younger than Paracelsus, was a man of a very different character. He had considerable refinement and discrimination, and ranked among the first scholars of his day. He is however most of all distinguished for the Memoirs he has left us of his life, which are characterised by a frankness and unreserve which are almost without a parallel. He had undoubtedly a considerable spice of madness in his composition. He says of himself, that he was liable to extraordinary fits of abstraction and elevation of mind, which by their intenseness became so intolerable, that he gladly had recourse to very severe bodily pain by way of getting rid of them. That in such cases he would bite his lips till they bled, twist his fingers almost to dislocation, and whip his legs with rods, which he found a great relief to him. That he would talk purposely of subjects which he knew were particularly offensive to the company he was in; that he argued on any side of a subject, without caring whether he was right or wrong; and that he would spend whole nights in gaming, often venturing as the stake he played for, the furniture of his house, and his wife's jewels.

Cardan describes three things of himself, which he habitually experienced, but respecting which he had never unbosomed himself to any of his friends. The first was, a capacity which he felt in himself of abandoning his body in a sort of extacy whenever he pleased. He felt in these cases a sort of splitting of the heart, as if his soul was about to withdraw, the sensation spreading over his whole frame, like the opening of a door for the dismissal of its guest. His apprehension was, that he was out of his body, and that by an energetic exertion he still retained a small hold of his corporeal figure. The second of his peculiarities was, that he saw, when he pleased, whatever he desired to see, not through the force of imagination, but with his material organs: he saw groves, animals, orbs, as he willed. When he was a child, he saw these things, as they occurred, without any previous volition or anticipation that such a thing was about to happen. But, after he had arrived at years of maturity, he saw them only when he desired, and such things as he desired. These images were in perpetual succession, one after another. The thing incidental to him which he mentions in the third place was, that he could not recollect any thing that ever happened to him, whether good, ill, or indifferent, of which he had not been admonished, and that a very short time before, in a dream. These things serve to shew of what importance he was in his own eyes, and also, which is the matter he principally brings it to prove, the subtlety and delicacy of his animal nature.

Cardan speaks uncertainly and contradictorily as to his having a genius or demon perpetually attending him, advising him of what was to happen, and forewarning him of sinister events. He concludes however that he had no such attendant, but that it was the excellence of his nature, approaching to immortality. He was much addicted to the study of astrology, and laid claim to great skill as a physician. He visited the court of London, and calculated the nativity of king Edward VI. He was sent for as a physician by cardinal Beaton, archbishop of St Andrews, whom, according to Melvile[a], he recovered to speech and health, and the historian appears to attribute the cure to magic. He calculated the nativity of Jesus Christ, which was imputed to him as an impious undertaking, inasmuch as it supposed the creator of the world to be subject to the influence of the stars. He also predicted his own death, and is supposed by some to have forwarded that event, by abstinence from food at the age of seventy-five, that he might not bely his prediction.

QUACKS, WHO IN COOL BLOOD UNDERTOOK TO OVERREACH MANKIND.

Hitherto we have principally passed such persons in review, as seem to have been in part at least the victims of their own delusions. But be-

---

[a] Memoirs, p. 14.

side these there has always been a numerous class of men, who, with minds perfectly disengaged and free, have applied themselves to concert the means of overreaching the simplicity, or baffling the penetration, of those who were merely spectators, and uninitiated in the mystery of the arts that were practised upon them. Such was no doubt the case with the speaking heads and statues, which were sometimes exhibited in the ancient oracles. Such was the case with certain optical delusions, which were practised on the unsuspecting, and were contrived to produce on them the effect of supernatural revelations. Such is the story of Bel and the Dragon in the book of Apocrypha, where the priests daily placed before the idol twelve measures of flour, and forty sheep, and six vessels of wine, pretending that the idol consumed all these provisions, when in fact they entered the temple by night, by a door under the altar, and removed them.

BENVENUTO CELLINI.

We have a story minutely related by Benvenuto Cellini in his Life, which it is now known was produced by optical delusion, but which was imposed upon the artist and his companions as altogether supernatural. It occurred a very short time before the death of pope Clement the Seventh in 1534, and is thus detailed. It took place in the Coliseum at Rome.

"It came to pass through a variety of odd accidents, that I made acquaintance with a Sicilian priest, who was a man of genius, and well versed in the Greek and Latin languages. Happening one day to have some conversation with him, where the subject turned upon the art of necromancy, I, who had a great desire to know something of the matter, told him, that I had all my life had a curiosity to be acquainted with the mysteries of this art. The priest made answer, that the man must be of a resolute and steady temper, who entered on that study. I replied, that I had fortitude and resolution enough to desire to be initiated in it. The priest subjoined, 'If you think you have the heart to venture, I will give you all the satisfaction you can desire.' Thus we agreed to enter upon a scheme of necromancy.

"The priest one evening prepared to satisfy me, and desired me to look for a companion or two. I invited one Vincenzio Romoli, who was my intimate acquaintance, and he brought with him a native of Pistoia who cultivated the art of necromancy himself. We repaired to the Coliseum; and the priest, according to the custom of conjurors, began to draw circles on the ground, with the most impressive ceremonies imaginable. He likewise brought with him all sorts of precious perfumes and fire, with some compositions which diffused noisome and bad odours. As soon as he was in readiness, he made an opening to the circle, and took us by the hand, and ordered the other necromancer, his partner, to throw perfumes into the fire at a proper time, intrusting the care of the fire and the perfumes to the rest; and then he began his incantations.

"This ceremony lasted above an hour and a half, when there appeared several legions of devils, so that the amphitheatre was quite filled with them. I was busy about the perfumes, when the priest, who knew that there was a sufficient number of infernal spirits, turned about to me, and said, 'Benvenuto, ask them something.' I answered, 'Let them bring me into company with my Sicilian mistress, Angelica.' That night we obtained no answer of any sort; but I received great satisfaction in having my curiosity so far indulged.

"The necromancer told me that it was requisite we should go a second time, assuring me that I should be satisfied in whatever I asked; but that I must bring with me a boy that had never known woman. I took with me my apprentice, who was about twelve years of age; with the same Vincenzio Romoli, who had been my companion the first time, and one Agnolino Gaddi, an intimate acquaintance, whom I likewise prevailed on to assist at the ceremony. When we came to the place appointed, the priest, having made his preparations as before with the same and even more striking ceremonies, placed us within the circle, which he had drawn with a more wonderful art and in a more solemn manner, than at our former meeting. Thus having committed the care of the perfumes and the fire to my friend Vincenzio, who was assisted by Gaddi, he put into my hands a pintacolo, or magical chart, and bid me turn it towards the places to which he should direct me; and under the pintacolo I held my apprentice. The necromancer, having begun to make his most tremendous invocations, called by their names a multitude of demons who were the leaders of the several legions, and questioned them, by the virtue and power of the eternal, uncreated God, who lives for ever, in the Hebrew language, as also in Latin and Greek; insomuch that the amphitheatre was filled, almost in an instant, with demons a hundred times more numerous than at the former conjuration. Vincenzio meanwhile was busied in making a fire with the assistance of Gaddi, and burning a great quantity of precious perfumes. I, by the direction of the necromancer, again desired to be in company with my Angelica. He then turning upon me said, 'Know, they have declared that in the space of a month you shall be in her company.'

"He then requested me to stand by him resolutely, because the legions were now above a thousand more in number than he had designed; and besides these were the most dangerous; so that, after they had answered my question, it behoved him to be civil to them, and dismiss them quietly. At the same time the boy under the pintacolo was in a terrible fright, saying, that there were in the place a million of fierce men who threatened to destroy us; and that, besides, there were four armed giants of enormous stature, who endeavoured to break into our circle. During this time, while the necromancer, trembling with fear, endeavoured by mild means to dismiss them in the best way he could, Vincenzio, who quivered like an aspen leaf, took care of the perfumes. Though I was as much afraid as any of them, I did my utmost to conceal it; so that I greatly contributed to inspire the rest with resolution: but the truth is, I gave myself over for a dead man, seeing the horrid fright the necromancer was in.

"The boy had placed his head between his knees; and said, 'In this attitude will I die; for we shall all surely perish.' I told him that those demons were under us, and what he saw was smoke and shadow; so bid him hold up his head and take courage. No sooner did he look up, than he cried out, 'The whole amphitheatre is burning, and the fire is just falling on us.' So, covering his eyes with his hands, he again exclaimed, that destruction was inevitable, and he desired to see no more. The necromancer intreated me to have a good heart, and to take care to burn proper perfumes; upon which I turned to Vincenzio, and bade him burn all the most precious perfumes he had. At the same time I cast my eyes upon Gaddi, who was terrified to such a degree, that he could scarcely distinguish objects, and seemed to be half dead. Seeing him in this condition, I said to him, 'Gaddi, upon these occasions a man should not yield to fear, but stir about to give some assistance; so come directly, and put on more of these perfumes.' Gaddi accordingly attempted to move; but the effect was annoying both to our sense of hearing and smell, and overcame the perfumes.

" The boy perceiving this, once more ventured to raise his head, and, seeing me laugh, began to take courage, and said, 'The devils are flying away with a vengeance.' In this condition we staid, till the bell rang for morning prayers. The boy again told us, that there remained but few devils, and those were at a great distance. When the magician had performed the rest of his ceremonies, he stripped off his gown, and took up a wallet full of books, which he had brought with him. We all went out of the circle together, keeping as close to each other as we possibly could, especially the boy, who placed himself in the middle, holding the necromancer by the coat, and me by the cloak.

" As we were going to our houses in the quarter of Banchi, the boy told us, that two of the demons whom we had seen at the amphitheatre, went on before us leaping and skipping, sometimes running upon the roofs of the houses, and sometimes on the ground. The priest declared that, as often as he had entered magic circles, nothing so extraordinary had ever happened to him. As we went along, he would fain have persuaded me to assist at the consecrating a book, from which he said we should derive immense riches. We should then ask the demons to discover to us the various treasures with which the earth abounds, which would raise us to opulence and power: but that those love-affairs were mere follies from which no good could be expected. I made answer, that I would readily have accepted his proposal if I had understood Latin. He assured me that the knowledge of Latin was nowise material; but that he could never meet with a partner of resolution and intrepidity equal to mine, and that that would be to him an invaluable acquisition." Immediately subsequent to this scene, Cellini got into one of those scrapes, in which he was so frequently involved by his own violence and ferocity; and the connection was never again renewed.

The first remark that arises out of this narrative is, that nothing is actually done by the supernatural personages which are exhibited. The magician reports certain answers as given by the demons; but these answers do not appear to have been heard from any lips but those of him who was the creator or cause of the scene. The whole of the demons therefore were merely figures, produced by the magic lantern (which is said to have been invented by Roger Bacon), or by something of that nature. The burning of the perfumes served to produce a dense atmosphere, that was calculated to exaggerate, and render more formidable and terrific, the figures which were exhibited. The magic lantern, which is now the amusement only of servant-maids, and boys at school in their holidays, served at this remote period, and when the power of optical delusions was unknown, to terrify men of wisdom and penetration, and make them believe that legions of devils from the infernal regions were come among them, to produce the most horrible effects, and suspend and invert the laws of nature. It is probable, that the magician, who carried home with him a "wallet full of books," also carried at the same time the magic lantern or mirror, with its lights, which had served him for his exhibition, and that this was the cause of the phenomenon, that they observed two of the demons which they had seen at the amphitheatre, going before them on their return, "leaping and skipping, sometimes running on the roofs of the houses, and sometimes on the ground ."

NOSTRADAMUS.

Michael Nostradamus, a celebrated astrologer, was born at St. Remi in Provence in the year 1503. He published a Century of Prophecies in obscure and oracular terms and barbarous verse,

* Brewster, Letters on Natural Magic, Letter IV.

and other works. In the period in which he lived the pretended art of astrological prediction was in the highest repute; and its professors were sought for by emperors and kings, and entertained with the greatest distinction and honour. Henry the Second of France, moved with his great renown, sent for Nostradamus to court, received much gratification from his visit, and afterward ordered him to Blois, that he might see the princes, his sons, calculate their horoscopes, and predict their future fortunes. He was no less in favour afterwards with Charles the Ninth. He died in the year 1566.

DOCTOR DEE.

Dr. John Dee was a man who made a conspicuous figure in the sixteenth century. He was born at London in the year 1527. He was an eminent mathematician, and an indefatigable scholar. He says of himself, that, having been sent to Cambridge when he was fifteen, he persisted for several years in allowing himself only four hours for sleep in the twenty-four, and two for food and refreshment, and that he constantly occupied the remaining eighteen (the time for divine service only excepted) in study. At Cambridge he superintended the exhibition of a Greek play of Aristophanes, among the machinery of which he introduced an artificial scarabæus, or beetle, which flew up to the palace of Jupiter, with a man on his back, and a basket of provisions. The ignorant and astonished spectators ascribed this feat to the arts of the magician; and Dee, annoyed by these suspicions, found it expedient to withdraw to the continent. Here he resided first at the university of Louvaine, at which place, his acquaintance was courted by the dukes of Mantua and Medina, and from thence proceeded to Paris, where he gave lectures on Euclid with singular applause.

In 1551 he returned to England, and was received with distinction by sir John Cheek, and introduced to secretary Cecil, and even to king Edward, from whom he received a pension of one hundred crowns *per annum*, which he speedily after exchanged for a small living in the church. In the reign of queen Mary he was for some time kindly treated; but afterwards came into great trouble, and even into danger of his life. He entered into correspondence with several of the servants of queen Elizabeth at Woodstock, and was charged with practising against Mary's life by enchantments. Upon this accusation, he was seized and confined; and, being after several examinations discharged of the indictment, was turned over to bishop Bonner to see if any heresy could be found in him. After a tedious persecution he was set at liberty in 1555, and was so little subdued by what he had suffered, that in the following year he presented a petition to the queen, requesting her co-operation in a plan for preserving and recovering certain monuments of classical antiquity.

The principal study of Dee however at this time lay in astrology; and accordingly, upon the accession of Elizabeth, Robert Dudley, her chief favourite, was sent to consult the doctor as to the aspect of the stars, that they might fix on an auspicious day for celebrating her coronation. Some years after we find him again on the continent; and in 1571, being taken ill at Louvaine, we are told the queen sent over two physicians to accomplish his cure. Elizabeth afterwards visited him at his house at Mortlake, that she might view his magazine of mathematical instruments and curiosities; and about this time employed him to defend her title to countries discovered in different parts of the globe. He says of himself, that he received the most advantageous offers from Charles V, Ferdinand, Maximilian II, and Rodolph II, emperors of Germany, and from the czar of Muscovy an offer of £2000 sterling *per annum*, upon condition that he would reside in his dominions. All these circumstances were solemnly attested by Dee in a Compendious Rehearsal of his Life and Studies for half-a-century, composed at a later period, and read by him at his house at Mortlake to two commissioners appointed by Elizabeth to enquire into his circumstances, accompanied with evidences and documents to establish the particulars.

* Appendix to Johannes Glastoniensis, edited by Hearne.

Had Dee gone no further than this, he would undoubtedly have ranked among the profoundest scholars and most eminent geniuses that adorned the reign of the maiden queen. But he was unfortunately cursed with an ambition that nothing could satisfy; and, having accustomed his mind to the wildest reveries, and wrought himself up to an extravagant pitch of enthusiasm, he pursued a course that involved him in much calamity, and clouded all his latter days with misery and ruin. He dreamed perpetually of the philosopher's stone, and was haunted with the belief of intercourse of a supramundane character. It is almost impossible to decide among these things, how much was illusion, and how much was forgery. Both were inextricably mixed in his proceedings; and this extraordinary victim probably could not in his most dispassionate moments precisely distinguish what belonged to the one, and what to the other.

As Dee was an enthusiast, so he perpetually interposed in his meditations prayers of the greatest emphasis and fervour. As he was one day in November 1582, engaged in these devout exercises, he says that there appeared to him the angel Uriel at the west window of his Museum, who gave him a translucent stone, or chrystal, of a convex form, that had the quality, when intently surveyed, of presenting apparitions, and even emitting sounds, in consequence of which the observer could hold conversations, ask questions and receive answers from the figures he saw in the mirror. It was often necessary that the stone should be turned one way and another in different positions, before the person who consulted it gained the right focus; and then the objects to be observed would sometimes shew themselves on the surface of the stone, and sometime in different parts of the room by virtue of the action of the stone. It had also this peculiarity, that only one person, having been named as seer, could see the figures exhibited, and hear the voices that spoke, though there might be various persons in the room. It appears that the person who discerned these visions must have his eyes and his ears uninterruptedly engaged in the affair, so that, as Dee experienced, to render the communication effectual, there must be two human beings concerned in the scene, one of them to describe what he saw, and to recite the dialogue that took place, and the other immediately to commit to paper all that his partner dictated. Dee for some reason chose for himself the part of the amanuensis, and had to seek for a companion, who was to watch the stone, and repeat to him whatever he saw and heard.

It happened opportunely that, a short time before Dee received this gift from on high, he contracted a familiar intercourse with one Edward Kelly of Worcestershire, whom he found specially qualified to perform the part which it was necessary to Dee to have adequately filled. Kelly was an extraordinary character, and in some respects exactly such a person as Dee wanted. He was just twenty-eight years younger than the memorable personage, who now received him as an inmate, and was engaged in his service at a stipulated salary of fifty pounds a year.

Kelly entered upon life with a somewhat unfortunate adventure. He was accused, when a young man, of forgery, brought to trial, convicted, and lost his ears in the pillory. This misfortune however by no means daunted him. He was assiduously engaged in the search for the philosopher's stone. He had an active mind, great enterprise, and a very domineering temper. Another adventure in which he had been engaged previously to his knowledge of Dee, was in digging up the body of a man, who had been buried only the day before, that he might compel him by incantations, to answer questions, and discover future events. There was this difference therefore between the two persons previously to their league. Dee was a man of regular manners and unspotted life, honoured by the great, and favourably noticed by crowned heads in different parts of the world; while Kelly was a notorious profligate, accustomed to the most licentious actions, and under no restraint from morals or principle.

One circumstance that occurred early in the acquaintance of Kelly and Dee it is necessary to mention. It serves strikingly to illustrate the ascendancy of the junior and impetuous party over his more gifted senior. Kelly led Dee, we are not told under what pretence, to visit the celebrated ruins of Glastonbury Abbey in Somersetshire. Here, as these curious travellers searched into every corner of the scene, they met by some rare accident with a vase containing a certain portion of the actual *elixir vitæ*, that rare and precious liquid, so much sought after, which has the virtue of converting the baser metals into gold and silver. It had remained here perhaps ever since the time of the highly-gifted St. Dunstan in the tenth century. This they carried off in triumph: but we are not told of any special use to which they applied it, till a few years after, when they were both on the continent.

The first record of their consultations with the supramundane spirits, was of the date of December 2, 1581, at Lexden Heath in the county of Essex; and from this time they went on in a regular series of consultations with and enquiries from these miraculous visitors, a great part of which will appear to the uninitiated extremely puerile and ludicrous, but which were committed to writing with the most scrupulous exactness by Dee, the first part still existing in manuscript, but the greater portion from 28 May 1583 to 1608, with some interruptions, having been committed to the press by Dr. Meric Casaubon in a well-sized folio in 1659, under the title of "A True and Faithful

Relation of what passed between Dr. John Dee and some Spirits, tending, had it succeeded, to a general alteration of most states and kingdoms of the world."

Kelly and Dee had not long been engaged in these supernatural colloquies, before an event occurred which gave an entirely new turn to their proceedings. Albert Alaski, a Polish nobleman, lord palatine of the principality of Siradia, came over at this time into England, urged, as he said, by a desire personally to acquaint himself with the glories of the reign of Elizabeth, and the evidences of her unrivalled talents. The queen and her favourite, the earl of Leicester, received him with every mark of courtesy and attention, and, having shewn him all the wonders of her court at Westminster and Greenwich, sent him to Oxford, with a command to the dignitaries and heads of colleges, to pay him every attention, and to lay open to his view all their rarest curiosities. Among other things worthy of notice, Alaski enquired for the celebrated Dr. Dee, and expressed the greatest impatience to be acquainted with him.

Just at this juncture the earl of Leicester happened to spy Dr. Dee among the crowd who attended at a royal levee. The earl immediately advanced towards him; and, in his frank manner, having introduced him to Alaski, expressed his intention of bringing the Pole to dine with the doctor at his house at Mortlake. Embarrassed with this unexpected honour, Dee no sooner got home, than he dispatched an express to the earl, honestly confessing that he should be unable to entertain such guests in a suitable manner, without being reduced to the expedient of selling or pawning his plate, to procure him the means of doing so. Leicester communicated the doctor's perplexity to Elizabeth; and the queen immediately dispatched a messenger with a present of forty angels, or twenty pounds, to enable him to receive his guests as became him.

A great intimacy immediately commenced between Dee and the stranger. Alaski, though possessing an extensive territory, was reduced by the prodigality of himself or his ancestors to much embarrassment; and on the other hand this nobleman appeared to Dee an instrument well qualified to accomplish his ambitious purposes. Alaski was extremely desirous to look into the womb of time; and Dee, it is likely, suggested repeated hints of his extraordinary power from his possession of the philosopher's stone. After two or three interviews, and much seeming importunity on the part of the Pole, Dee and Kelly graciously condescended to admit Alaski as a third party to their secret meetings with their supernatural visitors, from which the rest of the world were carefully excluded. Here the two Englishmen made use of the vulgar artifice, of promising extraordinary good fortune to the person of whom they purposed to make use. By the intervention of the miraculous stone they told the wondering traveller, that he should shortly become king of Poland, with the accession of several other kingdoms, that he should overcome many armies of Saracens and Paynims, and prove a mighty conqueror. Dee at the same time complained of the disagreeable condition in which he was at home, and that Burleigh and Walsingham were his malicious enemies. At length they concerted among themselves, that they, Alaski, and Dee and Kelly with their wives and families, should clandestinely withdraw out of England, and proceed with all practicable rapidity to Alaski's territory in the kingdom of Poland. They embarked on this voyage 21 September, and arrived at Siradia the third of February following.

At this place however the strangers remained little more than a month. Alaski found his finances in such disorder, that it was scarcely possible for him to feed the numerous guests he had brought along with him. The promises of splendid conquests which Dee and Kelly profusely heaped upon him, were of no avail to supply the deficiency of his present income. And the elixir they brought from Glastonbury was, as they said, so incredibly rich in virtue, that they were compelled to lose much time in making projection by way of trial, before they could hope to arrive at the proper temperament for producing the effect they desired.

In the following month Alaski with his visitors passed to Cracow, the residence of the kings of Poland. Here they remained five months, Dee and Kelly perpetually amusing the Pole with the extraordinary virtue of the stone, which had been brought from heaven by an angel, and busied in a thousand experiments with the elixir, and many tedious preparations which they pronounced to be necessary, before the compound could have the proper effect. The prophecies were uttered with extreme confidence; but no external indications were afforded, to shew that in any way they were likely to be realised. The experiments and exertions of the laboratory were incessant; but no transmutation was produced. At length Alaski found himself unable to sustain the train of followers he had brought out of England. With mountains of wealth, the treasures of the world promised, they were reduced to the most grievous straits for the means of daily subsistence. Finally the zeal of Alaski diminished; he had no longer the same faith in the projectors that had deluded him; and he devised a way of sending them forward with letters of recommendation to Rodolph II, emperor of Germany, at his imperial seat of Prague, where they arrived on the ninth of August.

Rodolph was a man, whose character and habits of life they judged excellently adapted to their purpose. Dee had a long conference with the emperor, in which he explained to him what wonderful things the spirits promised to this prince, in case he proved exemplary of life, and obedient to their suggestions, that he should be the greatest conqueror in the world, and should take captive the Turk in his city of Constantinople. Rodolph was extremely courteous in his reception, and sent away Dee with the highest hopes that he had at length found a personage with whom he should infallibly succeed to the extent of his wishes. He sought however a second interview, and was baffled. At one time the emperor was going to his country palace near Prague, and at another was engaged in the pleasures of the chace.

He also complained that he was not sufficiently familiar with the Latin tongue, to manage the conferences with Dee in a satisfactory manner in person. He therefore deputed Curtzius, a man high in his confidence, to enter into the necessary details with his learned visitor. Dee also contrived to have Spinola, the ambassador from Madrid to the court of the emperor, to urge his suit. The final result was that Rodolph declined any further intercourse with Dee. He turned a deaf ear to his prophecies, and professed to be altogether void of faith as to his promises respecting the philosopher's stone. Dee however was led on perpetually with hopes of better things from the emperor, till the spring of the year 1585. At length he was obliged to fly from Prague, the bishop of Placentia, the pope's nuncio, having it in command from his holiness to represent to Rodolph how discreditable it was for him to harbour English magicians, heretics, at his court.

From Prague Dee and his followers proceeded to Cracow. Here he found means of introduction to Stephen, king of Poland, to whom immediately he insinuated as intelligence from heaven, that Rodolph, the emperor, would speedily be assassinated, and that Stephen would succeed him in the throne of Germany. Stephen appears to have received Dee with more condescension than Rodolph had done, and was once present at his incantation and interview with the invisible spirits. Dee also lured him on with promises respecting the philosopher's stone. Meanwhile the magician was himself reduced to the strangest expedients for subsistence. He appears to have daily expected great riches from the transmutation of metals, and was unwilling to confess that he and his family were in the mean time almost starving.

When king Stephen at length became wearied with fruitless expectation, Dee was fortunate enough to meet with another and more patient dupe in Rosenburg, a nobleman of considerable wealth at Trebona in the kingdom of Bohemia. Here Dee appears to have remained till 1589, when he was sent for home by Elizabeth. In what manner he proceeded during this interval, and from whence he drew his supplies, we are only left to conjecture. He lured on his victim with the usual temptation, promising him that he should be king of Poland. In the mean time it is recorded by him, that, on the ninth of December, 1586, he arrived at the point of projection, having cut a piece of metal out of a brass warming-pan; and merely heating it by the fire, and pouring on it a portion of the elixir, it was presently converted into pure silver. We are told that he sent the warming-pan and the piece of silver to queen Elizabeth, that she might be convinced by her own eyes how exactly they tallied, and that the one had unquestionably been a portion of the other. About the same time it is said, that Dee and his associate became more free in their expenditure; and in one instance it is stated as an example, that Kelly gave away to the value of four thousand pounds sterling in gold rings on occasion of the celebration of the marriage of one of his maid-servants. On the twenty-seventh and thirtieth of July, 1587, Dee has recorded in his journal his gratitude to God for his unspeakable mercies on those days imparted, which has been interpreted to mean further acquisitions of wealth by means of the elixir.

Meanwhile perpetual occasions of dissention occurred between the two great confederates, Kelly and Dee. They were in many respects unfitted for each other's society. Dee was a man, who from his youth upward had been indefatigable in study and research, had the consciousness of great talents and intellect, and had been universally recognised as such, and had possessed a high character for fervent piety and blameless morals. Kelly was an impudent adventurer, a man of no principles and of blasted reputation; yet fertile in resources, full of self-confidence, and of no small degree of ingenuity. In their mutual intercourse the audacious adventurer often had the upper hand of the man who had lately possessed a well-earned reputation. Kelly frequently professed himself tired of enacting the character of interpreter of the Gods under Dee. He found Dee in all cases running away with the superior consideration; while he in his own opinion best deserved to possess it. The straitness of their circumstances, and the misery they were occasionally called on to endure, we may be sure did not improve their good understanding. Kelly once and again threatened to abandon his leader. Dee continually soothed him, and prevailed on him to stay.

Kelly at length started a very extraordinary proposition. Kelly, as interpreter to the spirits, and being the only person who heard and saw any thing, we may presume made them say whatever he pleased. Kelly and Dee had both of them wives. Kelly did not always live harmoniously with the partner of his bed. He sometimes went so far as to say that he hated her. Dee was more fortunate. His wife was a person of good family, and had hitherto been irreproachable in her demeanour. The spirits one day revealed to Kelly, that they must henceforth have their wives in common. The wife of Kelly was barren, and this curse could no otherwise be removed. Having started the proposition, Kelly played the reluctant party. Dee, who was pious and enthusiastic, inclined to submit. He first indeed started the notion, that it could only be meant that they should live in mutual harmony and good understanding. The spirits protested against this, and insisted upon the literal interpretation. Dee yielded, and compared his case to that of Abraham, who at the divine command consented to sacrifice his son Isaac. Kelly alleged that these spirits, which Dee had hitherto regarded as messengers from God, could be no other than servants of Satan. He persisted in his disobedience; and the spirits declared that he was no longer worthy to be their interpreter, and that another mediator must be found.

They named Arthur Dee, the son of the possessor of the stone, a promising and well-disposed boy of only eight years of age. Dee consecrated the youth accordingly to his high function by prayers and religious rites for several days together. Kelly took horse and rode away, protesting that they should meet no more. Arthur entered upon his office, April 15, 1587. The experiment proved abortive. He saw something; but not to the purpose. He heard no voices. At length Kelly, on the third day, entered the room unexpectedly, "by miraculous fortune," as Dee says, "or a divine fate," sate down between them, and immediately saw figures, and heard voices, which the little Arthur was not enabled to perceive. In particular he saw four heads inclosed in an obelisk, which he perceived to represent the two magicians and their wives, and interpreted to signify that unlimited communion in which they were destined to engage. The matter however being still an occasion of scruple, a spirit appeared, who by the language he used was plainly no other than the Saviour of the world, and took away from them the larger stone; for now it appears there were two stones. This miracle at length induced all parties to submit; and the divine command was no sooner obeyed, than the stone which had been abstracted, was found again under the pillow of the wife of Dee.

It is not easy to imagine a state of greater degradation than that into which this person had now fallen. During all the prime and vigour of his intellect, he had sustained an eminent part among the learned and the great, distinguished and honoured by Elizabeth and her favourite. But his unbounded arrogance and self-opinion could never be satisfied. And seduced, partly by his own weakness, and partly by the insinuations of a crafty adventurer, he became a mystic of the most dishonourable sort. He was induced to believe in a series of miraculous communications without common sense, engaged in the pursuit of the philosopher's stone, and no doubt imagined that he was possessed of the great secret. Stirred up by these conceptions, he left his native country, and became a wanderer, preying upon the credulity of one prince and eminent man after another, and no sooner was he discarded by one victim of credulity, than he sought another, a vagabond on the earth, reduced from time to time to the greatest distress, persecuted, dishonoured and despised by every party in their turn. At length by incessant degrees he became dead to all moral distinctions, and all sense of honour and self-respect. " Professing himself to be wise he became a fool, walked in the vanity of his imagination," and had his understanding under total eclipse. The immoral system of conduct in which he engaged, and the strange and shocking blasphemy that he mixed with it, render him at this time a sort of character that it is painful to contemplate.

Led on as Dee at this time was by the ascendancy and consummate art of Kelly, there was far from existing any genuine harmony between them; and, after many squabbles and heart-burnings, they appear finally to have parted in January 1589, Dee having, according to his own account, at that time delivered up to Kelly, the elixir and the different implements by which the transmutation of metals was to be effected.

Various overtures appear to have passed now for some years between Dee and queen Elizabeth, intended to lead to his restoration to his native country. Dee had upon different occasions expressed a wish to that effect; and Elizabeth in the spring of 1589 sent him a message, that removed from him all further thought of hesitation and delay. He set out from Trebona with three coaches, and a baggage train correspondent, and had an audience of the queen at Richmond towards the close of that year. Upon the whole it is impossible perhaps not to believe, that Elizabeth was influenced in this proceeding by the various reports that had reached her of his extraordinary success with the philosopher's stone, and the boundless wealth he had it in his power to bestow. Many princes at this time contended with each other, as to who should be happy enough by fair means or by force to have under his control the fortunate possessor of the great secret, and thus to have in his possession the means of inexhaustible wealth. Shortly after this time the emperor Rodolph seized and committed to prison Kelly, the partner of Dee in this inestimable faculty, and, having once enlarged him, placed him in custody a second time. Meanwhile Elizabeth is said to have made him pressing overtures of so flattering a nature that he determined to escape and return to his native country. For this purpose he is said to have torn the sheets of his bed, and twisted them into a rope, that by that means he might descend from the tower in which he was confined. But, being a corpulent man of considerable weight, the rope broke with him before he was half way down, and, having fractured one or both his legs, and being otherwise considerably bruised, he died shortly afterwards. This happened in the year 1595.

Dee (according to his own account, delivered to commissioners appointed by queen Elizabeth to enquire into his circumstances) came from Trebona to England in a state little inferior to that of an ambassador. He had three coaches, with four horses harnessed to each coach, two or three loaded waggons, and a guard, sometimes of six, and sometimes of twenty-four soldiers, to defend him from enemies, who were supposed to lie in wait to intercept his passage. Immediately on his arrival he had an audience of the queen at Richmond, by whom he was most graciously received. She gave special orders, that he should do what he would in chemistry and philosophy, and that no one should on any account molest him.

But here end the prosperity and greatness of this extraordinary man. If he possessed the power of turning all baser metals into gold, he certainly acted unadvisedly in surrendering this power to his confederate, immediately before his return to his native country. He parted at the same time with his gift of prophecy, since, though he brought away with him his miraculous stone, and at one time appointed one Bartholomew, and another one Hickman, his interpreters to look into the stone, to see the marvellous sights it was expected to disclose, and to hear the voices and report the words that issued from it, the experiments proved in both instances abortive. They wanted the finer sense, or the unparalleled effrontery and inexhaustible invention, which Kelly alone possessed.

The remainder of the voyage of the life of Dee was "bound in shallows and in miseries." Queen Elizabeth we may suppose soon found that her dreams of immense wealth to be obtained through his intervention were nugatory. Yet would she not desert the favourite of her former years. He presently began to complain of poverty and difficulties. He represented that the revenue of two livings he held in the church had been withheld from him from the time of his going abroad. He stated that, shortly after that period, his house had been broken into and spoiled by a lawless mob, instigated by his ill fame as a dealer in prohibited and unlawful arts. They destroyed or dispersed his library, consisting of four thousand volumes, seven hundred of which were manuscripts, and of inestimable rarity. They ravaged his collection of curious implements and machines. He enumerated the expences of his journey home by Elizabeth's command, for which he seemed to consider the queen as his debtor. Elizabeth in consequence ordered him at several times two or three small sums. But this being insufficient, she was prevailed upon in 1592 to appoint two members of her privy council to repair to his house at Mortlake to enquire into particulars, to whom he made a Compendious Rehearsal of half a hundred years of his life, accompanied with documents and vouchers.

It is remarkable that in this Rehearsal no mention occurs of the miraculous stone brought down to him by an angel, or of his pretensions respecting the transmutation of metals. He merely rests his claims to public support upon his literary labours, and the acknowledged eminence of his intellectual faculties. He passes over the years he had lately spent in foreign countries, in entire silence, unless we except his account of the particulars of his journey home. His representation to Elizabeth not being immediately productive of all the effects he expected, he wrote a letter to archbishop Whitgift two years after, lamenting the delay of the expected relief, and complaining of the " untrue reports, opinions and fables, which had for so many years been spread of his studies." He represents these studies purely as literary, frank, and wholly divested of mystery. If the " True Relation of what passed for many years between Dr. Dee and certain Spirits" had not been preserved, and afterwards printed, we might have been disposed to consider all that was said on this subject as a calumny.

The promotion which Dee had set his heart on, was to the office of master of St. Cross's Hospital near Winchester, which the queen had promised him when the present holder should be made a bishop. But this never happened. He obtained however in lieu of it the chancellorship of St. Paul's cathedral, 8 December 1594, which in the following year he exchanged for the wardenship of the college at Manchester. In this last office he continued till the year 1602 (according to other accounts 1604), during which time he complained of great dissentions and refractoriness on the part of the fellows; though it may perhaps be doubted whether equal blame may not fairly be imputed to the arrogance and restlessness of the warden. At length he receded altogether from public life, and retired to his ancient domicile at Mortlake. He made one attempt to propitiate the favour of king James; but it was ineffectual. Elizabeth had known him in the flower and vigour of his days; he had boasted the uniform patronage of her chief favourite; he had been recognised by the philosophical and the learned as inferior to none of their body; and he had finally excited the regard of his ancient mistress by his pretence to revelations, and the promises he held out of the philosopher's stone. She could not shake off her ingrafted prejudice in his favour; she could not find in her heart to cast him aside in his old age and decay. But then came a king, to whom in his prosperity and sunshine he had been a stranger. He wasted his latter days in dotage, obscurity and universal neglect. No one has told us how he contrived to subsist. We may be sure that his constant companions were mortification and the most humiliating privations. He lingered on till the year 1608; and the ancient people in the time of Antony Wood, nearly a century afterwards, pointed to his grave in the chancel of the church at Mortlake, and professed to know the very spot where his remains were desposited.

The history of Dee is exceedingly interesting, not only on its own account; not only for the eminence of his talents and attainments, and the incredible sottishness and blindness of understanding which marked his maturer years; but as strikingly illustrative of the credulity and superstitious faith of the time in which he lived. At a later period his miraculous stone which displayed such wonders, and was attended with so long a series of supernatural vocal communications would have deceived nobody: it was scarcely more ingenious than the idle tricks of the most ordinary conjurer. But at this period the crust of long ages of darkness had not yet been fully worn away. Men did not trust to the powers of human understanding, and were not familiarised with the main canons of evidence and belief. Dee passed six years on the continent, proceeding from the court of one prince or potent nobleman to another, listened to for a time by each, each regarding his oracular communications with astonishment and alarm, and at length irresolutely casting him off, when he found little or no difficulty in running a like career with another.

It is not the least curious circumstance respecting the life of Dee, that in 1659, half a century after his death, there remained still such an interest respecting practices of this sort, as to authorise the printing a folio volume, in a complex and elaborate form, of his communications with spirits. The book was brought out by Dr. Meric Casaubon, no contemptible name in the republic of letters. The editor observes respecting the hero and his achievements in the Preface, that, " though his carriage in certain respects seemed to lay in works of darkness, yet all was tendered by him to kings and princes, and by all (England alone excepted) was listened to for a good while with good respect, and by some for a long time embraced and entertained." He goes on to say, that " the fame of it made the pope bestir himself, and filled all, both learned and unlearned, with great wonder and astonishment." He adds, that, " as a whole it is undoubtedly not to be paralleled in its kind in any age or country." In a word the editor, though disavowing an entire belief in Dee's pretensions, yet plainly considers them with some degree of deference, and insinuates to how much more regard such undue and exaggerated pretensions are entitled, than the impious incredulity of certain modern Sadducees, who say that "there is no resurrection; neither angel, nor spirit." The belief in witchcraft and sorcery has undoutedly met with some degree of favour from this consideration, inasmuch as, by recognising the correspondence of human beings with the invisible world, it has one principle in common with the believers in revelation, of which the more daring infidel is destitute.

EARL OF DERBY.

The circumstances of the death of Ferdinand, fifth earl of Derby, in 1594, have particularly engaged the attention of the contemporary historians. Hesket, an emissary of the Jesuits and English Catholics abroad, was importunate with this nobleman to press his title to the crown, as the legal representative of his great-grandmother Mary, youngest daughter to king Henry the Seventh. But the earl, fearing, as it is said, that this was only a trap to ensnare him, gave information against Hesket to the government, in consequence of which he was apprehended, tried and executed. Hesket had threatened the earl that, *if he did not comply with his suggestion, he should live only a short time.* Accordingly, four months afterwards, the earl was seized with a very uncommon disease. A waxen image was at the same time found in his chamber with hairs in its belly exactly of the same colour as those of the earl*. The image was, by some zealous friend of lord Derby, burned; but the earl grew worse. He was himself thoroughly persuaded that he was bewitched. Stow has inserted in his Annals a minute account of his disease from day to day, with a description of all the symptoms.

KING JAMES'S VOYAGE TO NORWAY.

While Elizabeth amused herself with the supernatural gifts to which Dee advanced his claim, and consoled the adversity and destitution to which the old man, once so extensively honoured, was now reduced, a scene of a very different complexion was played in the northern part of the island. Trials for sorcery were numerous in the reign of Mary queen of Scots; the comparative darkness and ignorance of the sister kingdom rendered it a soil still more favourable than England to the growth of these gloomy superstitions. But the mind of James, at once inquisitive, pedantic and self-sufficient, peculiarly fitted him for the pursuit of these narrow-minded and obscure speculations. One combination of circumstances wrought up this propensity within him to the greatest height.

James was born in the year 1566. He was the

* Camden, anno 1693, 1694.

only direct heir to the crown of Scotland; and he was in near prospect of succession to that of England. The zeal of the Protestant Reformation had wrought up the anxiety of men's minds to a fever of anticipation and forecast. Consequently, towards the end of the reign of Elizabeth, a point which greatly arrested the general attention was the expected marriage of the king of Scotland. Elizabeth, with that petty jealousy which obscured the otherwise noble qualities of her spirit, sought to countermine this marriage, that her rival and expected successor might not be additionally graced with the honours of offspring. James fixed his mind upon a daughter of the king of Denmark. By the successful cabals of Elizabeth he was baffled in this suit; and the lady was finally married to the duke of Bavaria. The king of Denmark had another daughter; and James made proposals to this princess. Still he was counteracted; till at length he sent a splendid embassy, with ample powers and instructions, and the treaty was concluded. The princess embarked; but, when she had now for some time been expected in Scotland, news was brought instead, that she had been driven back by tempests on the coast of Norway. The young king felt keenly his disappointment, and gallantly resolved to sail in person for the port, where his intended consort was detained by the shattered condition of her fleet. James arrived on the twenty-second of October 1589, and having consummated his marriage, was induced by the invitation of his father-in-law to pass the winter at Copenhagen, from whence he did not sail till the spring, and, after having encountered a variety of contrary winds and some danger, reached Edinburgh on the first of May in the following year.

It was to be expected that variable weather and storms should characterise the winter-season in these seas. But the storms were of longer continuance and of more frequent succession, than was usually known. And at this period, when the proposed consort of James first, then the king himself, and finally both of them, and the hope of Protestant succession, were committed to the mercy of the waves, it is not wonderful that the process of the seasons should be accurately marked, and that those varieties, which are commonly ascribed to second causes, should have been imputed to extraordinary and supernatural interference. It was affirmed that, in the king's return from Denmark, his ship was impelled by a different wind from that which acted on the rest of his fleet.

It happened that, soon after James's return to Scotland, one Geillis Duncan, a servant-maid, for the extraordinary circumstances that attended certain cures which she performed, became suspected of witchcraft. Her master questioned her on the subject; but she would own nothing. Perceiving her obstinacy, the master took upon himself of his own authority, to extort confession from her by torture. In this he succeeded; and, having related divers particulars of witchcraft of herself, she proceeded to accuse others. The persons she accused were cast into the public prison.

One of these, Agnes Sampson by name, at first stoutly resisted the torture. But, it being more strenuously applied, she by and by became extremely communicative. It was at this period that James personally engaged in the examinations. We are told that he "took great delight in being present," and putting the proper questions. The unhappy victim was introduced into a room plentifully furnished with implements of torture, while the king waited in an apartment at a convenient distance, till the patient was found to be in a suitable frame of mind to make the desired communications. No sooner did he or she signify that they were ready, and should no longer refuse to answer, than they were introduced, fainting, sinking under recent sufferings which they had no longer strength to resist, into the royal presence. And here sat James, in envied ease and conscious "delight," wrapped up in the thought of his own sagacity, framing the enquiries that might best extort the desired evidence, and calculating with a judgment by no means to be despised, from the bearing, the turn of features, and the complexion of the victim, the probability whether he was making a frank and artless confession, or had still the secret desire to impose on the royal examiner, or from a different motive was disposed to make use of the treacherous authority which the situation afforded, to gratify his revenge upon some person towards whom he might be inspired with latent hatred and malice.

Agnes Sampson related with what solicitude she had sought to possess some fragment of the linen belonging to the king. If he had worn it, and it had contracted any soil from his royal person, this would be enough: she would infallibly, by applying her incantations to this fragment, have been able to undermine the life of the sovereign. She told how she with two hundred other witches had sailed in sieves from Leith to North Berwick church, how they had there encountered the devil in person, how they had feasted with him, and what obscenities had been practised. She related that in this voyage they had drowned a cat, having first baptised him, and that immediately a dreadful storm had arisen, and in this very storm the king's ship had been separated from the rest of his fleet. She took James aside, and, the better to convince him, undertook to repeat to him the conversation, the dialogue which had passed from the one to the other, between the king and queen in their bedchamber on the wedding-night. Agnes Sampson was condemned to the flames.

JOHN FIAN.

Another of the miserable victims on this occasion was John Fian, a schoolmaster at Tranent near Edinburgh, a young man, whom the ignorant populace had decorated with the style of doctor. He was tortured by means of a rope strongly twisted about his head, and by the boots. He was at length brought to confession. He told of a young girl, the sister of one of his scholars, with whom he had been deeply enamoured. He had proposed to the boy to bring him three hairs from the most secret part of his sister's body, possessing which he should be enabled by certain incantations to procure himself the love of the girl. The boy at his mother's instigation brought to Fian three hairs from a virgin heifer instead; and, applying his conjuration to them, the consequence had been that the heifer forced her way into his school, leaped upon him in amorous fashion, and would not be restrained from following him about the neighbourhood.

This same Fian acted an important part in the scene at North Berwick church. As being best fitted for the office, he was appointed recorder or clerk to the devil, to write down the names, and administer the oaths to the witches. He was actively concerned in the enchantment, by means of which the king's ship had nearly been lost on his return from Denmark. This part of his proceeding however does not appear in his own confession, but in that of the witches who were his fellow-conspirators.

He further said, that, the night after he made his confession, the devil appeared to him, and was in a furious rage against him for his disloyalty to his service, telling him that he should severely repent his infidelity. Acccording to his own account, he stood firm, and defied the devil to do his worst. Meanwhile the next night he escaped out of prison, and was with some difficulty retaken. He however finally denied all his former confessions, said that they were falshoods forced from him by mere dint of torture, and, though he was now once more subjected to the same treatment to such an excess as must necessarily have crippled him of his limbs for ever, he proved inflexible to the last. At length by the king's order he was strangled, and his body cast into the flames. Multitudes of unhappy men and women perished in this cruel persecution*.

KING JAMES'S DEMONOLOGY.

It was by a train of observations and experience like this, that James was prompted seven years after to compose and publish his Dialogues on Demonology in Three Books. In the Preface to this book he says, "The fearfull abounding at this

* Pitcairn, Trials in Scotland in Five Volumes, 4to.

time in this countrey, of these detestable slaves of the Diuel, the Witches or enchaunters, hath moved me (beloued Reader) to dispatch in post this following Treatise of mine, not in any wise (as I protest) to serue for a shew of my learning and ingine, but onely (moued of conscience) to preasse thereby, so farre as I can, to resolue the doubting hearts of many, both that such assaults of Satan are most certainely practised, and that the instruments thereof merits most seuerely to be punished."

In the course of the treatise he affirms, " that barnes, or wiues, or neuer so diffamed persons, may serue for sufficient witnesses and proofes in such trialls; for who but Witches can be prooves, and so witnesses of the doings of Witches*?" But, lest innocent persons should be accused, and suffer falsely, he tells us, " There are two other good helps that may be used for their trial: the one is, the finding of their marke [a mark that the devil was supposed to impress upon some part of their persons], and the trying the insensibleness thereof: the other is their fleeting on the water: for, as in a secret murther, if the dead carkasse be at any time thereafter handled by the murtherer, it will gush out of bloud, as if the bloud were crying to the heauen for revenge of the murtherer, God hauing appointed that secret supernaturall signe, for triall of that secret unnaturall crime, so it appears that God hath appointed (for a supernaturall

* King James's Works, p. 135.

signe of the monstrous impietie of Witches) that the water shall refuse to recciue them in her bosome, that haue shaken off them the sacred water of Baptisme, and wilfully refused the benefite thereof: No, not so much as their eyes are able to shed teares (threaten and torture them as ye please) while first they repent (God not permitting them to dissemble their obstinacie in so horrible a crime[b].)"

STATUTE, 1 JAMES I.

In consequence of the strong conviction James entertained on the subject, the English parliament was induced, in the first year of his reign, to supersede the milder proceedings of Elizabeth, and to enact that " if any person shall use, practice, or exercise any invocation or conjuration of any evil and wicked spirit, or shall consult, covenant with, entertain, employ, feed or reward any evil and wicked spirit, to or for any intent and purpose; or take up any dead man, woman, or child out of their grave, or the skin, bone, or any part of any dead person, to be used in any manner of witchcraft, sorcery or enchantment, or shall use any witchcraft, sorcery or enchantment, whereby any person shall be killed, destroyed, wasted, consumed, pined or lamed in his or her body, or any part thereof; that then every such offender, their

[b] King James's Works, p. 135, 136.

aiders, abettors and counsellors shall suffer the pains of death." And upon this statute great numbers were condemned and executed.

FORMAN AND OTHERS.

There is a story of necromancy which unfortunately makes too prominent a figure in the history of the court and character of king James the First. Robert earl of Essex, son of queen Elizabeth's favourite, and who afterwards became commander in chief of the parliamentary forces in the civil wars, married lady Frances Howard, a younger daughter of the earl of Suffolk, the bride and bridegroom being the one thirteen, the other fourteen years old at the time of the marriage. The relatives of the countess however, who had brought about the match, thought it most decorous to separate them for some time, and, while she remained at home with her friends, the bridegroom travelled for three or four years on the continent. The lady proved the greatest beauty of her time, but along with this had the most libertine and unprincipled dispositions.

The very circumstance that she had vowed her faith at the altar when she was not properly capable of choice, inspired into the wayward mind of the countess a repugnance to her husband. He came from the continent, replete with accomplishments; and we may conclude, from the figure he afterwards made in the most perilous times, not without a competent share of intellectual abilities. But the countess shrank from all advances on his part. He loved retirement, and woed the lady to scenes most favourable to the development of the affections: she had been bred in court, and was melancholy and repined in any other scene. So capricious was her temper, that she is said at the same time to have repelled the overtures of the accomplished and popular prince Henry, the heir to the throne.

It happened about this period that a beautiful young man, twenty years of age, and full of all martial graces, appeared on the stage. King James was singularly partial to young men who were distinguished for personal attractions. By an extraordinary accident this person, Robert Carr by name, in the midst of a court-spectacle, just when it was his cue to present a buckler with a device to the king, was thrown from his horse, and broke his leg. This was enough: James naturally became interested in the misfortune, attached himself to Carr, and even favoured him again and again with a royal visit during his cure. Presently the young man became an exclusive favourite; and no honours and graces could be obtained of the sovereign but by his interference.

This circumstance fixed the wavering mind of the countess of Essex. Voluptuous and self-willed in her disposition, she would hear of no one but

Carr. But her opportunities of seeing him were both short and rare. In this emergency she applied to Mrs. Turner, a woman whose profession it was to study and to accommodate the fancies of such persons as the countess. Mrs. Turner introduced her to Dr. Forman, a noted astrologer and magician, and he, by images made of wax, and various uncouth figures and devices, undertook to procure the love of Carr to the lady. At the same time he practised against the earl, that he might become impotent, at least towards his wife. This however did not satisfy the lady; and having gone the utmost lengths towards her innamorato, she insisted on a divorce in all the forms, and a legal marriage with the youth she loved. Carr appears originally to have had good dispositions; and, while that was the case, had assiduously cultivated the friendship of Sir Thomas Overbury, one of the most promising young courtiers of the time. Sir Thomas earnestly sought to break off the intimacy of Carr with lady Essex, and told him how utterly ruinous to his reputation and prospects it would prove, if he married her. But Carr, instead of feeling how much obliged he was to Overbury for this example of disinterested friendship, went immediately and told the countess what the young man said.

From this time the destruction of Overbury was resolved on between them. He was first committed to the Tower by an arbitrary mandate of

James for refusing an embassage to Russia, next sequestered from all visitors, and finally attacked with poison, which, after several abortive attempts, was at length brought to effect. Meanwhile a divorce was sued for by the countess upon an allegation of impotence; and another female was said to have been substituted in her room, to be subjected to the inspection of a jury of matrons in proof of her virginity. After a lapse of two years the murder was brought to light, the inferior criminals, Mrs. Turner and the rest, convicted and executed, and Carr, now earl of Somerset, and his countess, found guilty, but received the royal pardon.—It is proper to add, in order to give a just idea of the state of human credulity at this period, that, Forman having died at the time that his services were deemed most necessary, one Gresham first, and then a third astrologer and enchanter were brought forward, to consummate the atrocious projects of the infamous countess. It is said that she and her second husband were ultimately so thoroughly alienated from each other, that they resided for years under the same roof, with the most careful precautions that they might not by any chance come into each other's presence[a].

[a] Truth brought to Light by Time. Wilson, History of James I.

LATEST IDEAS OF JAMES ON THE SUBJECT.

It is worthy of remark however that king James lived to alter his mind extremely on the question of witchcraft. He was active in his observations on the subject; and we are told that "the frequency of forged possessions which were detected by him wrought such an alteration in his judgment, that he, receding from what he had written in his early life, grew first diffident of, and then flatly to deny, the working of witches and devils, as but falshoods and delusions[a]."

LANCASHIRE WITCHES.

A more melancholy tale does not occur in the annals of necromancy than that of the Lancashire witches in 1612. The scene of this story is in Pendlebury Forest, four or five miles from Man-

---

[a] Fuller, Church History of Britain, Book X, p. 74. See also Osborn's Works, Essay I: where the author says, he "gave charge to his judges, to be circumspect in condemning those, committed by ignorant justices for diabolical compacts. Nor had he concluded his advice in a narrower circle, as I have heard, than the denial of any such operations, but out of reason of state, and to gratify the church, which hath in no age thought fit to explode out of the common people's minds an apprehension of witchcraft." The author adds, that he "must confess James to have been the promptest man living in his dexterity to discover an imposture," and subjoins a remarkable story in confirmation of this assertion.

chester, remarkable for its picturesque and gloomy situation. Such places were not sought then as now, that they might afford food for the imagination, and gratify the refined taste of the traveller. They were rather shunned as infamous for scenes of depredation and murder, or as the consecrated haunts of diabolical intercourse. Pendlebury had been long of ill repute on this latter account, when a country magistrate, Roger Nowel by name, conceived about this time that he should do a public service, by rooting out a nest of witches, who rendered the place a terror to all the neighbouring vulgar. The first persons he seized on were Elizabeth Demdike and Ann Chattox, the former of whom was eighty years of age, and had for some years been blind, who subsisted principally by begging, though she had a miserable hovel on the spot, which she called her own. Ann Chattox was of the same age, and had for some time been threatened with the calamity of blindness. Demdike was held to be so hardened a witch, that she had trained all her family to the mystery; namely, Elizabeth Device, her daughter, and James and Alison Device, her grandchildren. In the accusation of Chattox was also involved Ann Redferne, her daughter. These, together with John Bulcock, and Jane his mother, Alice Nutter, Catherine Hewit, and Isabel Roby, were successively apprehended by the diligence of Nowel and one or two neighbouring magistrates, and were all of them by some means induced, some to make a more liberal, and others a more restricted confession of their misdeeds in witchcraft, and were afterwards hurried away to Lancaster Castle, fifty miles off, to prison. Their crimes were said to have universally proceeded from malignity and resentment; and it was reported to have repeatedly happened for poor old Demdike to be led by night from her habitation into the open air by some member of her family, when she was left alone for an hour to curse her victim, and pursue her unholy incantations, and was then sought, and brought again to her hovel. Her curses never failed to produce the desired effect.

These poor wretches had been but a short time in prison, when information was given, that a meeting of witches was held on Good Friday, at Malkin's Tower, the habitation of Elizabeth Device, to the number of twenty persons, to consult how by infernal machinations to kill one Covel, an officer, to blow up Lancaster Castle, and deliver the prisoners, and to kill another man of the name of Lister. The last was effected. The other plans by some means, we are not told how, were prevented.

The prisoners were kept in jail till the summer assizes; and in the mean time it fortunately happened that the poor blind Demdike died in confinement, and was never brought up to trial.

The other prisoners were severally indicted for

killing by witchcraft certain persons who were named, and were all found guilty. The principal witnesses against Elizabeth Device were James Device and Jennet Device, her grandchildren, the latter only nine years of age. When this girl was put into the witness-box, the grandmother, on seeing her, set up so dreadful a yell, intermixed with bitter curses, that the child declared that she could not go on with her evidence, unless the prisoner was removed. This was agreed to; and both brother and sister swore, that they had been present, when the devil came to their grandmother in the shape of a black dog, and asked her what she desired. She said, the death of John Robinson; when the dog told her to make an image of Robinson in clay, and after crumble it into dust, and as fast as the image perished, the life of the victim should waste away, and in conclusion the man should die. This evidence was received; and upon such testimony, and testimony like this, ten persons were led to the gallows, on the twentieth of August, Ann Chattox of eighty years of age among the rest, the day after the trials, which lasted two days, were finished. The judges who presided on these trials were sir James Altham and sir Edward Bromley, barons of the exchequer[x].

From the whole of this story it is fair to infer, that these old women had played at the game of

[x] Discovery of the Witches, 1612, printed by order of the Court.

commerce with the devil. It had flattered their vanity, to make their simpler neighbours afraid of them. To observe the symptoms of their rustic terror, even of their hatred and detestation, had been gratifying to them. They played the game so long, that in an imperfect degree they deceived themselves. Human passions are always to a certain degree infectious. Perceiving the hatred of their neighbours, they began to think that they were worthy objects of detestation and terror, that their imprecations had a real effect, and their curses killed. The brown horrors of the forest were favourable to visions; and they sometimes almost believed, that they met the foe of mankind in the night.—But, when Elizabeth Device actually saw her grandchild of nine years old placed in the witness-box, with the intention of consigning her to a public and an ignominious end, then the reveries of the imagination vanished, and she deeply felt the reality, that, where she had been somewhat imposing on the child in devilish sport, she had been whetting the dagger that was to take her own life, and digging her own grave. It was then no wonder that she uttered a preternatural yell, and poured curses from the bottom of her heart. It must have been almost beyond human endurance, to hear the cry of her despair, and to witness the curses and the agony in which it vented itself.

Twenty-two years elapsed after this scene, when a wretched man, of the name of Edmund Robinson, conceived on the same spot the scheme of making himself a profitable speculation from a similar source. He trained his son, eleven years of age, and furnished him with the necessary instructions. He taught him to say that one day in the fields he had met with two dogs, which he urged on to hunt a hare. They would not budge; and he in revenge tied them to a bush and whipped them; when suddenly one of them was transformed into an old woman and the other into a child, a witch and her imp. This story succeeded so well, that the father soon after gave out that his son had an eye that could distinguish a witch by sight, and took him round to the neighbouring churches, where he placed him standing on a bench after service, and bade him look round and see what he could observe. The device, however clumsy, succeeded, and no less than seventeen persons were apprehended at the boy's selection, and conducted to Lancaster Castle. These seventeen persons were tried at the assizes, and found guilty; but the judge, whose name has unfortunately been lost, unlike sir James Altham and sir Edward Bromley, saw something in the case that excited his suspicion, and, though the juries had not hesitated in any one instance, respited the convicts, and sent up a report of the affair to the government. Twenty-two years on this occasion had not elapsed in vain. Four of the prisoners were by the judge's recommendation sent for to the metropolis, and were examined first by the king's physicians, and then by Charles the First in person. The boy's story was strictly scrutinised. In fine he confessed that it was all an imposture; and the whole seventeen received the royal pardon[b].

LADY DAVIES.

Eleanor Tuchet, daughter of George lord Audley, married sir John Davies, an eminent lawyer in the time of James the First, and author of a poem of considerable merit on the Immortality of the Soul. This lady was a person of no contemptible talents; but what she seems most to have valued herself upon, was her gift of prophecy; and she accordingly printed a book of Strange and Wonderful Predictions. She professed to receive her prophecies from a spirit, who communicated to her audibly things about to come to pass, though the voice could be heard by no other person. Sir John Davies was nominated lord chief justice of the king's bench in 1626. Before he was inducted into the office, lady Eleanor, sitting with him on Sunday at dinner, suddenly burst into a passion of tears. Sir John asked her what made her weep. To which she replied, "These are your funeral tears." Sir John turned off the prediction with a merry answer. But in a very few days he was seized with an apoplexy, of which he presently

[b] History of Whalley, by Thomas Dunham Whitaker, p. 215.

died[a].—She also predicted the death of the duke of Buckingham in the same year. For this assumption of the gift of prophecy, she was cited before the high-commission-court and examined in 1634[b].

EDWARD FAIRFAX.

It is a painful task to record, that Edward Fairfax, the harmonious and elegant translator of Tasso, prosecuted six of his neighbours at York assizes in the year 1622, for witchcraft on his children. "The common facts of imps, fits, and the apparition of the witches, were deposed against the prisoners." The grand jury found the bill, and the accused were arraigned. But, we are told, "the judge, having a certificate of the sober behaviour of the prisoners, directed the jury so well as to induce them to bring in a verdict of acquittal[a]." The poet afterwards drew up a bulky argument and narrative in vindication of his conduct.

DOCTOR LAMB.

Dr. Lamb was a noted sorcerer in the time of Charles the First. The famous Richard Baxter, in his Certainty of the World of Spirits, printed in 1691, has recorded an appropriate instance of the mira-

---

[a] Wood, Athenæ Oxonienses, Vol. II, p. 507.
[b] Heylyn, Life of Laud.
[a] Hutchinson on Witchcraft.

culous performances of this man. Meeting two of his acquaintance in the street, and they having intimated a desire to witness some example of his skill, he invited them home with him. He then conducted them into an inner room, when presently, to their no small surprise, they saw a tree spring up in the middle of the apartment. They had scarcely ceased wondering at this phenomenon, when in a moment there appeared three diminutive men, with little axes in their hands for the purpose of cutting down this tree. The tree was felled; and the doctor dismissed his guests, fully satisfied of the solidity of his pretensions. That very night however a tremendous hurricane arose, causing the house of one of the guests to rock from side to side, with every appearance that the building would come down, and bury him and his wife in the ruins. The wife in great terror asked, "Were you not at Dr. Lamb's to-day?" The husband confessed it was true. "And did you not bring away something from his house?" The husband owned that, when the little men felled the tree, he had been idle enough to pick up some of the chips, and put them in his pocket. Nothing now remained to be done, but to produce the chips, and get rid of them as fast as they could. This ceremony performed, the whirlwind immediately ceased, and the remainder of the night became perfectly calm and serene.

Dr. Lamb at length became so odious by his

reputation for these infernal practices, that the populace rose upon him in 1640, and tore him to pieces in the streets.—Nor did the effects of his ill fame terminate here. Thirteen years after, a woman, who had been his servant-maid, was apprehended on a charge of witchcraft, was tried, and in expiation of her crime was executed at Tyburn.

URBAIN GRANDIER.

A few years previously to the catastrophe of Dr. Lamb, there occurred a scene in France which it is eminently to the purpose of this work to record. Urbain Grandier, a canon of the church, and a popular preacher of the town of Loudun in the district of Poitiers, was in the year 1634 brought to trial upon the accusation of magic. The first cause of his being thus called in question was the envy of his rival preachers, whose fame was eclipsed by his superior talents. The second cause was a libel falsely imputed to him upon cardinal Richelieu, who with all his eminent qualities had the infirmity of being inexorable upon the question of any personal attack that was made upon him. Grandier, beside his eloquence, was distinguished for his courage and resolution, for the gracefulness of his figure, and the extraordinary attention he paid to the neatness of his dress and the decoration of his person, which last circumstance brought upon him the imputation of being too much devoted to the service of the fair.

About this time certain nuns of the convent of Ursulines at Loudun were attacked with a disease which manifested itself by very extraordinary symptoms, suggesting to many the idea that they were possessed with devils. A rumour was immediately spread that Grandier, urged by some offence he had conceived against these nuns, was the author, by the skill he had in the arts of sorcery, of these possessions. It unfortunately happened, that the same capuchin friar who assured cardinal Richelieu that Grandier was the writer of the libel against him, also communicated to him the story of the possessed nuns, and the suspicion which had fallen on the priest on their account. The cardinal seized with avidity on this occasion of private vengeance, wrote to a counsellor of state at Loudun, one of his creatures, to cause a strict investigation to be made into the charge, and in such terms as plainly implied that what he aimed at was the destruction of Grandier.

The trial took place in the month of August 1634; and, according to the authorised copy of the trial, Grandier was convicted upon the evidence of Astaroth, a devil of the order of Seraphims, and chief of the possessing devils, of Easas, of Celsus, of Acaos, of Cedon, of Asmodeus of the order of thrones, of Alex, of Zabulon, of Naphthalim, of Cham, of Uriel, and of

Achas of the order of principalities, and sentenced to be burned alive. In other words, he was convicted upon the evidence of twelve nuns, who, being asked who they were, gave in these names, and professed to be devils, that, compelled by the order of the court, delivered a constrained testimony. The sentence was accordingly executed, and Grandier met his fate with heroic constancy. At his death an enormous drone fly was seen buzzing about his head; and a monk, who was present at the execution, attested that, whereas the devils are accustomed to present themselves in the article of death to tempt men to deny God their Saviour, this was Beelzebub, which in Hebrew signifies the God of flies, come to carry away to hell the soul of the victim[*].

ASTROLOGY.

The supposed science of astrology is of a nature less tremendous, and less appalling to the imagination, than the commerce with devils and evil spirits, or the raising of the dead from the peace of the tomb to effect certain magical operations, or to instruct the living as to the events that are speedily to befal them. Yet it is well worthy of attention in a work of this sort, if for no other reason, because it has prevailed in almost all nations and ages of the world, and has been assiduously

[*] Menagiana, Tom. II, p. 252, *et seqq.*

cultivated by men, frequently of great talent, and who were otherwise distinguished for the soundness of their reasoning powers, and for the steadiness and perseverance of their application to the pursuits in which they engaged.

The whole of the question was built upon the supposed necessary connection of certain aspects and conjunctions or oppositions of the stars and heavenly bodies, with the events of the world and the characters and actions of men. The human mind has ever confessed an anxiety to pry into the future, and to deal in omens and prophetic suggestions, and, certain coincidences having occurred however fortuitously, to deduce from them rules and maxims upon which to build an anticipation of things to come.

Add to which, it is flattering to the pride of man, to suppose all nature concerned with and interested in what is of importance to ourselves. Of this we have an early example in the song of Deborah in the Old Testament, where, in a fit of pious fervour and exaltation, the poet exclaims, " They fought from heaven; the stars in their courses fought against Sisera*."

The general belief in astrology had a memorable effect on the history of the human mind. All men in the first instance have an intuitive feeling of freedom in the acts they perform, and of consequence of praise or blame due to them in just pro-

* Judges, v, 20.

portion to the integrity or baseness of the motives by which they are actuated. This is in reality the most precious endowment of man. Hence it comes that the good man feels a pride and self-complacency in acts of virtue, takes credit to himself for the independence of his mind, and is conscious of the worth and honour to which he feels that he has a rightful claim. But, if all our acts are predetermined by something out of ourselves, if, however virtuous and honourable are our dispositions, we are overruled by our stars, and compelled to the acts, which, left to ourselves, we should most resolutely disapprove, our condition becomes slavery, and we are left in a state the most abject and hopeless. And, though our situation in this respect is merely imaginary, it does not the less fail to have very pernicious results to our characters. Men, so far as they are believers in astrology, look to the stars, and not to themselves, for an account of what they shall do, and resign themselves to the omnipotence of a fate which they feel it in vain to resist. Of consequence, a belief in astrology has the most unfavourable tendency as to the morality of man; and, were it not that the sense of the liberty of our actions is so strong that all the reasonings in the world cannot subvert it, there would be a fatal close to all human dignity and all human virtue.

WILLIAM LILLY.

One of the most striking examples of the ascendancy of astrological faith is in the instance of William Lilly. This man has fortunately left us a narrative of his own life; and he comes sufficiently near to our time, to give us a feeling of reality in the transactions in which he was engaged, and to bring the scenes home to our business and bosoms.

Before he enters expressly upon the history of his life, he gives us incidentally an anecdote which merits our attention, as tending strongly to illustrate the credulity of man at the periods of which we treat.

Lilly was born in the year 1602. When certain circumstances led his yet undetermined thoughts to the study of astrology as his principal pursuit, he put himself in the year 1632 under the tuition of one Evans, whom he describes as poor, ignorant, drunken, presumptuous and knavish, but who had a character, as the phrase was, for erecting a figure, predicting future events, discovering secrets, restoring stolen goods, and even for raising a spirit when he pleased. Sir Kenelm Digby was one of the most promising characters of these times, extremely handsome and graceful in his person, accomplished in all military exercises, endowed with high intellectual powers, and indefatigably inquisitive after knowledge. To render him the more remarkable, he was the eldest son of Everard Digby, who was the most eminent sufferer for the conspiracy of the Gunpowder Treason.

It was, as it seems, some time before Lilly became acquainted with Evans, that lord Bothwel and sir Kenelm Digby came to Evans at his lodgings in the Minories, for the express purpose of desiring him to shew them a spirit. Sir Kenelm was born in the year 1603; he must have been therefore at this time a young man, but sufficiently old to know what he sought, and to choose the subjects of his enquiry with a certain discretion. Evans consented to gratify the curiosity of his illustrious visitors. He drew a circle, and placed himself and the two strangers within the circle. He began his invocations. On a sudden, Evans was taken away from the others, and found himself, he knew not how, in Battersea Fields near the Thames. The next morning a countryman discovered him asleep, and, having awaked him, in answer to his enquiries told him where he was. Evans in the afternoon sent a messenger to his wife, to inform her of his safety, and to calm the apprehensions she might reasonably entertain. Just as the messenger arrived, sir Kenelm Digby came to the house, curious to enquire respecting the issue of the adventure of yesterday. Lilly received this story from Evans; and, having asked him how such an event came to attend on the experiment, was answered that, in practising the invocation, he had heedlessly omitted the necessary suffumigation, at which omission the spirit had taken offence

Lilly made some progress in astrology under Evans, and practised the art in minor matters with a certain success; but his ambition led him to aspire to the highest place in his profession. He made an experiment to discover a hidden treasure in Westminster Abbey; and, having obtained leave for that purpose from the bishop of Lincoln, dean of Westminster, he resorted to the spot with about thirty persons more, with divining rods. He fixed on the place according to the rules, and began to dig; but he had not proceeded far, before a furious storm came on, and he judged it advisable to "dismiss the demons," and desist. These supernatural assistants, he says, had taken offence at the number and levity of the persons present; and, if he had not left off when he did, he had no doubt that the storm would have grown more and more violent, till the whole structure would have been laid level with the ground.

He purchased himself a house to which to retire in 1636 at Hersham near Walton on Thames, having, though originally bred in the lowest obscurity, twice enriched himself in some degree by marriage. He came to London with a view to practise his favourite art in 1641; but, having received a secret monition warning him that he was not yet sufficiently an adept, he retired again into the country for two years, and did not finally commence his career till 1644, when he published a Prophetical Almanac, which he continued to do till about the time of his death. He then immediately began to rise into considerable notice. Mrs. Lisle, the wife of one of the commissioners of the great seal, took to him the urine of Whitlocke, one of the most eminent lawyers of the time, to consult him respecting the health of the party, when he informed the lady that the person would recover from his present disease, but about a month after would be very dangerously ill of a surfeit, which accordingly happened. He was protected by the great Selden, who interested himself in his favour; and he tells us that Lenthal, speaker of the house of commons, was at all times his friend. He further says of himself that he was originally partial to king Charles and to monarchy: but, when the parliament had apparently the upper hand, he had the skill to play his cards accordingly, and secured his favour with the ruling powers. Whitlocke, in his Memorials of Affairs in his Own Times, takes repeated notice of him, says that, meeting him in the street in the spring of 1645, he enquired of Lilly as to what was likely speedily to happen, who predicted to him the battle of Naseby, and notes in 1648 that some of his prognostications " fell out very strangely, particularly as to the king's fall from his horse about this time." Lilly applied to Whitlocke in favour of his rival, Wharton, the astrologer, and his prayer was granted, and again in behalf of Oughtred, the celebrated mathematician.

Lilly and Booker, a brother-astrologer, were sent for in great form, with a coach and four horses, to the head-quarters of Fairfax at Windsor, towards the end of the year 1647, when they told the general, that they were "confident that God would go along with him and his army, till the great work for which they were ordained was perfected, which they hoped would be the conquering their and the parliament's enemies, and a quiet settlement and firm peace over the whole nation." The two astrologers were sent for in the same state in the following year to the siege of Colchester, which they predicted would soon fall into possession of the parliament.

Lilly in the mean while retained in secret his partiality to Charles the First. Mrs. Whorwood, a lady who was fully in the king's confidence, came to consult him, as to the place to which Charles should retire when he escaped from Hampton Court. Lilly prescribed accordingly; but Ashburnham disconcerted all his measures, and the king made his inauspicious retreat to the isle of Wight. Afterwards he was consulted by the same lady, as to the way in which Charles should proceed respecting the negociations with the parliamentary commissioners at Newport, when Lilly advised that the king should sign all the propositions, and come up immediately with the commissioners to London, in which case Lilly did not doubt that the popular tide would turn in his favour, and the royal cause prove triumphant. Finally, he tells us that he furnished the saw and *aqua fortis*, with which the king had nearly removed the bars of the window of his prison in Carisbrook Castle, and escaped. But Charles manifested the same irresolution at the critical moment in this case, which had before proved fatal to his success. In the year 1649 Lilly received a pension of one hundred pounds *per annum* from the council of state, which, after having been paid him for two years, he declined to accept any longer. In 1659 he received a present of a gold chain and medal from Charles X king of Sweden, in acknowledgment of the respectful mention he had made of that monarch in his almanacs.

Lilly lived to a considerable age, not having died till the year 1681. In the year 1666 he was summoned before a committee of the house of commons, on the frivolous ground that, in his Monarchy or No Monarchy published fifteen years before, he had introduced sixteen plates, among which was one, the eighth, representing persons digging graves, with coffins, and other emblems significative of mortality, and, in the thirteenth, a city in flames. He was asked whether these things referred to the late plague and fire of London. Lilly replied in a manner to intimate that they did; but he ingenuously confessed that he had not known in what year they would happen. He said, that he had given these emblematical representations without any comment, that those who were competent might apprehend their meaning, whilst the rest of the world remained in the ignorance which was their appointed portion.

MATTHEW HOPKINS.

Nothing can place the credulity of the English nation on the subject of witchcraft about this time, in a more striking point of view, than the history of Matthew Hopkins, who, in a pamphlet published in 1647 in his own vindication, assumes to himself the surname of the Witch-finder. He fell by accident, in his native county of Suffolk, into contact with one or two reputed witches, and, being a man of an observing turn and an ingenious invention, struck out for himself a trade, which brought him such moderate returns as sufficed to maintain him, and at the same time gratified his ambition by making him a terror to many, and the object of admiration and gratitude to more, who felt themselves indebted to him for ridding them of secret and intestine enemies, against whom, as long as they proceeded in ways that left no footsteps behind, they felt they had no possibility of guarding themselves. Hopkins's career was something like that of Titus Oates in the following reign, but apparently much safer for the adventurer, since Oates armed against himself a very formidable party, while Hopkins seemed to assail a few only here and there, who were poor, debilitated, impotent and helpless.

After two or three successful experiments, Hopkins engaged in a regular tour of the counties of Norfolk, Suffolk, Essex and Huntingdonshire. He united to him two confederates, a man named John Stern, and a woman whose name has not been handed down to us. They visited every town in their route that invited them, and secured to them the moderate remuneration of twenty shillings and their expences, leaving what was more than this to the spontaneous gratitude of those who should deem themselves indebted to the exertions of Hopkins and his party. By this expedient they secured to themselves a favourable reception, and a set of credulous persons who would listen to their dictates as so many oracles. Being three of them, they were enabled to play the game into one another's hands, and were sufficiently strong to overawe all timid and irresolute opposition. In every town to which they came, they enquired for reputed witches, and having taken them into custody, were secure for the most part of a certain number of zealous abettors, who took care that they should have a clear stage for their experiments. They overawed their helpless victims with a certain air of authority, as if they had received a commission from heaven for the discovery of misdeeds. They assailed the poor creatures with a multitude of questions constructed in the most artful manner. They stripped them naked, in search for the devil's marks in different parts of their bodies, which were ascertained by running pins to the head into those parts, that, if they were genuine marks, would prove themselves such by their insensibility. They swam their victims in rivers and ponds, it being an undoubted fact, that, if the persons accused were true witches, the water, which was the symbol of admission into the Christian church, would not receive them into its bosom. If the persons examined continued obstinate, they seated them in constrained and uneasy attitudes, occasionally binding them with cords, and compelling them to remain so without food or sleep for twenty-four hours. They walked them up and down the room, two taking them under each arm, till they dropped down with fatigue. They carefully swept the room in which the experiment was made, that they might keep away spiders and flies, which were supposed to be devils or their imps in that disguise.

The most plentiful inquisition of Hopkins and his confederates was in the years 1644, 1645 and 1646. At length there were so many persons committed to prison upon suspicion of witchcraft, that the government was compelled to take in hand the affair. The rural magistrates before whom Hopkins and his confederates brought their victims, were obliged, willingly or unwillingly, to commit them for trial. A commission was granted to the earl of Warwick and others to hold a sessions of jail-delivery against them for Essex at Chelmsford. Lord Warwick was at this time the most popular nobleman in England. He was appointed by the parliament lord high admiral during the civil war. He was much courted by the independent clergy, was shrewd, penetrating and active, and exhibited a singular mixture of pious demeanour with a vein of facetiousness and jocularity. With him was sent Dr. Calamy, the most eminent divine of the period of the Commonwealth, to see (says Baxter*) that no fraud was committed, or wrong done to the parties accused. It may well be doubted however whether the presence of this clergyman did not operate unfavourably to the persons suspected. He preached before the judges. It may readily be believed, considering the temper of the times, that he insisted much upon the horrible nature of the sin of witchcraft, which could expect no pardon, either in this world or the world to come. He sat on the bench with the judges, and participated in their deliberations. In the result of this inquisition sixteen persons were hanged at Yarmouth in Norfolk, fifteen at Chelmsford, and sixty at various places in the county of Suffolk.

* Certainty of the World of Spirits.

Whitlocke in his Memorials of English Affairs, under the date of 1649, speaks of many witches being apprehended about Newcastle, upon the information of a person whom he calls the Witchfinder, who, as his experiments were nearly the same, though he is not named, we may reasonably suppose to be Hopkins; and in the following year about Boston in Lincolnshire. In 1652 and 1653 the same author speaks of women in Scotland, who were put to incredible torture to extort from them a confession of what their adversaries imputed to them.

The fate of Hopkins was such as might be expected in similar cases. The multitude are at first impressed with horror at the monstrous charges that are advanced. They are seized, as by contagion, with terror at the mischiefs which seem to impend over them, and from which no innocence and no precaution appear to afford them sufficient protection. They hasten, as with an unanimous effort, to avenge themselves upon these malignant enemies, whom God and man alike combine to expel from society. But, after a time, they begin to reflect, and to apprehend that they have acted with too much precipitation, that they have been led on with uncertain appearances. They see one victim led to the gallows after another, without stint or limitation. They see one dying with the most solemn asseverations of innocence, and another confessing apparently she knows not what,

what is put into her mouth by her relentless persecutors. They see these victims, old, crazy and impotent, harassed beyond endurance by the ingenious cruelties that are practised against them. They were first urged on by implacable hostility and fury, to be satisfied with nothing but blood. But humanity and remorse also have their turn. Dissatisfied with themselves, they are glad to point their resentment against another. The man that at first they hailed as a public benefactor, they presently come to regard with jealous eyes, and begin to consider as a cunning impostor, dealing in cool blood with the lives of his fellow-creatures for a paltry gain, and, still more horrible, for the lure of a perishable and short-lived fame. The multitude, we are told, after a few seasons, rose upon Hopkins, and resolved to subject him to one of his own criterions. They dragged him to a pond, and threw him into the water for a witch. It seems he floated on the surface, as a witch ought to do. They then pursued him with hootings and revilings, and drove him for ever into that obscurity and ignominy which he had amply merited.

CROMWEL.

There is a story of Cromwel recorded by Echard, the historian, which well deserves to be mentioned, as strikingly illustrative of the credulity which prevailed about this period. It takes its date from the morning of the third of September, 1651, when Cromwel gained the battle of Worcester against Charles the Second, which he was accustomed to call by a name sufficiently significant, his "crowning victory." It is told on the authority of a colonel Lindsey, who is said to have been an intimate friend of the usurper, and to have been commonly known by that name, as being in reality the senior captain in Cromwel's own regiment. "On this memorable morning the general," it seems, "took this officer with him to a woodside not far from the army, and bade him alight, and follow him into that wood, and to take particular notice of what he saw and heard. After having alighted, and secured their horses, and walked some little way into the wood, Lindsey began to turn pale, and to be seized with horror from some unknown cause. Upon which Cromwel asked him how he did, or how he felt himself. He answered, that he was in such a trembling and consternation, that he had never felt the like in all the conflicts and battles he had ever been engaged in : but whether it proceeded from the gloominess of the place, or the temperature of his body, he knew not. 'How now?' said Cromwel, 'What, troubled with the vapours? Come forward, man.' They had not gone above twenty yards further, before Lindsey on a sudden stood still, and cried out, 'By all that is good I am seized with such unaccountable terror and astonishment, that it is impossible for me to stir one step further.' Upon which Cromwel called him, 'Faint-hearted fool!' and bade him, 'stand there, and observe, or be witness.' And then the general, advancing to some distance from him, met a grave, elderly man with a roll of parchment in his hand, who delivered it to Cromwel, and he eagerly perused it. Lindsey, a little recovered from his fear, heard several loud words between them: particularly Cromwel said, 'This is but for seven years; I was to have had it for one-and-twenty; and it must, and shall be so.' The other told him positively, it could not be for more than seven. Upon which Cromwel cried with great fierceness, 'It shall however be for fourteen years.' But the other peremptorily declared, 'It could not possibly be for any longer time; and, if he would not take it so, there were others that would.' Upon which Cromwel at last took the parchment: and, returning to Lindsey with great joy in his countenance, he cried, 'Now, Lindsey, the battle is our own! I long to be engaged.' Returning out of the wood, they rode to the army, Cromwel with a resolution to engage as soon as possible, and the other with a design to leave the army as soon. After the first charge, Lindsey deserted his post, and rode away with all possible speed day and night, till he came into the county of Norfolk, to the house of an intimate friend, one Mr. Thoroughgood, minister of the parish of Grimstone. Cromwel, as soon as he missed him, sent all ways after him, with a promise of a great reward to any that should bring him alive or dead. When Mr. Thoroughgood saw his friend Lindsey come into his yard, his horse and himself much tired, in a sort of a maze, he said, 'How now, colonel? We hear there is likely to be a battle shortly: what, fled from your colours?' 'A battle,' said the other; 'yes there has been a battle, and I am sure the king is beaten. But, if ever I strike a stroke for Cromwel again, may I perish eternally! For I am sure he has made a league with the devil, and the devil will have him in due time.' Then, desiring his protection from Cromwel's inquisitors, he went in, and related to him the story in all its circumstances." It is scarcely necessary to remind the reader, that Cromwel died on that day seven years, September the third, 1658.

Echard adds, to prove his impartiality as an historian, "How far Lindsey is to be believed, and how far the story is to be accounted incredible, is left to the reader's faith and judgment, and not to any determination of our own."

DOROTHY MATELEY.

I find a story dated about this period, which, though it does not strictly belong to the subject of necromancy or dealings with the devil, seems well to deserve to be inserted in this work. The topic of which I treat is properly of human credulity; and this infirmity of our nature can scarcely be more forcibly illustrated than in the following example. It is recorded by the well-known John Bunyan, in a fugitive tract of his, entitled the Life and Death of Mr. Badman, but which has since been inserted in the works of the author in two volumes folio. In minuteness of particularity and detail it may vie with almost any story which human industry has collected, and human simplicity has ever placed upon record.

"There was," says my author, "a poor woman, by name Dorothy Mateley, who lived at a small village, called Ashover, in the county of Derby. The way in which she earned her subsistence, was by washing the rubbish that came from the lead-mines in that neighbourhood through a sieve, which labour she performed till the earth had passed the sieve, and what remained was particles and small portions of genuine ore. This woman was of exceedingly low and coarse habits, and was noted to be a profane swearer, curser, liar and thief; and her usual way of asserting things was with an imprecation, as, 'I would I might sink into the earth, if it be not so,' or, 'I would that God would make the earth open and swallow me up, if I tell an untruth.'

"Now it happened on the 23rd of March, 1660, [according to our computation 1661], that she was washing ore on the top of a steep hill about a quarter of a mile from Ashover, when a lad who was working on the spot missed two-pence out of his pocket, and immediately bethought himself of charging Dorothy with the theft. He had thrown off his breeches, and was working in his drawers. Dorothy with much seeming indignation denied the charge, and added, as was usual with her, that she wished the ground might open and swallow her up, if she had the boy's money.

"One George Hopkinson, a man of good report in Ashover, happened to pass at no great distance at the time. He stood a while to talk to the woman. There stood also near the tub a little child, who was called to by her elder sister to come away. Hopkinson therefore took the little girl by the hand to lead her to her that called her. But he had not gone ten yards from Dorothy, when he heard her crying out for help, and turning back, to his great astonishment he saw the woman, with her tub and her sieve, twirling round and round, and sinking at the same time in the earth. She sunk about three yards, and then stopped, at the same time calling lustily for assistance. But at that very moment a great stone fell upon her head, and broke her skull, and the earth fell in and covered her. She was afterwards digged up, and found about four yards under ground, and the boy's two pennies were discovered on her person, but the tub and the sieve had altogether disappeared."

WITCHES HANGED BY SIR MATTHEW HALE.

One of the most remarkable trials that occur in the history of criminal jurisprudence, was that of Amy Duny and Rose Cullender at Bury St. Edmund's in the year 1664. Not for the circumstances that occasioned it; for they were of the coarsest and most vulgar materials. The victims were two poor, solitary women of the town of Lowestoft in Suffolk, who had by temper and demeanour rendered themselves particularly obnoxious to their whole neighbourhood. Whenever they were offended with any one, and this frequently happened, they vented their wrath in curses and ill language, muttered between their teeth, and the sense of which could scarcely be collected; and ever and anon they proceeded to utter dark predictions of evil, which should happen in revenge for the ill treatment they received. The fishermen would not sell them fish; and the boys in the street were taught to fly from them with horror, or to pursue them with hootings and scurrilous abuse. The principal charges against them were, that the children of two families were many times seized with fits, in which they exclaimed that they saw Amy Duny and Rose Cullender coming to torment them. They vomited, and in their vomit were often found pins, and once or twice a two-penny nail. One or two of the children died; for the accusations spread over a period of eight years, from 1656 to the time of the trial. To back these allegations, a waggoner appeared, whose waggon had been twice overturned in one morning, in consequence of the curses of one of the witches, the waggon having first run against her hovel, and materially injured it. Another time the waggon stuck fast in a gate-way, though the posts on neither side came in contact with the wheels; and, one of the posts being cut down, the waggon passed easily along.

This trial, as I have said, was no way memorable for the circumstances that occasioned it, but for the importance of the persons who were present, and had a share in the conduct of it. The judge who presided was sir Matthew Hale, then chief baron of the exchequer, and who had before rendered himself remarkable for his undaunted resistance to one of the arbitrary mandates of Cromwel, then in the height of his power, which was addressed to Hale in his capacity of judge. Hale was also an eminent author, who had treated upon the abstrusest subjects, and was equally distinguished for his piety and inflexible integrity. Another person, who was present, and accidentally took part in the proceedings, was sir Thomas Browne, the superlatively eloquent and able author of the Religio Medici. (He likewise took a part on the side of superstition in the trial of the Lancashire witches in 1634.) A judge also who assisted at the trial was Keeling, who afterwards occupied the seat of chief justice.

Sir Matthew Hale apparently paid deep attention to the trial, and felt much perplexed by the evidence. Seeing sir Thomas Browne in court, and knowing him for a man of extensive information and vast powers of intellect, Hale appealed to him, somewhat extrajudicially, for his thoughts on what had transpired. Sir Thomas gave it as his opinion that the children were bewitched, and inforced his position by something that had lately occured in Denmark. Keeling dissented from this, and inclined to the belief that it might all be practice, and that there was nothing supernatural in the affair.

The chief judge was cautious in his proceeding. He even refused to sum up the evidence, lest he might unawares put a gloss of his own upon any thing that had been sworn, but left it all to the jury. He told them that the Scriptures left no doubt that there was such a thing as witchcraft, and instructed them that all they had to do was, first, to consider whether the children were really bewitched, and secondly, whether the witchcraft was sufficiently brought home to the prisoners at the bar. The jury returned a verdict of guilty; and the two women were hanged on the seventeenth of March 1664, one week after their trial. The women shewed very little activity during the trial, and died protesting their innocence[*].

[*] Trial of the Witches executed at Bury St. Edmund's.

This trial is particularly memorable for the circumstances that attended it. It has none of the rust of ages: no obscurity arises from a long vista of years interposed between. Sir Matthew Hale and sir Thomas Browne are eminent authors; and there is something in such men, that in a manner renders them the contemporaries of all times, the living acquaintance of successive ages of the world. Names generally stand on the page of history as mere abstract idealities; but in the case of these men we are familiar with their tempers and prejudices, their virtues and vices, their strength and their weakness.

They proceed in the first place upon the assumption that there is such a thing as witchcraft, and therefore have nothing to do but with the cogency or weakness of evidence as applied to this particular case. Now what are the premises on which they proceed in this question? They believe in a God, omniscient, all wise, all powerful, and whose "tender mercies are over all his works." They believe in a devil, awful almost as God himself, for he has power nearly unlimited, and a will to work all evil, with subtlety, deep reach of thought, vigilant, "walking about, seeking whom he may devour." This they believe, for they refer to "the Scriptures, as confirming beyond doubt that there is such a thing as witchcraft." Now what office do they assign to the devil, "the prince of the power of the air," at whose mighty attributes, combined with his insatiable malignity, the wisest of us might well stand aghast? It is the first law of sound sense and just judgment,

> ———————————— *servetur ad imum,*
> *Qualis ab incoepto processerit, et sibi constet ;*

that every character which we place on the scene of things should demean himself as his beginning promises, and preserve a consistency that, to a mind sufficiently sagacious, should almost serve us in lieu of the gift of prophecy. And how is this devil employed according to sir Matthew Hale and sir Thomas Browne? Why in proffering himself as the willing tool of the malice of two doting old women. In afflicting with fits, in causing them to vomit pins and nails, the children of the parents who had treated the old women with barbarity and cruelty. In judgment upon these women sit two men, in some respects the most enlightened of an age that produced Paradise Lost, and in confirmation of this blessed creed two women are executed in cool blood, in a country which had just achieved its liberties under the guidance and the virtues of Hampden.

What right we have in any case to take away the life of a human being already in our power, and under the forms of justice, is a problem, one of the hardest that can be proposed for the wit of man to solve. But to see some of the wisest of men, sitting in judgment upon the lives of two human creatures in consequence of the forgery and tricks of a set of malicious children, as in this case undoubtedly it was, is beyond conception deplorable. Let us think for a moment of the inexpressible evils which a man encounters when dragged from his peaceful home under a capital accusation, of his arraignment in open court, of the orderly course of the evidence, and of the sentence awarded against him, of the "damned minutes and days he counts over" from that time to his execution, of his being finally brought forth before a multitude exasperated by his supposed crimes, and his being cast out from off the earth as unworthy so much as to exist among men, and all this being wholly innocent. The consciousness of innocence a hundred fold embitters the pang. And, if these poor women were too obtuse of soul entirely to feel the pang, did that give their superiors a right to overwhelm and to crush them?

WITCHCRAFT IN SWEDEN.

The story of witchcraft, as it is reported to have passed in Sweden in the year 1670, and has many times been reprinted in this country, is on several accounts one of the most interesting and deplorable that has ever been recorded. The scene lies in Dalecarlia, a country for ever memorable as having witnessed some of the earliest adventures of Gustavus Vasa, his deepest humiliation, and the first commencement of his prosperous fortune.

The Dalecarlians are represented to us as the simplest, the most faithful, and the bravest of the sons of men, men undebauched and unsuspicious, but who devoted themselves in the most disinterested manner for a cause that appeared to them worthy of support, the cause of liberty and independence against the cruelest of tyrants. At least such they were in 1520, one hundred and fifty years before the date of the story we are going to recount.—The site of these events was at Mohra and Elfdale in the province that has just been mentioned.

The Dalecarlians, simple and ignorant, but of exemplary integrity and honesty, who dwelt amidst impracticable mountains and spacious mines of copper and iron, were distinguished for superstition among the countries of the north, where all were superstitious. They were probably subject at intervals to the periodical visitation of alarms of witches, when whole races of men became wild with the infection without any one's being well able to account for it.

In the year 1670, and one or two preceding years, there was a great alarm of witches in the town of Mohra. There were always two or three witches existing in some of the obscure quarters of this place. But now they increased in number, and shewed their faces with the utmost audacity. Their mode on the present occasion was to make a journey through the air to Blockula, an imaginary scene of retirement, which none but the witches and their dupes had ever seen. Here they met with feasts and various entertainments, which it seems had particular charms for the persons who partook of them. The witches used to go into a field in the environs of Mohra, and cry aloud to the devil in a peculiar sort of recitation, " Antecessor, come and carry us to Blockula!" Then appeared a multitude of strange beasts, men, spits, posts, and goats with spits run through their entrails and projecting behind that all might have room. The witches mounted these beasts of burthen or vehicles, and were conveyed through the air over high walls and mountains, and through churches and chimneys, without perceptible impediment, till they arrived at the place of their destination. Here the devil feasted them with various compounds and confections, and, having eaten to their hearts' content, they danced, and then fought. The devil made them ride on spits, from which they were thrown; and the devil beat them with the spits, and laughed at them. He then caused them to build a house to protect them against the day of judgment, and presently overturned the walls of the house, and derided them again. All sorts of obscenities were reported to follow upon these scenes. The devil begot on the witches sons and daughters: this new generation intermarried again, and the issue of this further conjunction appears to have been toads and serpents. How all this pedigree proceeded in the two or three years in which Blockula had ever been heard of, I know not that the witches were ever called on to explain.

But what was most of all to be deplored, the devil was not content with seducing the witches to go and celebrate this infernal sabbath; he further insisted that they should bring the children of Mohra along with them. At first he was satisfied, if each witch brought one; but now he demanded that each witch should bring six or seven for her quota. How the witches managed with the minds of the children we are at a loss to guess. These poor, harmless innocents, steeped to the very lips in ignorance and superstition, were by some means kept in continual alarm by the wicked, or, to speak more truly, the insane old women, and said as their prompters said. It does not appear that the children ever left their beds, at the time they reported they had been to Blockula. Their parents watched them with fearful anxiety. At a certain time of the night the children were seized with a strange shuddering, their limbs were agitated, and their skins covered with a profuse perspiration. When they came to themselves, they related that they had been to Blockula, and the strange things they had seen, similar to what had already been described by the women. Three hundred children of various ages are said to have been seized with this epidemic.

The whole town of Mohra became subject to

the infection, and were overcome with the deepest affliction. They consulted together, and drew up a petition to the royal council at Stockholm, intreating that they would discover some remedy, and that the government would interpose its authority to put an end to a calamity to which otherwise they could find no limit. The king of Sweden was at that time Charles the Eleventh, father of Charles the Twelfth, and was only fourteen years of age. His council in their wisdom deputed two commissioners to Mohra, and furnished them with powers to examine witnesses, and to take whatever proceedings they might judge necessary to put an end to so unspeakable a calamity.

They entered on the business of their commission on the thirteenth of August, the ceremony having been begun with two sermons in the great church of Mohra, in which we may be sure the damnable sin of witchcraft was fully dilated on, and concluding with prayers to Almighty God that in his mercy he would speedily bring to an end the tremendous misfortune, with which for their sins he had seen fit to afflict the poor people of Mohra. The next day they opened their commission. Seventy witches were brought before them. They were all at first stedfast in their denial, alleging that the charges were wantonly brought against them, solely from malice and ill will. But the judges were earnest in pressing them, till at length first one, and then another, burst into tears, and confessed all. Twenty-three were prevailed on thus to disburthen their consciences; but nearly the whole, as well those who owned the justice of their sentence, as those who protested their innocence to the last, were executed. Fifteen children confessed their guilt, and were also executed. Thirty-six other children (who we may infer did not confess), between the ages of nine and sixteen, were condemned to run the gauntlet, and to be whipped on their hands at the church-door every Sunday for a year together. Twenty others were whipped on their hands for three Sundays[a].

This is certainly a very deplorable scene, and is made the more so by the previous character which history has impressed on us, of the simplicity, integrity, and generous love of liberty of the Dalecarlians. For the children and their parents we can feel nothing but unmingled pity. The case of the witches is different. That three hundred children should have been made the victims of this imaginary witchcraft is doubtless a grievous calamity. And that a number of women should have been found so depraved and so barbarous, as by their incessant suggestions to have practised on the minds of these children, so as to have robbed them of sober sense, to have frightened them into fits and disease, and made them believe the most odious impossibilities, argued a most degenerate

---

[a] Narrative translated by Dr. Horneck, *apud* Satan's Invisible World by Sinclair, and Sadducismus Triumphatus by Glanville.

character, and well merited severe reprobation, but not death. Add to which, many of these women may be believed innocent, otherwise a great majority of those who were executed, would not have died protesting their entire freedom from what was imputed to them. Some of the parents no doubt, from folly and ill judgment, aided the alienation of mind in their children which they afterwards so deeply deplored, and gratified their senseless aversion to the old women, when they were themselves in many cases more the real authors of the evil than those who suffered.

WITCHCRAFT IN NEW ENGLAND.

As a story of witchcraft, without any poetry in it, without any thing to amuse the imagination, or interest the fancy, but hard, prosy, and accompanied with all that is wretched, pitiful and withering, perhaps the well known story of the New England witchcraft surpasses every thing else upon record. The New Englanders were at this time, towards the close of the seventeenth century, rigorous Calvinists, with long sermons and tedious monotonous prayers, with hell before them for ever on one side, and a tyrannical, sour and austere God on the other, jealous of an arbitrary sovereignty, who hath " mercy on whom he will have mercy, and whom he will he hardeneth." These men, with long and melancholy faces, with a drawling and sanctified tone, and a carriage that would "at once make the most severely disposed merry, and the most cheerful spectators sad," constituted nearly the entire population of the province of Massachuset's Bay.

The prosecutions for witchcraft continued with little intermission principally at Salem, during the greater part of the year 1692. The accusations were of the most vulgar and contemptible sort, invisible pinchings and blows, fits, with the blastings and mortality of cattle, and wains stuck fast in the ground, or losing their wheels. A conspicuous feature in nearly the whole of these stories was what they named the "spectral sight;" in other words, that the profligate accusers first feigned for the most part the injuries they received, and next saw the figures and action of the persons who inflicted them, when they were invisible to every one else. Hence the miserable prosecutors gained the power of gratifying the wantonness of their malice, by pretending that they suffered by the hand of any one whose name first presented itself, or against whom they bore an ill will. The persons so charged, though unseen by any but the accuser, and who in their corporal presence were at a distance of miles, and were doubtless wholly unconscious of the mischief that was hatching against them, were immediately taken up, and cast into prison. And what was more monstrous and incredible, there stood at the bar the prisoner on trial for his life, while the witnesses were permitted to swear that his spectre had haunted them, and afflicted them with all manner of injuries. That the poor prosecuted wretch stood astonished at what was alleged against him, was utterly overwhelmed with the charges, and knew not what to answer, was all of it interpreted as so many presumptions of his guilt. Ignorant as they were, they were unhappy and unskilful in their defence; and, if they spoke of the devil, as was but natural, it was instantly caught at as a proof how familiar they were with the fiend that had seduced them to their damnation.

The first specimen of this sort of accusation in the present instance was given by one Paris, minister of a church at Salem, in the end of the year 1691, who had two daughters, one nine years old, the other eleven, that were afflicted with fits and convulsions. The first person fixed on as the mysterious author of what was seen, was Tituba, a female slave in the family, and she was harassed by her master into a confession of unlawful practices and spells. The girls then fixed on Sarah Good, a female known to be the victim of a morbid melancholy, and Osborne, a poor man that had for a considerable time been bed-rid, as persons whose spectres had perpetually haunted and tormented them: and Good was twelve months after hanged on this accusation.

A person, who was one of the first to fall under

the imputation, was one George Burroughs, also a minister of Salem. He had, it seems, buried two wives, both of whom the busy gossips said he had used ill in their life-time, and consequently, it was whispered, had murdered them. This man was accustomed foolishly to vaunt that he knew what people said of him in his absence; and this was brought as a proof that he dealt with the devil. Two women, who were witnesses against him, interrupted their testimony with exclaiming that they saw the ghosts of the murdered wives present (who had promised them they would come), though no one else in the court saw them; and this was taken in evidence. Burroughs conducted himself in a very injudicious way on his trial; but, when he came to be hanged, made so impressive a speech on the ladder, with fervent protestations of innocence, as melted many of the spectators into tears.

The nature of accusations of this sort is ever found to operate like an epidemic. Fits and convulsions are communicated from one subject to another. The "spectral sight," as it was called, is obviously a theme for the vanity of ignorance. "Love of fame," as the poet teaches, is an "universal passion." Fame is placed indeed on a height beyond the hope of ordinary mortals. But in occasional instances it is brought unexpectedly within the reach of persons of the coarsest mould; and many times they will be apt to seize it with proportionable avidity. When too such things are talked of, when the devil and spirits of hell are made familiar conversation, when stories of this sort are among the daily news, and one person and another, who had a little before nothing extraordinary about them, become subjects of wonder, these topics enter into the thoughts of many, sleeping and waking: " their young men see visions, and their old men dream dreams."

In such a town as Salem, the second in point of importance in the colony, such accusations spread with wonderful rapidity. Many were seized with fits, exhibited frightful contortions of their limbs and features, and became a fearful spectacle to the bystander. They were asked to assign the cause of all this; and they supposed, or pretended to suppose, some neighbour, already solitary and afflicted, and on that account in ill odour with the townspeople, scowling upon, threatening, and tormenting them. Presently persons, specially gifted with the " spectral sight," formed a class by themselves, and were sent about at the public expence from place to place, that they might see what no one else could see. The prisons were filled with the persons accused. The utmost horror was entertained, as of a calamity which in such a degree had never visited that part of the world. It happened, most unfortunately, that Baxter's Certainty of the World of Spirits had been published but the year before, and a number of copies had been sent out to New England. There seemed a strange coincidence and sympathy between vital Christianity in its most honourable sense, and the fear of the devil, who appeared to be "come down unto them, with great wrath." Mr. Increase Mather, and Mr. Cotton Mather, his son, two clergymen of highest reputation in the neighbourhood, by the solemnity and awe with which they treated the subject, and the earnestness and zeal which they displayed, gave a sanction to the lowest superstition and virulence of the ignorant.

All the forms of justice were brought forward on this occasion. There was no lack of judges, and grand juries, and petty juries, and executioners, and still less of prosecutors and witnesses. The first person that was hanged was on the tenth of June, five more on the nineteenth of July, five on the nineteenth of August, and eight on the twenty-second of September. Multitudes confessed that they were witches; for this appeared the only way for the accused to save their lives. Husbands and children fell down on their knees, and implored their wives and mothers to own their guilt. Many were tortured by being tied neck and heels together, till they confessed whatever was suggested to them. It is remarkable however that not one persisted in her confession at the place of execution.

The most interesting story that occurred in this affair was of Giles Cory, and Martha, his wife. The woman was tried on the ninth of September, and hanged on the twenty-second. In the interval, on the sixteenth, the husband was brought up for trial. He said, he was not guilty; but, being asked how he would be tried? he refused to go through the customary form, and say, "By God and my country." He observed that, of all that had been tried, not one had as yet been pronounced not guilty; and he resolutely refused in that mode to undergo a trial. The judge directed therefore that, according to the barbarous mode prescribed in the mother-country, he should be laid on his back, and pressed to death with weights gradually accumulated on the upper surface of his body, a proceeding which had never yet been resorted to by the English in North America. The man persisted in his resolution, and remained mute till he expired.

The whole of this dreadful tragedy was kept together by a thread. The spectre-seers for a considerable time prudently restricted their accusations to persons of ill repute, or otherwise of no consequence in the community. By and by however they lost sight of this caution, and pretended they saw the figures of some persons well connected, and of unquestioned honour and reputation, engaged in acts of witchcraft. Immediately the whole fell through in a moment. The leading inhabitants presently saw how unsafe it would be to trust their reputations and their lives to the mercy of these profligate accusers. Of fifty-six bills of indictment that were offered to the grand-jury on the third of January, 1693, twenty-six only were found true bills, and thirty thrown out. On the twenty-six bills that were found, three persons only were pronounced guilty by the petty jury, and these three received their pardon from the government. The prisons were thrown open; fifty confessed witches, together with two hundred persons imprisoned on suspicion, were set at liberty, and no more accusations were heard of. The "afflicted," as they were technically termed, recovered their health; the "spectral sight" was universally scouted; and men began to wonder how they could ever have been the victims of so horrible a delusion[a].

[a] Cotton Mather, Wonders of the Invisible World; Calef, More Wonders of the Invisible World; Neal, History of New England.

CONCLUSION.

THE volume of records of supposed necromancy and witchcraft is sufficiently copious, without its being in any way necessary to trace it through its latest relics and fragments. Superstition is so congenial to the mind of man, that, even in the early years of the author of the present volume, scarcely a village was unfurnished with an old man or woman who laboured under an ill repute on this score; and I doubt not many remain to this very day. I remember, when a child, that I had an old woman pointed out to me by an ignorant servant-maid, as being unquestionably possessed of the ominous gift of the " evil eye," and that my impulse was to remove myself as quickly as might be from the range of her observation.

But witchcraft, as it appears to me, is by no means so desirable a subject as to make one unwilling to drop it. It has its uses. It is perhaps right that we should be somewhat acquainted with this repulsive chapter in the annals of human nature. As the wise man says in the Bible, " It is good for us to resort to the house of those that mourn;" for there is a melancholy which is attended with beneficial effects, and " by the sadness of the countenance the heart is made better." But I feel no propensity to linger in these dreary abodes, and would rather make a speedy exchange for the dwellings of healthfulness and a certain hilarity. We will therefore with the reader's permission at length shut the book, and say, "Lo, it is enough."

There is no time perhaps at which we can more fairly quit the subject, than when the more enlightened governments of Europe have called for the code of their laws, and have obliterated the statute which annexed the penalty of death to this imaginary crime.

So early as the year 1672, Louis XIV promulgated an order of the council of state, forbidding the tribunals from proceeding to judgment in cases where the accusation was of sorcery only[a].

In England we paid a much later tribute to the progress of illumination and knowledge; and it was not till the year 1736 that a statute was passed, repealing the law made in the first year of James I, and enacting that no capital prosecution should for the future take place for conjuration, sorcery and enchantment, but restricting the punishment of persons pretending to tell fortunes and discover stolen goods by witchcraft, to that appertaining to a misdemeanour.

As long as death could by law be awarded

[a] Menagiana, Tom II, p. 264. Voltaire, Siécle de Louis XIV, Chap. xxxi.

against those who were charged with a commerce with evil spirits, and by their means inflicting mischief on their species, it is a subject not unworthy of grave argument and true philanthropy, to endeavour to detect the fallacy of such pretences, and expose the incalculable evils and the dreadful tragedies that have grown out of accusations and prosecutions for such imaginary crimes. But the effect of perpetuating the silly and superstitious tales that have survived this mortal blow, is exactly opposite. It only serves to keep alive the lingering folly of imbecile minds, and still to feed with pestiferous clouds the thoughts of the ignorant. Let us rather hail with heart-felt gladness the light which has, though late, broken in upon us, and weep over the calamity of our forefathers, who, in addition to the inevitable ills of our sublunary state, were harassed with imaginary terrors, and haunted by suggestions,

> Whose horrid image did unfix their hair,
> And make their seated hearts knock at their ribs,
> Against the use of nature.

THE END.

LONDON:
BAYLIS AND LEIGHTON, JOHNSON'S COURT, FLEET-STREET.

ERRATA.

Page 27, line 14, *read* "for the most part."
100, note b, *dele* Plinius.
111, line penult. *read* "himself."
129, line 6, *dele* and.
143, line 14, *read* "Cerberus."
243, line 11, *read* "adherent."
294, line 14, *read* "flagitious."
302, line 21, *read* "taskmaster."
359, line 9, *read* "no where."

NEW WORKS JUST PUBLISHED

BY

F. J. MASON,

444, WEST STRAND, LONDON.

1.

In one Volume, royal 18mo. Price 6s. in cloth, uniform with the Standard Novels, &c.

DOUGLAS D'ARCY:

Or, some Passages in the Life of an Adventurer.

2.

In one Volume, post 8vo., with Plates, price 12s.

THE ROYAL PARISIAN PASTRY-COOK AND CONFECTIONER.

From the Original Edition of the celebrated Carême. Edited by JOHN PORTER, late Cook to the Marquis Camden, the Senior United Service and Travellers' Clubs, and now of the Oriental. To which is added, all the recent Improvements in Confectionery.

3.

In 8vo., price 4s., boards,

THE ART OF WINE-MAKING, IN ALL ITS BRANCHES.

By the Author of the "ART OF BREWING." The First and Second Parts of which were published under the superintendence of the Society for the Diffusion of Useful Knowledge.

Also,

Price 2s., 8vo., sewed,

THE ART OF BREWING; PARTS III. AND IV.

BY THE SAME AUTHOR.

4.

In 2 vols. 8vo., in cloth, price 18s.

THE MIRROR OF TIME,

From the Creation to the present hour, containing the Anniversaries of Eminent Persons, Leading Events, Institutions and Festivals, interspersed with appropriate Extracts from the best Writers, and exhibiting numerous Important and curious Facts, Sacred, Historical, Political, and Domestic, in every period and state of the World; the whole arranged in the form of a Diurnal Chronology, with a copious Index.

Works published by F. J. Mason.

5.

The Second Edition, in two thick Volumes 8vo., in whole cloth, price 1l. 1s.

INDIA;

OR FACTS SUBMITTED TO ILLUSTRATE THE CHARACTER AND CONDITION OF THE NATIVE INHABITANTS,

With Suggestions for Reforming the present System of Government.

By R. RICKARDS, Esq.

*** This valuable and interesting Work is replete with sound practical information on all matters connected with British India, developing the various bearings of that vital question which now occupies the attention of our Statesmen, Merchants, and all, indeed, who consider our mighty Empire in the East as worth preserving.

6.

Price 3s. 6d. neatly bound in cloth, or 6s. in roan, with tuck, gilt edges; or in morocco extra, for presents, 7s. 6d.

THE LITTLE LEXICON;

OR,

MULTUM IN PARVO OF THE ENGLISH LANGUAGE.

Carefully revised, with Additions from "The Treasury of Knowledge."

BY SAMUEL MAUNDER.

"If this volume is small enough to be called a toy (for it is about the length of the 'forefinger of an alderman') it is well enough done to be thought a very useful abridgment of Dr. Johnson's Great Dictionary."—Literary Gazette.

Also, of a similar size and price, and by the same Author,

THE LITTLE GAZETTEER;

A GEOGRAPHICAL DICTIONARY IN MINIATURE:

Describing the Situation, Extent, and other Topographical Features, with the natural and artificial Productions, of every Country in the World; including the most recent Discoveries.

7.

Price 7s. 6d. cloth boards,

THE PRINCIPLES OF ENGLISH COMPOSITION,

Illustrated by Examples, with Critical Remarks, by DAVID BOOTH, Author of "The Analytical Dictionary." The Second Edition, containing a Supplementary ESSAY ON STYLE, which may be had separately, price 1s. 6d.

8.

In Quarto, price 7s. 6d., Part V. of

BOOTH'S ANALYTICAL DICTIONARY OF THE ENGLISH LANGUAGE;

In which the Words are explained in the order of their natural affinity, independent of alphabetical arrangement; and the signification of each is traced from its etymology: the whole exhibiting, in one continued Narrative, the Origin, History, and Modern Usage of the existing Vocabulary of the English Tongue.

9.

In the Press, in two volumes Post 8vo.

COUNTRY SKETCHES;

OR, PICTURES OF RURAL LIFE.

www.ingramcontent.com/pod-product-compliance
Lightning Source LLC
Chambersburg PA
CBHW052336230426
43664CB00041B/1705